The
Save t

The Plot to Save the Planet

HOW VISIONARY ENTREPRENEURS

AND CORPORATE TITANS ARE

CREATING REAL SOLUTIONS

TO GLOBAL WARMING

Brian Dumaine

CROWN
BUSINESS
NEW YORK

Published in the United States by Crown Business,
an imprint of the Crown Publishing Group,
a division of Random House, Inc., New York.
www.crownpublishing.com

CROWN BUSINESS is a trademark and CROWN and the Rising Sun colophon
are registered trademarks of Random House, Inc.

Library of Congress Cataloging-in-Publication Data
Dumaine, Brian.
The plot to save the planet: how visionary entrepreneurs and corporate titans
are creating real solutions to global warming / Brian Dumaine.—1st ed.
p.   cm.
Includes bibliographical references and index.
1. Economic development—Environmental aspects.   2. Industrial
management—Environmental aspects.   3. Renewable energy sources—
Economic aspects.   I. Title.
HD75.6.D84   2008
658.4'083—dc22   2008000277

ISBN 978-0-307-40618-7

Printed in the United States of America

Printed on 100 percent postconsumer recycled paper

Design by Nancy B. Field

10   9   8   7   6   5   4   3   2   1

First Edition

To Caroline, Paul, and Sophia with love

Contents

Plotters

Racing to Create the Green Wealth Machine

WE ARE IN A RACE AGAINST TIME. Newspaper and magazine articles, television specials, and film documentaries all predict a terrible future: global warming will bring to the world melting ice sheets, flooded coastal regions, powerful hurricanes, droughts, and dislocated populations. In a recent study, the Pentagon described the famine, widespread rioting, and even war we can expect as nations defend their dwindling food, water, and energy supplies.[1] And the effects will not fall evenly: poor people will suffer most. Sectors of the economy heavily dependent on fossil fuels—autos, utilities, chemicals, construction, and others—will have to transform themselves. In the words of the early-twentieth-century economist Joseph Schumpeter, we are heading for an age of "creative destruction" unlike any since the Industrial Revolution.

The debate is over; the climate is disastrously changing because human beings turn out so much carbon dioxide and other greenhouse gases.[2] And the pace of the atmosphere's decline is much faster than the scientific community believed it would be. In late 2007, Rajendra Pachauri, director of the Nobel Prize–winning Intergovernmental Panel on Climate Change (IPCC), said, "What we do in the next two to three years will determine our future. This is the defining moment."[3] According to a recent IPCC report, the world must stabilize emissions of greenhouse gases by 2015, begin to reduce them shortly thereafter, and largely free itself of carbon-emitting technologies by midcentury.

There are also urgent practical reasons to take quick action. A green economy will lessen our dependence on foreign oil and the political risks that go with it. In any case, the world's oil supply will not last forever. North Sea and American reserves are already shrinking. Further dwindling of reserves will drive prices up and world economies way down.

Is there any good news? There is: a new, rapidly growing network of investors, entrepreneurs, corporate mavericks, and environmental activists is emerging. They hail from places such as the United States, Japan, Germany, China, and Brazil. Together they are marshaling the technology, the capital, and the management necessary to construct a new green economy. For these pioneers, the goal is to make money but to do it without spilling into the atmosphere the greenhouse gases that cause global warming. They are building what promises to be the biggest, most profitable industry of the twenty-first century—green technology.

To succeed, these innovators must find cheap, clean replacements for fossil fuels that enable economic growth without exacerbating global warming or severely eroding our standard of living. We're looking for tomorrow's oil substitute, the life blood of prosperity—but without the carbon. For the first time environmentalists are working closely with big business. For example, the Environmental Defense Fund, one of America's most influential advocacy groups, has added a staff position in Bentonville, Arkansas, to advise Wal-Mart on reducing its greenhouse gas emissions. GE has invited top environmentalists to join its Ecomagination Board. Also for the first time, venture capitalists are assembling scientists and engineers from disciplines as diverse as genetics, microprocessing, and logistics to devise cross-disciplinary formulas for the next generation of fuels. When Craig Venter, the man who was instrumental in mapping the human genome, decides to dedicate his latest efforts to biofuels, it's clear that something new is brewing.

In this book, we'll meet the people who are creating the new business models and the cutting-edge technologies that are driving innovations like solar and wind energy, clean cars, practical biofuels, and energy-smart offices and homes. Some of this work, at this point in our history, may appear impractical, or too expensive, or counterproductive. But, though no single program is likely to solve the problem, taken together these emerging technologies are our best chance to reach a carbon-free future.

And such ventures may yield astounding financial opportunities. As John Doerr, a leading venture capitalist and an early backer of Sun Microsystems, Yahoo!, and Google, puts it, "Green tech is bigger than the Internet. It could be the biggest economic opportunity of the twenty-first century."[4] Energy is a $6 trillion global industry, and we're talking about the emergence of a global, powerhouse industry that will take its place.

The boom is under way. While Europe holds the lead in the installation of solar, wind, and other sources of clean power, the United States has recently become the leader in green-tech investment. According to Ernst & Young, by the end of 2006, $100 billion had been invested in renewable technologies worldwide, with America, for the first time, leading the pack. The markets for technologies such as wind and solar are growing at more than 30 percent a year, and the consulting firm predicts that global investment in renewable energy could reach $750 billion over the next decade.[5] As impressive as these numbers are, it is prudent to remember that green technology is in its infancy: from 2002 to 2006 ExxonMobil alone invested $80 billion in oil and gas exploration and refining. The green-tech revolution will have to grow many times over before it takes a meaningful place in the world economy. But there is real hope for rapid change given the recent steep trajectories of the computer, telecommunications, and Internet industries.

A Green Economy

What will a green economy look like? First, cars will radically change. Toyota predicts that in the near future we'll be driving plug-in hybrid cars that are competitively priced and get at least 60 miles per gallon of gasoline. The company announced early in 2008 that such hybrids will reach the market by 2010. At least fifteen new electric car companies are vying to capture the market. As we will see, Tesla Motors is developing an electric sports car powered by lithium batteries that can accelerate from zero to 60 in four seconds, with a life of more than 200 miles between charges. For clean sources of energy to power these cars, desert solar plants are currently under development by a number of start-ups including BrightSource in California. Other entrepreneurs as well as big companies are at work on clean-power technologies from windmills to wave and tide power generators that harness the tremendous energy trapped in the world's oceans.

Genetic engineers are perfecting techniques to produce ethanol economically and from sources other than corn, such as prairie grass and wood chips. Bioengineers are modifying plants to make them self-fertilizing and resistant to drought and pests. They are adding man-made microbes to this biomass, creating a fuel potentially cleaner and cheaper than corn ethanol. In fact, if plans go as predicted, non-corn ethanol may eventually capture a significant portion of the $300 billion annual U.S. wholesale gasoline market.

Richard Branson has pledged the next ten years' profits from Virgin Airlines, an estimated $3 billion, to create the clean fuel of the future. Though he says he believes that this is "the right thing to do," he adds, "I'm not doing it purely as a charity, I'm saying that if we can come up with the right fuels we'll sell those fuels."[6] Branson has also created the Virgin Earth Challenge, a $25 million prize to anyone who can devise a commercially viable design that reduces man-made greenhouse gases from the atmosphere.

America's 619 coal plants account for about half the nation's CO_2 emissions from energy generation. In an odd twist, Duke Energy, one of the largest coal plant operators in the country, is leading the way toward less power consumption and less reliance upon coal. Duke and eight other major utilities have adopted the radical "Save A Watt" program, under which utilities will charge customers for installing solar panels and energy efficient appliances and windows in their homes. Because of the resulting power savings, the homeowner will end up paying less because he uses less energy.

GE plans to invest $1.5 billion a year in clean technologies and has developed a coal technology that would make it feasible to store CO_2 emissions underground. Such technologies are still more expensive than the methods they will replace and are almost certainly out of the reach of fast-developing, power-consuming nations such as China and India. A solution may be forthcoming from a company like GreenFuel Technologies that takes smoke emitted from a coal plant and runs it through giant translucent sacks filled with pond algae, thereby transforming up to 40 percent of the carbon into raw material for clean biofuels.

We will also examine the challenges of constructing home and office buildings that are easier on the environment. New structures in the twenty-first century promise to be energy misers compared with those we occupy today. A good current model is New York City's Bank of America Tower, which uses half the energy of a conventional office building, has a superefficient air-conditioning system, features low-energy lighting, and is constructed of concrete made with recycled materials. The building costs only 3 to 4 percent more to build than a conventional skyscraper, yet its green features should pay for themselves in energy savings after only a few years.

Our homes and commercial buildings account for a significant portion of all the heat-trapping gases we generate. Can we power them with clean energy? Martin Roscheisen, the founder of Nanosolar, thinks so. He is one of a number of entrepreneurs developing a new kind of solar power called "thin film." As we will see, Nanosolar believes its foil could be layered onto a conventional roof shingle that would generate electricity for your house when the sun hits it. The cost of powering a house would be less than traditional methods. Is this just a tinkerer's pipe dream? As of this writing, Nanosolar has started to produce thin solar sheets at its factory in Silicon Valley.

Wind power now is as cheap as electricity generated from natural gas and is fast overtaking coal, the least expensive method of generating electricity. Electric utilities such as American Electric Power, FPL Energy, TXU, and Xcel Energy are ramping up their wind energy investments. Billionaire Warren Buffett, the CEO of Berkshire Hathaway, has invested heavily in windmill farms in the Midwest.

We seem to be amassing the technology, talent, capital, and business savvy to turn the world's energy industries upside down. Such change is not unprecedented. We moved from an agricultural society to an industrial one in less than a hundred years. When the United States needed to build its war machine during World War II, the federal government transformed Detroit from a car-making center to a military manufacturing behemoth in under three years. That is the kind of effort we need now. Some environmentalists and politicians say that combating global warming will take the equivalent of an Apollo moon shot, which rallied the American people around an important cause. But the analogy is imprecise. The race to the moon was pursued irrespective of cost. The transition to a green economy must be accomplished by finding a cost-competitive substitute for petroleum. That's a tougher challenge. Plus we must marshal forces to fight an invisible enemy whose effects mostly won't be felt or seen for decades.

Climate change is not solely an American problem. Carbon emitted from Chinese coal plants warms the entire globe. Arctic melting will cause flooding in Boston Harbor and on a Pacific atoll. Water is scarce in Africa and Arizona. We need prompt international action and a worldwide resolve to curb greenhouse gas emissions. Most parts of the current Kyoto Protocol expire in 2012. It should be replaced with a treaty that sets tough greenhouse gas targets and includes both the United States and China. This will be a diplomatic high-wire act. The developing world believes that it has the right to use fossil fuels to build its economy—just as we did. As a result, the United States remains reluctant to join a new protocol without the compliance of the developing nations. And yet, if no one takes the initiative to change, what kind of world will our children inherit?

As we will later explore, one of the most politically palatable ways to curb emissions is what has come to be called a carbon cap and trade system: the world's nations agree to ratchet down annually the total amount of carbon emitted globally and require companies to buy permits to burn fossil fuels. Coal, oil, and gas will thereby become more expensive as companies pay for pollution-control technologies to meet lower greenhouse gas levels. The good news is that by keeping the price of fossil fuels high, a cap and trade agreement will cut dramatically the time it will take for solar, wave, and wind to become more affordable. Also, a well-designed system could provide economic incentives for Western nations and corporations to provide clean technology to developing nations.

In the long run, wringing the greenhouse gas out of our economies may actually save money. The costs of a haphazard, laissez-faire approach will be enormous. But if the private sector, aided by a global cap and trade system, can keep driving down the cost of clean energy, the world's economies may prosper as new green businesses and jobs outweigh the losses in the traditional energy industries.

According to Princeton's Stephen Pacala and Robert Socolow, two centuries of burning fossil fuels to heat our homes, run our factories, and power our cars has raised the amount of carbon in our atmosphere by 35 percent to 380 parts per million. If the world economy keeps growing at its present rate, the amount of carbon in our atmosphere will triple by midcentury and cause catastrophic and irreversible climate changes, such as the disappearance of the Greenland ice cap.[7] That would mean sea levels would rise more than 20 feet to submerge islands and the world's coastal cities.

The scientific community believes we can avert catastrophe if the level of greenhouse gas in the atmosphere fifty years from now has risen only slightly from its current concentrations. Can that happen if, as predicted, the world's population grows from 6 to 9 billion by 2050? Can that happen if the demand for energy jumps 50 percent by 2030, as we expect it will? Estimates vary, but most experts agree that the rich nations of the world must cut their greenhouse gas by as much as 80 percent by 2050 to avoid the worst consequences of climate change.

No one can predict precisely how the world will reach that goal. Pacala and Socolow have done the best work in this area, devising a road map to show that there are at least fifteen different solutions that could, in some combination, get us to a world that emits dramatically less greenhouse gas. The challenge is to deploy these technologies and strategies on a large scale. In the United States, strides made in energy efficiency—smart grids, LED lighting, more recycling, better building designs—could get the nation roughly halfway to that goal. The rest must come from improvements in our power plants and cars. Plug-in hybrid and all electric vehicles will cut the amount of greenhouse gases emitted. Solar, wind and wave, hydro, and geothermal technologies should be able to contribute significantly, perhaps supplying as much as 25 percent of our electricity by midcentury and even more if battery technology can be developed to store power on cloudy or windless days. Nuclear power, which exudes no greenhouse gas and currently provides the United States with 20 percent of its power, will, for better or worse, play a role. Coal now supplies half our electricity. There is no question about it. It must be cleaned up. Carbon-capture technologies, where the CO_2 emitted from coal plants is buried beneath the ground, should eventually become feasible. New approaches, such as using algae to eat the carbon in coal exhaust, may also become commercially viable. Will we be able to develop the technologies fast enough to meet this goal?

This book attempts to answer these questions. But its investigations have also raised questions of social and economic equity. The United States, with less than 5 percent of the world's population, emits a quarter of the planet's greenhouse gas. The American consumer who lives in a McMansion, drives an SUV, and watches a plasma TV drinks up five times the energy as his counterpart in the rest of the world. And that discrepancy is even worse when you factor less-developed nations into the equation. Nearly 2 billion people today, or a third of the world's population, have no access to affordable power. If China, India, Indonesia, and Brazil are to grow and prosper, they need a source of energy. For the earth to survive, the United States, Europe, Japan, and other rich countries must rely on energy from cleaner sources.

While this book is international in scope, it focuses on the United States, largely because we are the biggest greenhouse gas producers in the world and among the last of the industrial nations to press hard for change. Japan is already one of the globe's most energy-efficient countries; France gets 78 percent of its electricity from nuclear power, which emits no greenhouse gas; Germany has been investing billions to build a solar and wind economy; and the Swedish government aims to cut its nation's greenhouse gas levels by 30 percent from 1990 levels (that's more than the European Union goal of 20 percent) by using mostly wind, hydro, nuclear power, and biomass to generate its energy.

What would a carbon-free America look like? We would conserve more. We would use renewable energy wherever possible. We would quickly clean up coal technology. We would explore the controlled use of nuclear energy. We would put an end to deforestation. We would increase government R&D spending to encourage the creation of new green technology at affordable prices.

Throughout the world small and large companies are working on clean tech. The pages ahead focus on the entrepreneurs and mavericks inside big corporations who are working on solutions, on those who have the best backing or the most promising technologies. Not all of them will succeed, and others not profiled here may leap to the forefront of their fields. The point is not to make bets on a horse race, but to show the ways in which existing technology may be used to solve the grave problem of global warming. We hear gloomy predictions every day. Perhaps here we can also discern some hope.

1

Big Energy

We Can Put Seawalls
Around New York

WHAT ARE THE OBSTACLES to cleaning up our planet? First, we must confront the idea that the American economy is inextricably entwined with the oil industry. Probably the most vivid illustration of this challenge came in the summer of 1979. Gasoline shortages were so severe that American drivers waited for as long as four or five hours to fill their tanks. The turmoil of the Iranian revolution had caused a slowdown in that nation's oil production and helped push world prices to record highs. In the United States, stations closed on weekends for lack of supply. On the nightly news, viewers watched incidents of name-calling, fistfights, and worst. In Freemansburg, Pennsylvania, the wife of a gas-station owner was struck by a car that had been waiting in line. As the husband held his bleeding wife in his arms, motorists filled up and sped off without paying. Miami police arrested two thieves who drove into a gas station, parked over an underground tank, dropped a hose through a hole in the floorboard of their van, and pumped the precious liquid into a 350-gallon storage tank hidden in the back of their vehicle.[1]

Despite the high prices and fuel shortages, when a cardigan-clad President Carter asked citizens to turn down their thermostats and drive less, he was accused of fostering "an age of malaise." Americans were vividly made aware of the risks of having an oil-dependent economy.

After Ronald Reagan defeated Jimmy Carter in 1980, oil prices began to fall, eventually reaching precrisis levels. America was once again hooked on oil. One of Reagan's first symbolic gestures was to tear out the White House solar panels that Carter had installed. The oil crisis had presented an opportunity to transition to an economy driven by alternative energy. Solar and wind companies were being created. The Carter administration had invested heavily in synthetic fuels. But with the return of cheap oil, there seemed to be no appetite to move to unproven technologies.

The new president was sending a clear signal to the nation: the way to solve the energy crisis was not to develop clean technologies to replace fossil fuels; instead, the answer lay in finding and producing *more* coal and oil. Americans wanted sprawling suburban houses, big cars, and limitless air-conditioning. To meet those needs, a consortium of powerful politicians and industrialists, with remarkable efficiency, spent the next two decades turning an already oil-dependent nation into the planet's largest consumer of fossil fuels, one that used nearly five times more than the world average.

Corporate giants such as ExxonMobil, Chevron, and ConocoPhillips created an infrastructure of tankers, pipelines, refineries, and gas stations so efficient that Americans can own 243 million cars and trucks[2]—more than two vehicles for every three citizens—and fill them up anywhere in the country in less than five minutes. Americans, in fact, consume more than a gallon of gasoline a day for every man, woman, and child. And that is in addition to the coal and natural gas we use.

Dominion in Virginia, Duke Energy in North Carolina, FPL Energy in Florida, and Pacific Gas & Electric (PG&E) in California built hundreds of coal or natural gas plants to heat America's homes, cool its office towers, and run its factories. They helped to make our economy the largest in the world. Despite occasional blackouts, these power companies have been a model of industrial efficiency, providing electricity twenty-four hours a day during heat waves, droughts, storms, deep freezes, and blizzards.

Such abundance doesn't come cheap. Over the last fifty years, the energy industry has invested hundreds of billions of dollars in power plants, refineries, and gas stations. As a result, American oil companies and utilities represent a staggering worldwide economic force. As of 2006, Fortune 500 oil companies alone generated nearly $1 trillion in sales and $88 billion in profits,[3] and employed 299,000 people. America's utilities generated $330 billion in sales and $24 billion in profits, and supported 400,000 jobs. That does not take into account the automotive industry, which depends on an unlimited stream of oil. The U.S. motor vehicles and parts industry chalked up $580 billion in sales in 2006 and employed 1.5 million people. In all, big oil, big power, and big auto represent roughly 15 percent of the U.S. economy and employ 2.2 million people, more than enough to populate the city of Houston.

The world's thirst for energy grows each day. If we continue on our current course, the global oil, utility, and auto industries will produce and burn ever more fossil fuel and emit enough greenhouse gases to irrevocably change our climate. A private equity conference for the energy industry, held at New York City's staid Union League Club in 2007, presented a stark picture of the world's future need for oil and coal.[4] John Rice, vice chairman of GE, was the keynote speaker that day. His division builds power plants and equipment; it also provides financial services for the energy industry and has annual revenues of $47 billion. Rice said, "We've never seen anything like the current global energy demand, and there are no signs of it abating. Demand is strong in China, India, South America, and the Middle East. In places such as China and Saudi Arabia, the governments don't want blackouts or brownouts because the populations there won't tolerate it. People see that the 'haves' have power and they want it too. Politicians who don't address this will be voted out of office. Some two billion people in the world don't have access to affordable power. All this will require big energy infrastructure investments."

One participant estimated that in the United States alone $700 billion had been invested in energy to date and predicted that $800 billion more would be invested by 2020 in coal and nuclear power plants, in oil refineries, and in other fossil fuel infrastructure. As I listened to these numbers, I turned to a private equity banker sitting beside me and asked, "What about global warming?"

"We're going to keep looking for oil and building coal plants unless people want to stop driving their cars and live in the dark and in cold houses," he replied.

I pressed on. "What about melting ice sheets and rising sea levels?"

Without missing a beat, he said, "We can put seawalls around New York and the shores of New Jersey. We can afford to do that. The Dutch have lived that way for hundreds of years; they built walls to keep themselves safe from the sea."

"But," I said, "global warming is going to hit the Southern Hemisphere the hardest. The Pentagon is analyzing how to deal with the millions of refugees displaced by floods and famine who might head north toward the U.S. border."

"Well," said the banker, "I'm not saying it's going to be pretty, but we can live with it."

To avoid such a bleak scenario, today's small scrappy clean-energy start-ups must grow big enough to compete against Exxon-Mobil and other huge conglomerates. In the meantime, Rex Tillerson, Exxon's CEO, is determined to keep the world's oil wells gushing far into the twenty-first century. A growing number of environmentalists, scientists, politicians, and investors are attacking big oil, urging these companies to pursue green energy on a massive scale. So far, there has been no significant response—though, for example, Britain's BP now stands for "beyond petroleum." BP, Royal Dutch Shell, Chevron, and other members of the big-oil fraternity have invested in biofuels, wind power, and solar power. Shell has put $40 million into Iogen, a maker of biofuels headquartered in Ontario, Canada. Yet it is hard to give too much credence to the sincerity of companies whose wealth derives from fossil fuels. John Melo, who ran BP's massive gasoline distribution system in the United States before he defected to a biofuel start-up, explains big oil's indifference to alternative energy: "The refiners care about one thing. They care about processing crude and making more products. They don't care, and, as a matter of fact, they're not very interested in what's happening to renewable fuels. If anything, that is a distraction, something that gets in their way, and it shows up very, very actively in the attitude and in the investment choices they make."

ExxonMobil's case illustrates what he is talking about. Up until late 2006, the company's leaders scoffed at the notion of global warming. Public documents show that Exxon gave money to organizations that publish papers, run Web sites, and write letters contending that global warming isn't happening, or isn't proven, or isn't connected to human activity. The company says it has since stopped funding such organizations. At a 2006 energy conference Tillerson finally admitted, "We know our climate is changing, the average temperature of the earth is rising, and greenhouse gas emissions are increasing."

But he is adamant about not investing any meaningful portion of the company's massive R&D budget in alternative fuels. In a 2007 *Fortune* magazine interview, Tillerson said, "We're only going to invest our shareholders' money where we think they can get the kind of returns they expected when they invested their money with ExxonMobil."[5] It is clear that Tillerson simply doesn't believe he can get the same kind of returns by investing in solar, biofuels, and other types of alternative energy that he can by pumping oil. The company is worried that if oil prices drop dramatically, as they did in the 1980s, alternative energy would turn out to be a bad investment. The company would rather put its scientists to work figuring out how to reduce CO_2 emissions from oil and gas by improving gas mileage in cars, for example.

But there is more to worry about. While new sources of fossil fuel such as tar sands and oil shale might help meet our future energy needs, they would exacerbate global warming. Royal Dutch Shell, ConocoPhillips, Chevron, and Imperial Oil, which is owned largely by ExxonMobil, have received permits for massive tar sands projects in Alberta, Canada. This plentiful, carbon-rich fuel can be found in an area the size of Florida in the western United States and Canada. Geologists estimate that tar sands constitute the second largest oil reserve in the world after what lies beneath Saudi Arabia. But mining these vast fields will lead to environmental degradation. Furthermore, processing and burning a barrel of tar sands emits as much as 40 percent more carbon dioxide than a barrel of oil. Oil shale, which can also be converted to fuel, generates twice as much greenhouse gas as oil.[6]

Converting the world's electric grid to clean energy won't be easy, either. Most large utility companies have plans to build new CO_2-spewing coal plants. In the United States alone, power producers have 150 such plants on the drawing boards. Coal plants provide half of America's electricity,[7] and the country has at least a two-hundred-year supply of coal, now the cheapest fuel used to generate power. Without government incentives to clean up its act, the utility industry will keep building dirty coal plants. A few companies are working on a technology that enables the carbon from coal plants to be buried and stored underground (see chapter 7). But this expensive, difficult technology isn't likely to be pursued under current market conditions. If burning carbon is free, why would a utility pay to put it underground?

The Hail Mary Pass

The size of our global warming problem requires a large-scale solution. To meet that challenge, a small group of scientists and entrepreneurs is pursuing what they call geoengineering. In the fall of 2007 they met at the American Academy of Arts and Sciences in Cambridge, Massachusetts, to discuss ways to mitigate climate change by altering the environment. Geoengineering ideas included seeding the oceans in order to increase algae uptake of CO_2, injecting chemicals into the upper atmosphere to cool the poles, blocking sunlight by making clouds more reflective, and stationing heat-deflecting mirrors in space.

These schemes, however, are the scientific equivalent of a Hail Mary pass—to be pursued only after all other earth-bound solutions have failed. After all, tinkering with a complex system such as the biosphere can generate unintended consequences, and not necessarily positive ones. One of the more popular ideas is to use the oceans to gobble up the excess carbon in the atmosphere. Plankton absorb the carbon dioxide: increase their number and you increase the amount of greenhouse gas that gets sucked out of the air. German researchers testing the waters off the Raune fjord in southern Norway added increasing amounts of carbon to the water and found that plankton were able to consume 39 percent more of it than they normally do without draining the waters of nutrients. British scientists James Lovelock and Chris Rapley have proposed to float in the ocean giant pipes that would pump cold, nutrient-rich water from the depths. This would trigger more algae to bloom on the surface and suck greenhouse gas from the air.[8] Climos, a small California firm, wants to pour tons of iron dust into international waters.[9] Iron is known to spur plankton growth, which in turn would absorb more atmospheric CO_2.

These projects have drawn criticism from environmentalists and members of the scientific community who believe that the law of unintended consequences might come into play. Such planetary engineering could be harmful, even devastating, to the marine ecosystem—runaway algae growth could starve huge sections of the ocean of oxygen. The UN's Intergovernmental Panel on Climate Change said that ocean fertilization and other geoengineering schemes are "largely speculative and with the risk of unknown side effects."

If the oceans aren't a solution, what about tinkering with the atmosphere? Nobel Prize winner Paul Crutzen of Germany's Max Planck Institute proposes firing into the upper atmosphere heavy artillery shells that explode and release sulfur. In another scenario he suggests dropping the sulfur particles from overhead balloons. The model for this scheme is the 1991 eruption of Mount Pinatubo in the Philippines. The huge plume of sulfur dioxide that was released cooled the earth by almost 1 degree Fahrenheit the following year.[10]

Roger Angel, University of Arizona Regents Professor and director of the Steward Observatory Mirror Laboratory, wants to place into orbit a cloud of small disks that would reflect the sun's heat back into space. Angel received a NASA grant to explore his plan to launch trillions of transparent sheets two feet in diameter and $1/5,000$ of an inch thick to a point in space where they would be held in place by the equal pull of the earth's and sun's gravitation. Together they would form a cylindrical cloud some sixty thousand miles long. He estimates that the cloud would reduce the sunlight on Earth's surface by 2 percent, enough to offset the warming produced by a doubling of atmospheric carbon dioxide. Building such a cloud would be an expensive, daunting task. NASA would have to launch a stack of Angel's transparent sheets every five minutes for ten years to put the whole structure in place.[11] However, Angel argues that space mirrors "could be developed and deployed in about twenty-five years at a cost of a few trillion dollars. With care, the solar shade should last about fifty years. So the average cost is about $100 billion a year, or about two-tenths of one percent of the global domestic product."

Both Angel and Crutzen stress that their plans are emergency options, to be used only if all earthbound options fail. Our climate is a very complex system, and it would be difficult to gauge the consequences of lowering the earth's temperature even a couple of degrees. Who would decide what the ideal temperature is? Would we design an environment that would most benefit the Russians, the Chinese, or the Americans? Anyone who has argued with a spouse over what temperature to set the air-conditioning knows the trouble this could cause.

To hedge our bets, we should encourage scientists to pursue these imaginative lines of research. In the meantime, some of their earthbound colleagues are trying to design an economy that will allow people to prosper without increasing global warming.

2

Green Is
the Color of
Growth

Nothing Happens
Without Money

SOME REVOLUTIONS START SMALL. Both Apple and HP began in their founders' garages. Intel was born when a handful of engineers left their jobs and rented office space in Mountain View, California. The idea for the Internet was hatched when several small networks decided to band together to share information. Now hundreds of green-tech companies are being launched throughout the world, with some destined to become leaders in the new green economy.

To succeed they must battle big oil, big autos, and big coal. That won't be easy, nor will it happen overnight. The global energy system is enormous. Forty thousand gallons of oil are consumed every second. Chevron CEO David O'Reilly, who oversees one of the world's largest oil companies and has directed it to invest in alternatives such as geothermal and solar, doesn't believe the transition to a green economy will happen anytime soon. "[It's] very long term, a century out, maybe 50 years out. With new technology and changes in the capital structure—maybe some changes will occur. But in the next 25 years, it's unlikely there will be significant change."[1]

Creative Destruction:
A Beautiful Thing

The same venture capitalists who provided the money to create the computer industry and the Internet strongly disagree with O'Reilly. They believe green tech will be to the energy industry what the steamship was to clippers, what television was to radio, what the Internet has been to traditional media—a disruptive force that destroys old business models and ushers in the new. At play is Joseph Schumpeter's theory of creative destruction, which the economist likened to a Darwinian process where new, better technologies push out the old. The creation of new green businesses can happen within conglomerates such as Toyota, GE, and Sharp, but innovation is much more likely to come from small companies because change is much harder in large organizations.

The legendary Harvard professor Theodore Levitt once explained that the railroads in the early twentieth century were prospering and that the Pennsylvania Railroad was considered the best-managed institution in the country. Levitt argued that the railroads should have known they were in the transportation business and not just railroading. When times changed, the railroads were crushed by new competition from big trucks and then jumbo jets, because they were, in Levitt's words, "imperturbably self-confident." Even after the evidence of change was clear, railroad executives and their investors thought they would last forever.

Old-line energy companies that do not adapt to change in a carbon-scarce world will shed jobs, if not go out of business altogether. Displaced oil drillers and coal miners will need to be retrained. The good news is that opportunities to engage in new kinds of work will abound. Over the next decade or two the new green economy will create hundreds of thousands of new jobs and will generate as much, if not more, wealth than did computers and the Internet.

Creating new sources of clean energy will require the latest in computer technology and genetic engineering, which suggests that the future U.S. capitals of energy and autos will eventually migrate from Houston and Detroit to Silicon Valley and other green-tech clusters like Austin and Boston. So far California has taken the lead. As of 2006 the state had more green-tech start-ups than any other: 124.[2] A solar conference attended by eight hundred investors and engineers in 2005 attracted more than six thousand in San Jose the next year.

Another reason for optimism: record amounts of venture capital (VC) are flowing into green tech. According to the consulting group Clean Edge, clean-energy investments rose from 1 percent of total American venture investing in 1999 to $2.9 billion, or nearly 10 percent, in 2006. The Cleantech Capital Group, a Michigan-based research firm, predicts that by 2009 it will grow to $10 billion, some ten times what the Department of Energy currently spends on alternative energy research. Most of the money is coming from veteran VC firms. But new money is flowing from all sources. Hedge fund giant Steven Cohen, who runs his $10 billion firm, SAC Capital Partners, from his offices in Greenwich, Connecticut, has invested in the Palo Alto solar start-up Nanosolar, which has developed a radical new process for solar energy. Even Google has gotten into the act. The company says it will invest hundreds of millions in renewable energy technologies like solar, geothermal, and wind power that it predicts will be cheaper than coal-generated power.

Follow the Money

One company leading the charge is VantagePoint Venture Partners in San Bruno, California. A rapidly growing share of the

$4 billion in assets it manages has been invested in green technology, including solar and biofuel start-ups as well as Tesla Motors, the electric car company. Stephan Dolezalek, leader of Vantage-Point's Clean Tech Group, is a Silicon Valley veteran who has successfully invested in numerous high-tech and biotech firms for over twenty years. While he is admittedly in business to make money, he believes he can do so while addressing the issue of global inequality.

"It's called the 'single earth' phenomenon," he explains as he stands up from the company conference table at which we are talking. He points to a large whiteboard. "There's one planet here," he says, drawing a large circle, "and you've got six and a half billion people who want to share the resources of this planet. What's the resource allocation of fuel, of food, per person? The main question will be: who can afford what?"

As of this writing, 2 billion people have no access to affordable electricity. The world population, if it continues at its current pace, is expected to grow to 9 billion by 2050. Economists predict that demand for energy will rise by 50 percent from current levels by 2030. Clean alternative energy is still too expensive for many residents of the developing world. If the cost of solar, wave, and wind power does not drop dramatically, people in the poorer nations will consume enough coal and oil to greatly exacerbate global warming.

"Long term," Dolezalek continues, "we can go one of two ways. We can continue to go down the path of a world of haves and have-nots. If the paths diverge too much, the have-nots will wreak enough havoc on the haves that the outcome is bad. The other path is let's figure out how to share all the resources in a more equitable way."

The key, Dolezalek believes, is to think globally about our resources: "China says to us, 'We haven't put all that carbon into the air. You did. Give us thirty years to do our share of polluting while you clean up your mess, and in thirty years we'll clean up ours.' It's not an unfair argument. The question is, 'When does it become in my interest to solve their problem?' And, for those of us who live on the West Coast, China's problem has already blown across the ocean and become part of our problem with air pollution in L.A. and acid rain in the ocean."

The way to build a more equitable world, Dolezalek says (by now the whiteboard is filled with a myriad of crisscrossing lines), is to develop clean and affordable energy for everyone. If business can present alternatives that are cheaper than fossil fuel, China can grow and reduce its pollution. More Africans, South Asians, and South Americans can afford to light their homes and run their businesses.

This vision presents a huge business opportunity, of course. Dolezalek's partner, Bill Green, argues that the big oil companies are pursuing alternative energy in only a halfhearted way. In fact, Exxon is basically not pursuing it at all, claiming that it will stick with what it knows best: oil.

If Exxon and its colleagues were doing more work on alternative energy, there would be fewer opportunities for the venture capitalists. Indeed, there is a good possibility that when the large oil companies are finally ready to go green—and circumstances will eventually force them in that direction—they will have to rely on the technology today's investors are sponsoring.

Can anything stop this drive toward the next generation of cheap, green energy? One fear is that the price of oil, which rose to more than $100 a barrel in early 2008, will fall. When it is financially convenient, OPEC turns the spigot that fuels the world on and off. Or the world economy slows and demand for energy drops. Oil floods the market, the price drops, and the pursuit of alternative fuels seems less urgent. There is a good chance that if oil remains above $50 a barrel, investors will continue to invest in alternative technologies because they would have a better shot at becoming cost competitive with fossil fuels. But if oil prices drop precipitously, the investment stream moving into clean energy may well dry up.

VantagePoint and other VC firms believe the companies they are backing can drive the price of solar power and biofuels

down enough to be cheaper than coal and oil. That means placing bets only on technologies that promise to stand on their own
economically—even if oil falls as low as $30 a barrel, which could
happen if the world's economies go into recession. Designing
green energy sources that are cheaper than fossil fuels won't be
easy. One out of every ten venture investments will fail. The same
will hold true for green-tech start-ups.

Among others, VantagePoint is backing Miasolé, a solar energy company that believes its radical "thin film" technology will
produce electricity at rates that can compete with fossil fuels. Its
CIGS solar cells use less than 1 percent of the semiconductor material required by traditional crystalline silicon cells, which yields
an inherent cost advantage. Its cells weigh 80 percent less per watt
than conventional flat-plate, glass modules. The company has
raised more than $56 million to bring its thin-film solar, which
could be layered over roof shingles or on the sides of buildings, to
market. Ramping up to commercial production levels, however,
has proved difficult. VantagePoint also owns part of BrightSource,
a California company that is building a massive solar farm in the
Mojave Desert designed to generate electricity at competitive
rates. It is planning a 400-megawatt solar installation in the desert
that uses a field of mirrors to concentrate the sun's heat and make
steam to power an electrical generator. If successful, just two
BrightSource plants will generate as much electricity in one year
as all the rooftop solar panels currently installed in the United
States. These and other promising technologies are discussed later
in the book.

Ironically, there is a danger that green tech is attracting *too
many* venture dollars and will end up in a bubble like Dutch tulips
and Internet stocks. A major problem is that most small start-up
companies cannot grow fast enough to keep up with the technology or the competition or changing market exigencies. They often
cannot perform well enough to justify the large investments behind them. "We hope there will be a soft landing," Stephan
Dolezalek says, "but there never is."

Corn ethanol companies, for example, have raised money at valuations that don't take into account when the technology will be available and affordable. If corn ethanol doesn't deliver, investment in a more promising technology called cellulosic ethanol, which uses renewable resources like prairie grass or wood chips, will likely be tainted. "The trouble is that most investors aren't smart enough to tell the difference," explains Dolezalek. "We saw this with cell phone development. Companies raise a lot of money, start burning through it fast, and then say, 'Uh-oh, the market has moved two years out on me.'" When that happens investors cool to the entire category, even though the technology itself remains attractive. To hedge its bets, VantagePoint invests in a portfolio of green-tech companies at different stages of development. If the market for green investments does crash, the firm claims it will have companies ready to go public when investor bullishness returns.

Even so, Dolezalek and Green are convinced that the green-tech market is moving in the right direction and will someday be a huge generator of wealth. They see the creation of high-end jobs as engineers, software designers, and marketing experts help launch green start-ups. Then there are the green-collar jobs. Construction workers will be needed to build giant solar farms in the desert and to install solar panels on the roofs of millions of homes and businesses. An army of service technicians will be called on to maintain these products, too.

FEAR OF A GREEN-TECH bubble hasn't damped the enthusiasm of other VC firms. Venerable Sand Hill Road names like Draper Fisher Jurvetson and Kleiner Perkins Caufield & Byers are also playing a leading role in the field. At Kleiner Perkins, John Doerr, with Al Gore as his new business partner, is on a crusade to battle global warming. Doerr's firm had invested $200 million in alternative energy as of 2007, including stakes in EEStor, a Cedar Park, Texas, start-up working on a revolutionary new power pack for

cars, and Amyris Biotechnologies, a Bay Area producer of genetically engineered biofuels.

Driving some of these VCs is the growing sense that the world
is running out of time to mitigate the effects of global warming.
You might call it the "I'm doing it for my children" philosophy.
Consider what happened at a recent TED conference, an annual
gathering in Monterey, California, of leaders in technology, enter-
tainment, and design. TED challenges all attendees to give the
"talk of their life" in eighteen minutes. A session in the spring of
2007 was dominated by discussions of the environment. John
Doerr started his presentation by recalling a conversation he'd had
with his fifteen-year-old daughter. She told him that his generation was responsible for global warming and asked him what he
was going to do about it. After describing his green investments to
the audience, Doerr said, "I'm scared. I don't think we're gonna
make it." In a choked voice, he added that in twenty years he
wanted to be able to tell his daughter that the problem of global
warming has been fixed.

Doerr has assembled a phantom organization called the
Greentech Innovation Network (GIN) designed to ramp up the
speed at which alternative technology is launched. The formula is
one Doerr has long used in Silicon Valley. For thirty-five years he
has been assembling networks of seasoned entrepreneurs and
technical experts to master new industries such as computer networking, personal computers, and the Internet. He uses people he
calls "spiders," leaders who have woven a web of connections with
experts in green tech and policy. Doerr asked them to identify the
best and the brightest in their fields. For the first GIN meeting, in
May 2006, Doerr invited sixty experts to convene in California
and trade ideas.

At that first meeting Doerr learned a great deal about both the
sources of pollution and the technology and financing that would
be required to implement possible solutions. He also discovered
that breakthroughs are most likely to emerge at the intersection of

disciplines—where, for example, physics overlaps with chemistry, biology, and engineering. New specialties like nanotechnology— creating products on a molecular level—were explored. Transportation was a crucial issue, with particular focus on automobiles.

The group also took political action. Eight GIN attendees traveled to Sacramento to lobby undecided legislators to vote in favor of the Global Warming Solutions Act. Seven of these eight ended up voting in favor, and California became the first state to mandate a 25 percent reduction of CO_2 by 2020. Doerr estimates that the law will generate 83,000 new jobs, create $4 billion in annual income, and reduce CO_2 by 174 million tons a year. Now Doerr and his spiders are lobbying in Washington for greenhouse gas regulation. In the fall of 2007, Doerr recruited former vice president Al Gore to join his firm. Gore's political connections can only help Kleiner Perkins push its agenda in the nation's capital.[3]

The Corner of Wall and Green Streets

The potential wealth to be created by the green-tech revolution has also been noted outside Silicon Valley. Back East, Citibank, despite its troubles in the subprime mortgage market, has pledged $50 billion to invest in or loan to green-related businesses. The Carlyle Group, a huge private equity firm, is heavily invested in clean technology. With close ties to two Bush administrations, to global military contractors, and to oil and gas interests in the Middle East, Carlyle nonetheless sees potential for big returns in the clean-energy sectors. Goldman Sachs, arguably the world's most successful investment bank, has put billions of its own capital to work, investing in alternative energy companies like First Solar, GridPoint, and SunEdison.

Goldman Sachs has been a leader on Wall Street in integrating environmental considerations into its strategy and core businesses. Its foray into conservation and environmental awareness had unusual origins. In 2002, by way of its distressed-debt business, Goldman ended up owning roughly 700,000 acres of property in Tierra del Fuego, Chile, an area the size of Yellowstone National Park. Goldman employees on the trading desk weren't sure what to do with this asset. One suggested a logging operation. Another suggested selling it. Someone else proposed another idea—maximizing the land's value by purchasing it for conservation.

The tract turned out to be ecologically important. It was a significant carbon sink—its foliage stored significant amounts of greenhouse gases, and if the peat-rich land were mined, it would release tremendous amounts of carbon into the atmosphere.

Rather than split up and sell these lands in individual parcels, Goldman's senior management and its board agreed that the best way to maximize the value of the land was to conserve it. In December 2003, title to the land was acquired by the Goldman Sachs Charitable Fund, and in 2004, Goldman announced a partnership with the Wildlife Conservation Society (WCS) to endow the land, ensuring that it would remain protected in perpetuity for the people of Chile. Goldman and WCS worked with the government of Chile to obtain support for the nature reserve, and created an advisory council including some of Chile's most distinguished experts to manage the lands, educate the local community, conduct scientific research, and promote sustainable development of ecotourism. As part of the conservation plan, the reserve was recently expanded through the purchase of adjacent property.

Though the land and endowment cost relatively little by Wall Street standards, Goldman was under some pressure from certain shareholders and members of the business press who believed a public company shouldn't use its funds to support an environmental agenda. The most vocal criticism came from the Free Enterprise Action Fund, a small, right-wing mutual fund whose stated philosophy is as follows: "Left-wing social and political activists are harnessing the power, resources and influence of publicly owned corporations to advance their social and political agendas."[4]

The fund criticized Goldman for not maximizing profits by pursuing large-scale sustainable forestry in the region. "Shareholders and the environment lost out in the Chilean land deal," said Tom Borelli of Action Fund Management, which advises the fund.[5]

Mark Tercek, who then ran Goldman's mergers and acquisitions division and is now the head of the firm's environmental strategy team, notes, "Yes, we took a lot of heat for that. But when we did it, everyone inside the company felt great. It was the right thing to do."

Protecting land in Chile also has an intangible business payback. When Goldman is perceived to be at the forefront of an issue as crucial as global warming and climate change, it helps tremendously in recruiting smart, young talent. That's a huge competitive advantage in any business, but especially so in investment banking. Goldman for years has been a top pick among college graduates, but its Tierra del Fuego activities, it soon discovered, made it even more desirable.

The Chilean deal also sent a message to Goldman's more than 25,000 employees that the top management of the company was serious about the firm's environmental impact. Thoughout the course of the deal, Goldman executives began meeting with some of the world's top environmentalists, who applauded the firm's decision to protect land in Chile but also called on the company to employ its people, resources, and expertise to address other environmental problems. In November 2005, Goldman published its environmental policy framework. In it the firm acknowledged the broad scientific consensus that man-made emissions are largely responsible for climate change and stated that though voluntary action is important, it is insufficient to deal with the problem.

As a result of this position—radical for its time and place—each Goldman business unit was asked to come up with a green strategy. In its principal investing division, Goldman earmarked $1 billion of its own money for clean and renewable energy projects—and so far has exceeded that goal more than two times over. Many competitors watch closely what Goldman does and when the firm was seen investing in green technologies, a wave of capital followed.

Goldman, as a major global commodities trader, is now trading carbon credits and providing related services in the European market and is one of its biggest players. The company also became the largest minority investor in the Chicago Climate Exchange PLC, the owner of the Chicago Climate Exchange and the European Climate Exchange, voluntary markets to trade carbon credits. This is not philanthropy. If the U.S. Congress passes carbon "cap and trade" legislation, Wall Street players who have expertise in the area stand to make significant trading fees from buying and selling emissions allowances and related financial and risk management products.

Goldman's investment research division also evaluates the companies that it follows on the basis of their environmental, social, and governance performance. At first their own research team complained that there was no indication that any of its customers wanted such information. And some of the companies Goldman followed were surprised and even annoyed by the questions the analysts began asking: What is your carbon footprint? What measures are you taking to reduce the use of fossil fuel in your operations? What steps are you taking to protect your company from the adverse effects of global warming? The companies answered them anyhow. As a result, many institutional investors and businesses alike came to see the value of this information in making investment and strategic decisions.

One of the most visible impacts of Goldman's new environmental strategy was seen in its vaunted investment banking division. Goldman makes billions of dollars in advising governments and big companies on their biggest transactions. The firm tries to integrate environmental issues and opportunities into its regular dialogue with clients and also considers these factors when evaluating its participation in new transactions. Some of Goldman's clients have pushed back, but as Mark Tercek explains: "We tell them we care about the environment, but that you should care more than us because if we see something—and we're just being good investment bankers—that troubles us, it should trouble you even more. And our smartest clients get that."

As an example of this philosophy, in 2007, two of the largest private equity firms, TPG Capital and Kohlberg, Kravis, Roberts & Co. (KKR), along with Goldman's merchant bank, decided to buy TXU, a Dallas utility. Goldman's investment bankers advised the buyers on the deal. Previously, TXU had announced a plan to build eleven new pulverized coal–fired plants, which would double the amount of greenhouse gas the utility emitted. The company had become a prime target of the environmental community, which charged that the new coal plants would contribute to global warming, as well as local communities, who worried that the new plants would pollute the air and pose a health hazard. The Environmental Defense Fund set up a Web site, stoptxu.com; the media covered developments in great detail; and TXU came under intense and highly critical scrutiny for the plan. Its share price suffered.

TPG, KKR, and Goldman Sachs recognized an opportunity, but realized that if a leveraged buyout were to be successful, environmental concerns would have to be a central part of the deal. TPG cofounder David Bonderman, who was on the board of the World Wildlife Fund, and William K. Reilly, a TPG advisor and former EPA administrator, reached out to Environmental Defense and the Natural Resources Defense Council, some of TXU's biggest environmental critics, for their views on a proposed new strategy. The environmentalists, the bankers, and the private equity sponsors devised a new plan for TXU, which included cutting the number of new coal plants from eleven to three, making new investments in alternative energy and demand management, and developing a Climate Advisory Board comprised of representatives from the business, utility, environmental, and local communities. The $45 billion leveraged buyout is the largest in history—a major victory for the buyers, shareholders, and the environment.

Some critics have argued that the private equity investors made little sacrifice in pushing for the new plan as part of the buy-out deal. With carbon regulations tightening at the state level and increasing public pressure on the company, it's not likely that those eleven plants would ever have been built. TXU will now have to replace some of the coal plants with power that will probably be more expensive. But the old coal plants that TXU already owns, because they can generate power cheaply, should become more valuable over time, and the private equity investors are likely to recoup a good economic return on them if they resell the utility four or five years from now.

GOLDMAN SACHS IS NOT the only firm on Wall Street to think green is good business. A growing number of big money managers believe that corporate America must change the way it does business if it is to thrive in an era of global warming. They are triggering seismic changes in corporate boardrooms around the country. The global management consultancy McKinsey and Company now advises twenty of the Fortune 100 on how to build corporate sustainability programs.

What's driving these behemoths? As concerns about global warming grow, corporations are coming under attack by both government and environmental groups; it is, in fact, likely that climate change will become the next big legal battlefield. In 2006, for instance, the state of California filed a lawsuit against six automakers, charging that greenhouse gases from their vehicles have caused billions of dollars in damages. The suit contended that California must spend millions of dollars to deal with reduced snowpack, beach erosion, ozone pollution, and the impact on endangered animals and fish.

California is not alone. Eight states, as well as New York City, sued five electricity generators to reduce greenhouse gas emissions. As of 2004, the five being sued—American Electric Power,

Cinergy (now Duke Energy), Southern Tennessee Valley Authority, and Xcel Energy—owned or operated 174 power plants that accounted for 10 percent of America's CO_2 emissions.

In addition, there is growing shareholder pressure. More and more big institutional investors believe that those corporations that fail to adapt to global warming will soon see their shares pummeled. McKinsey, in a report called "Preparing for a Low Carbon Future," argues that the first companies to respond to climate change could not only protect their share price but also create a long-term competitive advantage.[6] McKinsey cites big institutional investors such as Calpers, the California state pension fund, and the city and state of New York pension funds that are pressuring companies to report their carbon footprint—the amount of carbon they and their suppliers emit. The Carbon Disclosure Project, a group representing 39 institutional investors who control $41 trillion in assets, sends letters to 2,400 of the world's top corporations asking them to explain their emissions policies and strategies. The group then publishes the response or lack of one from each company and lets investors decide where to put their money.

Most of the 117 members of Ceres, an organization that studies the risks and opportunities of climate change and files shareholder resolutions to force companies to change their ways, are investment funds and public-interest groups representing $400 billion in assets. These include the New York State Teachers' Retirement System, the Union of Concerned Scientists, and the AFL-CIO. Ceres had filed a resolution with TXU regarding its plan to build eleven new pulverized coal–burning power plants in Texas. The Investor Network on Climate Risk, a Ceres project, has sixty members, including the Florida State Treasury and the Rockefeller Brothers Fund, representing more than $4 trillion in assets. The network's mission is to increase the financial market's awareness of climate risks. As the authors of the McKinsey report write: "Rising input costs—for energy or transportation, say—will affect companies of every stripe, from retailers that consume energy in their stores to consumer product companies that design packaging. Investors will increasingly hold them responsible for managing emissions. Managers who fail to respond to calls for more transparency and better planning will face greater public censure or even charges of breaches of duty. They might also find the share price of their companies discounted in the capital markets."[7]

The bottom line: emitting carbon is going to become more expensive, and shareholders will demand to know how executives plan to manage these costs. As the price of oil, gas, and coal rise, there will be clear winners and losers. The first to feel the pressure will be utilities, oil, cement, and steel companies that discharge large amounts of carbon. In a study of the European market, McKinsey found that industries relatively unaffected by foreign competition will be in a much better position to pass higher carbon control costs along to customers. European makers of flat steel—used, say, for manufacturing cars—are under intense pressure from foreign competitors and would have a hard time raising their prices high enough to pay for reducing carbon emissions.

Companies working hard to lower their carbon footprint will also hold a competitive edge. PG&E in California and FPL in Florida have been investing heavily in wind, solar, and nuclear power. That means they won't have high revamping costs to clean up their power generation. Obviously they will be less affected by rising carbon-control costs than companies like American Electric Power, Southern Tennessee Valley Authority, and Xcel Energy that are more heavily dependent on coal.

Many corporations fear that global warming itself will drive their operating expenses sky-high, as rising insurance premiums raise the cost of doing business. While science does not definitively support the idea that global warming causes hurricanes like Katrina, it does suggest that the warming increases the intensity of these storms. As carbon concentrations in our atmosphere grow, scientists expect more severe and more numerous hurricanes, torrential rains, and droughts. The United Nations Environment Program and the insurer Swiss Re predict that annual losses from extreme weather events such as heat waves and floods will increase from $55 billion in 2003 to $300 billion in 2050.

Many of the world's top corporations, including Du Pont, GE, Toyota, and Wal-Mart, have developed a comprehensive, imaginative, and intimidatingly ambitious program to address these concerns by cutting their own carbon footprints and by developing products that use less or no fossil fuel. Some corporations, Wal-Mart for one, see green changes as an opportunity to slash energy costs and drive more dollars to the bottom line. Wal-Mart CEO Lee Scott told *Fortune* magazine in a 2006 interview, "To me, there can't be anything good about putting all these chemicals in the air. There can't be anything good about the smog you see in cities. There can't be anything good about putting chemicals in these rivers in Third World countries so that somebody can buy an item for less money in a developed country. Those things are just inherently wrong, whether you are an environmentalist or not."[8]

Scott should know. Wal-Mart remains one of the largest producers of greenhouse gas in the country. According to *Fortune*, the retailer is the biggest private user of electricity in America: each of its 2,435 supercenters uses an average of 1.5 million kilowatts annually; together they use enough energy to power a small African nation. Wal-Mart has the nation's second-largest private fleet of trucks, and its vehicles travel a billion miles a year.[9]

The company wants to cut back on its energy use not only because it's the right thing to do but also because it is a way to save money—a philosophy that has been deeply ingrained in the corporate culture ever since Sam Walton founded the chain in 1962. Wal-Mart's environmental campaign to spread its new green image also helps to distract public attention from controversial issues such as the low wages it pays or the large percentage of Wal-Mart employees and their children who have no health insurance or are on Medicare. Add to that a recent California court case in which the company is being sued by former employees for gender discrimination.

When asked about its green program, Wal-Mart points to its new "green" supercenters, one near Bentonville, Arkansas, and one in suburban Denver. At the Bentonville store skylights let in enough natural light that the fluorescent fixtures can be turned off a lot of the time. For those times when the lights are necessary, the company has installed superefficient LED lighting that could, as they become more affordable, cut electricity bills by as much as 80 percent. Motion sensors control the lights in the freezers: they switch on only when a customer is within arm's reach. Overall, the company estimates that this store could save as much as $100,000 in annual electricity costs.[10]

The Denver store, which opened in 2005, gets some of its energy from wind turbines and from solar panels mounted on its roof. Dirty cooking oil from the deli and used motor oil from the lube department are recycled to heat the store. Some of the display cases are made from recycled bamboo. Spoiled food gets composted into fertilizer and resold for garden use. But no more green Wal-Marts have been built. The company won't explain, but it seems reasonable to conclude that the green technologies do not yet provide a return on Wal-Mart's investment.

During Wal-Mart's 2007 Live Better Sustainability Summit, Lee Scott told his suppliers that the company is aiming for zero waste. It also plans to consume 100 percent renewable energy. To start down that road, Scott has set some tough mileposts. He challenged his 1.8 million employees to figure out how to boost the efficiency of Wal-Mart's vehicle fleet by 25 percent over three years, and then double it within ten years. Wal-Mart believes it will save $26 million a year in fuel costs for its fleet of 7,200 trucks by equipping them with auxiliary air-conditioning and heating units so that during drivers' rest and sleep breaks the big truck diesel engines would not be left idling. They must cut energy use in Wal-Mart stores by 30 percent and reduce solid waste from U.S. stores by 25 percent.[11]

But even if the retailer succeeds in emitting less carbon, its plan to build a thousand or more new stores over the next decade is likely to create a net increase in the amount of greenhouse gas in our atmosphere. Stacy Mitchell, a senior researcher with the New Rules Project, a program of the Institute for Local Self-Reliance, conducted a study of the impact of Wal-Mart stores on the environment.[12] The problem, she argues, is that Wal-Mart destroyed tens of thousands of neighborhood and downtown businesses that were within walking distance of their customers. The big box stores with their vast parking lots encourage shoppers to drive miles just to pick up a quart of milk. She found that Americans now travel on average 50 percent more vehicle miles each year for shopping than they did in 1990.

The other problem Mitchell noted is that the amount of store space in the United States is vast and continues to grow: "Since Wal-Mart opened its first store in 1962, the amount of retail store space per capita in the U.S. has grown tenfold. America now has five to six times as much store space as other industrialized nations. Wal-Mart alone has more than 300 empty stores nationwide. Most were abandoned after the company opened larger stores in the same market. Wal-Mart's annual report says that it plans to 'relocate' (i.e., vacate) up to 150 stores in 2007."[13]

In a recent advisory report to real estate investors, PricewaterhouseCoopers declared, "The most over-retailed country in the world hardly needs more shopping outlets of any kind." Yet the building and the consumption of fossil fuels to construct these superstores continues. As Wal-Mart abandons old stores and builds hundreds of new ones, it will surely increase the total amount of carbon it emits, even if those stores are energy efficient.

Wal-Mart, then, is as much a part of the problem as of the solution. The best outcome would be for Wal-Mart to stop growing. That is not going to happen. The most we can hope for is that the retailer will use its enormous leverage to make itself and its thousands of suppliers limit the amount of greenhouse gas they emit as they grow.

Wal-Mart's daily operations account for only 8 percent of its overall carbon footprint; the remainder is emitted by its sixty thousand suppliers who provide Styrofoam coolers, broccoli grown with petrochemical fertilizers, and paper towels that have their origins in forests around the world. If the company has any chance of becoming remotely sustainable, it must also press its suppliers to embrace a low-carbon diet as well.

Such a move will help, but ultimately big corporate consumers of energy such as Wal-Mart will not be able to keep growing without a radical shift in the kinds of energy we use. That will happen once entrepreneurs along with a handful of mavericks inside of big companies provide the affordable solar power, viable electric vehicles, and smart-energy buildings to allow these corporate behemoths to grow in a sustainable fashion.

Ecomagination

Where will companies like Wal-Mart find this clean energy? GE thinks it has some answers. This global conglomerate, with sales of $207 billion, runs businesses ranging from industrial machinery to wind turbines, finance, and media—it owns NBC. In 2005 GE launched Ecomagination, a program to get the entire organization focused on the challenge of building cleaner jet engines, locomotives, and coal turbines and of inventing entirely new products such as energy-efficient LED lighting systems that discharge less greenhouse gas. While still in its early stages, the Ecomagination program is showing results for GE and could act as a template for how all big corporations can adapt to the new green economy and avoid the crush of the oncoming wave of creative destruction.

• • •

ECOMAGINATION WAS BORN during one of CEO Jeff Immelt's "growth playbook" meetings. Every year he meets with all his division heads to do long-term strategic planning. Each of the division heads lays out what is likely to impact his or her business over the next three to five years. At the growth playbook meeting in 2004, Immelt heard a common theme: whichever energy-consuming business they were running, all his executives told him that regulations on emissions will become more stringent, that environmental leadership is going to count, and that the company is going to have to address these issues, especially because their customers were feeling the same pressures. They also stressed that energy costs will continue to be high and that energy security is increasingly important to GE's customers. Finally, they argued that in the future many of the world's precious resources were going to be scarcer. As one executive put it: "We're living in a world where GDPs are growing rapidly and growing in places where there is a scarcity of resources such as water. At the same time the world population will grow by three billion. The basic scenario is that we are facing an economy of scarcity."

Immelt and his management team then agreed to commit to Ecomagination. They would identify their most promising green technologies. They would boost research spending for green technology. They would be publicly transparent about their environmental initiatives. At the same time, Immelt decided to reduce GE's own greenhouse gas emissions by 1 percent from 2004 levels by 2012. This doesn't sound like much, but the company points out that, based on its projected growth, its emissions would have otherwise risen 40 percent over that period. Already this drive for increased efficiency helped save the company $70 million in energy costs in 2006 and $100 million in 2007. Says Immelt, "We basically applied GE operational tenets to an initiative that was socially responsible and economic at the same time."[14]

Next, Immelt needed someone to lead the Ecomagination charge. In early 2005 he appointed Lorraine Bolsinger, a GE veteran. Bolsinger can best be described as a high-energy multi-tasker. Throughout her career at GE, Bolsinger, who has a degree in biomechanical engineering, has worked her way up through engineering, project management, sales, and marketing, giving her a broad view of the business.

One of the tenets of Ecomagination is transparency, and Bolsinger felt that the world should know about GE's dramatic change in strategy sooner rather than later. Some inside GE thought this to be a risky move, because it was too early to show any material results from Ecomagination. If the company announced the project, the environmental community could argue that Ecomagination was nothing more than the next wave of corporate greenwash—a lot of talk without much substance. Wanting to position GE as a leader in the environmental movement, Bolsinger gave the launch a green light.

On the evening of May 9, 2005, the company announced Ecomagination to the world with great fanfare. At a tony cocktail party on Pennsylvania Avenue, not far from the White House, Immelt schmoozed with senators and industry leaders who munched on organic appetizers and downed cabernets from Shafer, whose vineyard ran on solar panels made by GE. Immelt told the crowd of gathered luminaries that "it's no longer a zero-sum game—things that are good for the environment are also good for business" and vowed that GE was embarking on this initiative "not because it is trendy or moral, but because it will accelerate [economic] growth." Bolsinger then played an Ecomagination television ad, part of a $90 million marketing campaign that would run throughout the year. One of the spots attempted to make coal sexy again. It featured scantily clad models dusted with soot and shoveling coal in a dingy mine as a voiceover announces, "Now, thanks to emissions-reducing technologies from GE, the power of coal is getting more beautiful every day."[15] Jonathan Lash, president of the WRI and a chairman of President Clinton's Council on Sustainable Development, remarked that the GE initiative "is enough to make even a gloomy environmentalist hopeful." He went on to call Immelt "not only a visionary, but in the absence of coherent national policies . . . encouraging energy efficiency and use of renewable energy, he is just plain gutsy."[16]

How is the ecomagination program working internally? Bolsinger says most managers went along with it—after all, they were the ones who had originally asked Immelt to go green. But she did meet resistance from a handful of managers who were themselves getting pushback from customers who didn't want global warming to get so much play. "When a company like GE moves into an area like this," explains Bolsinger, "it gives it more voice, gives it more press, gives it more publicity. Some of our customers may have been concerned about that. If you're a coal-burning utility you might not want to shed a lot of light on it, but they sure weren't mad at us because we were going to produce more efficient products. If anything it was, 'Hey, give us a voice in what you're doing. Because we're going to have to afford it and deploy it.' "

Immelt also created an Ecomagination board, which meets monthly to try to keep pace with the latest ideas and opportunities in the battle against global warming. The meetings' agendas are set by Lorraine Bolsinger and Mark Little, a GE senior vice president in charge of the company's global research center. CEO Jeff Immelt presides. Outside board members include Eileen Claussen of the Pew Center on Global Climate Change; Jonathan Lash, president of the World Resources Institute (WRI); architect William McDonough; and MIT energy expert Ernie Moniz.

Bolsinger described to me a typical meeting: "We discuss what new trends, new emerging markets, and emerging regulations we should be thinking about and then how to apply our technology not so much in the next six months but over the next three to ten years. Are we suited for that space, are we ready for it? Is there something we should be doing with technology? Should we be investing more R&D money so we can develop it ourselves, or should we be partnering with a venture capitalist who can help us get smart on the technology?" Among other areas, the board pinpointed wind, solar, and low-energy lighting as promising areas of growth. In one session, the Ecomagination board was exploring how GE could construct greener airports and buildings, and to find ways to incorporate in the company's solar panels and green lighting systems. At one point, board member McDonough suggested, "Why not make everything from the baggage carousels to the e-ticket machines to the security X-ray machines run off solar power?"

The green brainpower that GE has gathered on its Ecomagination board allows Immelt to send a message to his employees that the company is open to outside thinking and should pursue new green opportunities. The other purpose of the board is to act as a watchdog, to see how well GE lives up to the environmental goals it has set for itself. Is the company, in fact, on its way to becoming truly green, or is the program nothing more than marketing "greenwash"? CEO Immelt, of course, says he's sincere in his quest to become green. His critics say that GE is a major perpetuator of a carbon-based economy and, no matter how it tinkers with the details, can't possibly be considered a green company. Who is right?

It is a steep challenge for any old-line, industrial business to transform itself into a low-carbon and eventually a zero-carbon player. Yet companies like GE have to start somewhere. Given the resources that Immelt is directing toward Ecomagination, the company so far seems to be laying a solid groundwork for the future. The CEO says he will grow GE's green product lines to $20 billion in revenues by 2010, up from $10 billion in 2005. More significant, over the same period, the plan is to double GE's R&D spending on green tech to $1.5 billion.

Though GE's stock, as of this writing, has remained basically flat from the time Immelt took over from Jack Welch in 2001, some investors seem pleased with the Ecomagination strategy. "We use GE as a constant example, because it shows that there's a market for building renewable infrastructure," says Anne Kelley, the director of corporate governance at Ceres, the Boston-based group of investors and environmentalists that works on climate change.[17]

GE has already become the largest wind turbine manufacturer in the world, with $4 billion in annual sales. It has started selling low-energy light-emitting diodes (LED) for commercial uses such as in store signs. A chain of two hundred stores that replaces the neon in existing signs with 250 feet of red LEDs could save about $67,000 per year in energy costs and reduce annual CO_2 emissions by 1.14 million pounds, which is equivalent to the CO_2 absorbed each year by 142 acres of trees. GE says LEDs for home use, which consume up to 80 percent less energy than fluorescent bulbs, will be ready for market within two or three years.

One of the biggest criticisms of Ecomagination arises from environmentalists who believe that GE has simply taken products it was making anyway and put a green label on them. There seems to be some truth to that charge. Initially, as part of the program, Bolsinger and her team identified some seventeen products that generated about $6 billion in revenues in 2004. These included compact fluorescent lightbulbs, wind turbines, and solar cells, as well as some not-so-identifiable green products like locomotives, jet engines, and clothes dryers. GE says that each product labeled green has passed a two-step certification process developed by a New York City consulting firm called GreenOrder. First, Ecomagination products have to be substantially and measurably better in terms of operating performance than what's currently available from either GE or its competitors. Second, they have to be substantially and measurably better in terms of environmental performance. These are the products Immelt said the company would grow to $20 billion in sales by 2010.

"There's no magic in the $20 billion target," explains

Bolsinger. "Let's make the target big and bold enough so it matters and then figure out how to get it done. If we made it too easy people would just say it's business as usual. And if we make it so big that we're going to fail, that's crazy." Environmentalists say that these products may be marginally better than the old models, but they are still far from friendly to the ecosystem.

One of the products that made the cut is GE's Evolution locomotive. Here's why critics have a hard time swallowing Ecomagination. GE says that this new engine is 3 percent more efficient than the model it replaces, and that it will save the burning of roughly 10,000 gallons of diesel fuel a year, or nearly 190,000 gallons over its life span. That sounds great, until you realize that each of these locomotives still burns about 350,000 gallons a year. Imagine long freight trains headed to Wal-Mart warehouses. It certainly doesn't sound like the kind of technology that will help the United States get anywhere near the target of cutting greenhouse gas by 80 percent by 2050.

When I asked Bolsinger how she justified putting a product like a greenhouse gas–spewing locomotive under the Ecomagination banner, she was quick to defend her decision: "Unless you're going to say we're going to stop the world, that we're going to stop flying, that we're going to stop transferring freight, unless we're going to stop making electricity . . . that's a different question. I don't think anyone believes we're going to get an 80 percent reduction in greenhouse gas by 2010. That's a goal for 2050. So it's going to take some breakthrough, transformational technologies to make that happen. In the meantime, how are we going to cope over the next twenty years? It all comes down to CO_2, and when you're talking CO_2 you're talking fuel efficiency."

Over the long haul, Immelt believes that GE will be able to create transformational technologies that will put a real dent in greenhouse gas emissions. "Ecomagination was one way to show the organization that it was OK to stick your neck out, even if it makes customers a little bit uncomfortable. We just kept saying:

'Here's where we're going. Here's why we think it's good for both of us. And it's going to come someday anyhow, so let's get ahead of it.' "[18]

What Immelt has in mind is GE's next-generation locomotive, a prototype hybrid engine that rolled into L.A.'s Union Station in May 2007. The 4,400-horsepower hybrid diesel-electric behemoth carries a series of innovative batteries that capture and store the energy dissipated during braking. The energy stored in the batteries will reduce fuel consumption and emissions by as much as 10 percent compared with most of the freight locomotives in use today. As efficient as that sounds, the GE hybrid will still not provide what it takes to meet those 80 percent reductions in greenhouse gas by 2050. The key will be how soon business figures out how to make a low-carbon biofuel to run those giant engines. But it is a start.

One of the first big customers for GE's Evolution locomotive is China, which has plans for one of the most modern and efficient locomotive fleets in the world. The Chinese may care about cleaning up their environment, but they will not buy a technology that hurts them economically. GE and other major corporations have to figure out how to make green products more affordable for international markets. China burns tremendous amounts of coal. One way to reduce the greenhouse gas emissions thus produced would be for China to buy GE's highly efficient combined-cycle gas turbines. The problem is that they cost about 15 percent more than the traditional coal power plants that China is now building at a rate of two a week. Does that mean that China will turn away from these products? The GE executives who met with Chinese CEOs in 2007 report that they found them surprisingly open to adopting new green technologies and to finding a way for energy efficiency and environmental safeguards to proceed hand in hand. When the Chinese told GE it had to make gas turbines more affordable, the answer was "It will get more affordable when we build ten. The first one will never be affordable." The good news is the Chinese have started to license gasification technology to power ammonia and methane plants, a small but important step.

Eventually the world will have to use advanced turbines to replace older coal plant designs for a simple but crucial reason: it is very difficult to retrofit a traditional coal plant to sequester CO_2; the new gas turbine plants can do the job much more efficiently. As Bolsinger explains, "Let's say it's ten years away before we are really seriously sequestering CO_2 on any scale. The problem is that in ten years you will have built a whole lot of old-technology coal plants without the capability to sequester carbon, and you have to make the bet now." The sooner GE can drive down the costs of its gas turbine systems—which is part of its Ecomagination mandate—the sooner the Chinese may come to believe that green tech makes economic sense.

The catch? If you use cheap labor in Asia, Africa, and South America, you can make cheaper products, but that will likely cost future American manufacturing jobs. The hope is that the designing, installation, and servicing of these inexpensive green products will create new opportunities for workers in the United States. GE apparently is already moving green manufacturing offshore. CEO Immelt says, "We've actually made these emerging markets the source of new innovation. You know, the next generation of innovation is going to come from the emerging markets back to the U.S. Think about it—health care, water, and energy at super low costs and super efficiency. You're not going to do that here. You're going to do that in India. You're going to do that in China. You're going to do that in the Middle East. We have to use the emerging markets as a framework for the next generation of innovation."[19]

WITHIN THE ENVIRONMENTAL COMMUNITY, some worry about the strengthening ties between big businesses such as GE and environmental groups. The concern is that if the two traditionally antagonistic groups become partners, the green community will have a hard time serving as watchdog. Such criticisms are off the mark. The environmental community is full of smart, serious people who aren't likely to be hoodwinked by a big company. As we've seen, the cooperation between the Environmental Defense Fund and the utility TXU led to the scrapping of eight polluting coal plants. The partnership between Goldman Sachs and the Wildlife Conservation Fund resulted in the creation of a valuable preserve in Tierra del Fuego. The campaigns of investor groups such as Ceres and the Investor Network on Climate Risk have led to corporations taking action to reduce their carbon footprints. "The NGO community," says Bolsinger, "wants to know and scrutinize what you're really doing. I would also ask, 'What did we accomplish before we started working together?' I'd say the answer is 'not much.' "

3

How Less Is More

A Radical Business Model
for Fighting Global Warming

AL GORE IS A SERIOUS ENVIRONMENTALIST who is doing an impressive job in raising our consciousness of global warming. To accomplish this important task, however, he must use jet planes that belch greenhouse gas to travel around the world. Adding to his carbon production, the former vice president owns a home in Nashville, a condo in San Francisco, and a farm in Carthage, Tennessee, that consume heat, hot water, and electricity.

The work he has done has earned him a Nobel Prize, and it almost certainly requires extensive travel. He has to live in a house somewhere, and owning a second home is hardly rare for wealthy Americans. Gore also points out that he uses renewable energy and buys carbon offsets to mitigate his impact on our climate. For example, he may pay to plant enough trees to suck out of the atmosphere the same amount of CO_2 that he puts in when he flies to Sri Lanka. But offsets aren't a reliable way of reducing global warming. Gore's trees would have to live a long time to make a significant difference in carbon reduction. And who can be sure they've been planted in the first place? And there's simply not room on Earth to plant enough trees to offset the greenhouse gas we emit.

I'm not criticizing missionaries for saving the globe, nor advocating a damper on travel. But conservation is the low-hanging fruit for healing our ailing planet. Everyone wants to live a rich, abundant life, and there's nothing wrong with doing that. In fact, it is a goal society should strive to achieve for as many citizens as possible.

But we won't be able to achieve this without advances in technology. It's important to recognize that we're not going to save our way out of this problem. U.S. population is projected to grow by 34 percent between 2005 and 2050. Real GDP is projected to more than triple over that time period, which means a dramatic increase in energy demand, which is likely to offset a good portion of any gains in energy efficiency. That doesn't mean, however, that we can be cavalier about the earth's limited resources, especially as the world's population is expected to grow from 6 billion to 9 billion over the next fifty years. Using the world's resources and then buying carbon offsets may soothe your conscience, but it is not a solution. The hedge fund millionaire who flies his private jet to Aspen to stay two weeks a year in his "green" 10,000-square-foot vacation home ten miles from town is not helping the climate. The health-conscious jogger who sips Asian bottled water should note the required energy to produce and ship each bottle to the United States. And the organic-minded shopper who buys raspberries in the middle of winter should understand that they have traveled from Chile in a plane that was spewing CO_2 all along the five-thousand-mile route.

In the summer of 2007, an article in the Sunday style section of the *New York Times* pointed out that green had become the new black: trend-conscious consumers were buying the latest organically grown jeans and expensive Lexus hybrid luxury sedans. Paul Hawken, a longtime environmental activist, complained about the growing popularity of so-called sustainable products, whether jeans or furniture built with wood from replanted forests. "Green consumerism is an oxymoronic phrase," he said. He blamed the news media and marketers for turning environmentalism into fashion and distracting us from serious issues. "We turn toward the consumption part because that's where the money is," Hawken said. "We tend not to look at the 'less' part. So you get these anomalies like . . . 'green' fashion shows. Fashion is the deliberate inculcation of obsolescence."[1] In other words, you would do more for global warming if you kept your old jeans and didn't buy new ones every season—even those made of organically grown cotton.

Wal-Mart, as noted in the last chapter, has embarked on a green campaign to reduce its energy use and save money. That is certainly an admirable goal, but don't be fooled into thinking that Wal-Mart is a green company. Wal-Mart and many other big consumer companies face a dilemma. Can an organization that promotes endless consumption, that exists to sell as much as it can as cheaply as it can, ever be green? Many of the products Wal-Mart sells are made of petroleum-based plastics and transported from China on fossil fuel–belching cargo ships. They are designed to be bought cheaply, used briefly, thrown away, and then bought again. That's the opposite of sustainability. Even if the company manages to reduce the amount of carbon used to deliver and sell paper towels but ends up selling three times as many each year, it will amount to a net loss in the battle against global warming. That is a shame when the use of a dish towel would serve as well, even after factoring in the energy used in washing it. If a product is good for business but bad for the environment, it's likely that Wal-Mart will keep selling it.

You can't, however, blame Wal-Mart and other consumer companies for making and selling these products. After all, consumers want them, and Wal-Mart is in the business of maximizing returns for its shareholders. What must happen is that all of us need to find comfortable ways of living that have the least impact on the environment. In the streets of Stockholm, Copenhagen, and Paris, many residents ride bicycles, use public transit, carry cloth sacks for their groceries rather than use plastic or paper bags, and try to buy local produce as much as possible. They don't seem to be suffering. If consumers learn to do without the products of a throwaway society, Wal-Mart will not be able to sell them.

So cutting consumption is the first task. A new study by the consulting firm McKinsey and Company estimates that the United States could cut its energy use by 28 percent and its greenhouse gas by a similar amount through efficiency. That would go a long way in meeting that target of an 80 percent reduction in greenhouse gas by 2050. And we could do that without incurring extra costs to the economy. In fact, Diana Farrell, the director of McKinsey's Global Institute, says that businesses and consumers could enjoy at least a 10 percent return on their investment when buying energy-efficient appliances, lightbulbs, and insulation. "There are spectacular opportunities to achieve through energy productivity," she says. If we were to switch to more energy-efficient appliances, improve the insulation in our homes, live closer to our jobs or telecommute more, eat as much locally grown food as possible, and use cloth sacks to carry home our groceries, we'd have gone a long way toward tackling climate change without having to dramatically change our lives.

That would be a noble start, but though our intentions may be good, either we don't understand the math or we don't have the capital to make energy improvements today for a payback that will come tomorrow. Forty percent of our carbon footprint comes from existing homes and office buildings. Most of our houses could be better insulated. Tighter windows also would help. We should install fluorescent lightbulbs throughout the house. Solar panels on the roof would help cut greenhouse gas as would a more efficient air-conditioning system and appliances.

Why don't we all rush out and make such changes? Typically, solar panels alone would cost more than $30,000, and it might take another $30,000 to upgrade to double-paned energy-efficient windows. Such costs would be hard to undertake in the first place and might be difficult to recoup for most Americans, who, on average, move every seven years. We have not yet reached the point where appraisers and real estate agents are trained to sell the value of energy improvements to prospective buyers. At best they might point to the solar panel on the roof with no inkling of the dollar value of their savings.

What Duke Energy *Doesn't* Do

The advantages may be hard to quantify because energy efficiency is all about what it *doesn't* do. It is, in its essence, the substitution of cleverness for energy. If we use more fluorescent bulbs, more insulation, more efficient appliances, we will not need hundreds of new greenhouse gas–spewing power plants. Oil and gas fields will be developed more slowly because windows will leak less heat. The cleanest, greenest power plant is the one that is never built. But how do we create the incentives to do this?

Jim Rogers, the CEO of Duke Energy in Charlotte, North Carolina, may seem like a strange person to ask. Duke is one of the largest utilities in the country with 4 million customers and annual revenues of $15 billion. It operates twenty coal-fired power plants and is the third-largest producer of carbon emissions in the United States.

Rogers first became concerned with the environment in the 1970s, when, fresh out of law school, he took a job as an assistant attorney general in Kentucky and acted as the state's consumer advocate fighting rate increases from the utility companies. At one point, a utility wanted to put scrubbers on their coal plants to cut smog. The law at that time didn't require scrubbers on coal plants, but the CEO of the company thought that was the right thing to do. He put the scrubber on the back end of the plant and applied to get it included in an electricity rate raise. As Kentucky's consumer advocate, Rogers opposed the price hike. As he recalls, "I said, 'No way! I don't care if you clean up the air. The law doesn't require it, and if you were to do something good to clean up the air, let the investors pay for that, not the customers.' " Rogers lost the case because the state utility commission approved of the utility's attempt to reduce air pollution. "It was a real eye-opener," Rogers now says.

In the 1980s Rogers left the practice of law and joined the utility industry, eventually becoming the CEO of Cinergy, the Cincinnati power company, in the mid-1990s. At the time, Cinergy was burning more than 20 million tons of coal each year, making it among the highest consumers in the power industry. Rogers confronted the issue straight on: in his 2004 annual report he invited a group of twenty-three prominent business, political, and environmental leaders, as well as some Cinergy customers and employees, to write essays on the dangers of global warming. The group concluded that global warming was real and that something had to be done immediately. Rogers then called on his industry to take major action to hasten the development of clean-energy technology. As he wrote, "To simply avoid this debate and fail to understand the implications of the regulation of CO_2 and greenhouse gas on our company is not an option."

Never before had a utility taken such a bold and public stance on the issue. In 2006 Cinergy acquired Duke for $9 billion and Rogers, as the new CEO of the combined companies, set his environmental program into action. He committed to making his utility a source of reduced carbon emission through carbon sequestration technology—Duke has a pilot program under way—and through the application of state-of-the-art coal-burning technology. As one example, Duke will be the first utility in the country to install GE's new superefficient coal turbine that cuts greenhouse gas significantly over traditional coal plants. In 2006 he became one of the founders of the United States Climate Action Partnership (USCAP), the consortium of environmental and business leaders calling for a national carbon cap and trade system aimed at reducing CO_2 emissions nationwide.

Next Rogers found a way to tackle global warming that also

will make money for Duke: it is a new initiative called "Save A Watt." If widely adopted, this radical business model might help the United States become one of the most energy-efficient countries on the planet. President Bill Clinton, at his Global Initiative annual meeting in the fall of 2007, called the Rogers plan "a simple, brilliant idea that has the capacity to fundamentally transform what we're doing in the United States."

Save A Watt, as it has been described, shifts the burden of making homes more energy efficient from the individual to the utility. "If you have to count on people doing twenty things in their homes to be more energy efficient," says Rogers, "it probably isn't going to happen, even if you increase the rates 30 or 40 percent, because a person's utility bill is such a small percentage of his disposable income. However, if I'm motivated to go do that, and I have four million customers, I can make a difference."

The difference Duke and other utilities could make is in the amount of greenhouse gas they emit. A McKinsey study called "The Supply Curve" concluded that there has been chronic underinvestment in energy efficiency in the United States and that utilities are in a position to invest billions more in conservation before they hit diminishing returns on their investments. Rogers believes "you could get huge CO_2 reductions before you have to put carbon-capture sequestration to work, before you have to build more coal plants, more nuclear plants. And so when I saw this curve, it was eye opening. I said to myself, 'My goodness, there is so much that we can do on energy efficiency. What we need to do is figure out a way to go get it.' "

Rogers does not look like the radical thinker he is. With graying hair and conservative attire, he has the casual demeanor of a Southern gentleman. Sitting in his corner office of Duke headquarters, I noticed that Rogers was taking notes—something I've rarely seen during an interview with a CEO. He explained, "I used to be a newspaper reporter and I'm a lawyer by training, so I take notes."

Despite his manner, Rogers has faced his industry head-on. The fact is that utilities make money when they build more power plants. They ask their state utility board for the right to charge their electric customers for the cost of a new plant with a profit built in. Rogers's breakthough? What if the utilities got paid for generating *less* electricity? As he explains, "Essentially what I am proposing is that I eventually go beyond your meter and into your house. I might put in a more efficient refrigerator. I might be able to put a chip in your air conditioner to make it use less energy, I might put solar panels on your roof and double-paned windows in your house."

It would make sense for Duke to pay for these improvements because it has a lower cost of capital and a longer time horizon than its customers. While it might not pay for a home owner to buy new energy-efficient windows that have a twenty- or thirty-year payback in energy savings, things would work differently under Rogers's scheme. The improvements in the home would not come free to consumers. They would be in effect borrowing the money for their windows or air conditioners from the utility and would pay it down each month on their power bills. Duke might also install certain devices like solar panels and own and maintain them as it would a power plant. Duke's customers would be charged their proportionate share of its costs: they would pay 90 percent of what it would have cost to build a new power plant to generate the amount of electricity saved through energy efficiency. The customer's cost of each watt of electricity would go up—but less than if Duke had had to build a new power plant to meet demand. And overall, the customer's utility bill should be lower because of the energy-saving devices Duke has installed in her home. If a customer doesn't want the utility to fiddle with her house, she can simply opt out of the Save A Watt program.

Rogers explains another potential benefit of Save A Watt: creating new markets for entrepreneurs who are inventing green technology. "We install energy-saving equipment for our first million customers and if a better technology comes along, then we'll install it for the next million, and then another technology comes along that we'll use for the next million. So all of a sudden, you get this huge sucking sound. The guys in their garages experimenting with new technologies and ways to do things that are more energy efficient now have a demand for their product. The point is that capital and technology will come together and change the world."

Already Duke has installed smart meters in 500 homes in Charlotte, North Carolina, and 10,000 in Cincinnati that allow the company to monitor electricity use and encourage conservation. It says it will have 160,000 homes in its markets hooked up by late 2009. Duke may install more efficient lighting in homes in a few years—light-emitting diode (LED) systems, which use up to 80 percent less energy than flourescent bulbs.

David Mohler, Duke's chief technology officer, believes that the first phase of Save A Watt will conserve over the next few years the equivalent in power of two new coal-fired plants in the Carolinas alone. "That's two greenhouse gas facilities that don't need to be built," says Mohler, "and that's the cleanest form of electricity you can create."

Duke still has to persuade regulators in each state to buy into the Save A Watt program, and there's no guarantee they will go along. Utility boards, by nature, are conservative, and the tradition has been to allow for rate hikes only for new plants that are badly needed. But if Rogers can demonstrate, as he thinks he can, that, through conservation, customers will actually spend less for power, he may get the approval he needs.

Rogers has already received support from within his own industry. In 2007, when he presented his Save A Watt plan at the Clinton Global Initiative, seven CEOs of major utility companies, representing 22 million customers, stood beside him to demonstrate their approval. These leaders have formed the Institute for Energy Efficiency and have pledged to increase their annual spending for CO_2 reduction by $500 million to $1.5 billion. If they achieve their goal, it will be the equivalent of taking 6 million cars off America's roads each year.

• • •

EVEN IF WE DO TAKE ADVANTAGE of programs such as Save A Watt and make our homes more snug and energy efficient, the food, clothing, and furniture that we buy still contribute to global warming. Getting consumers to switch to green products represents an enormous business opportunity. Already roughly 35 million Americans buy so-called earth-friendly products: low-energy lightbulbs from GE and Phillips, organic honey from local farmers, and Priuses from Toyota. Whole Foods is one of the fastest-growing supermarket chains in the country. Although only a small percentage of its produce is locally grown, the company is making an effort to train and support local farmers. Home Depot now offers some 2,500 products under its new Eco Options program, and Toyota has become the largest car company in the world. The trend will only grow.

Yet, despite earth-friendly labels, most products today are not green. Our food requires petrochemical fertilizers and farm machinery that end up generating 12 percent of all the anthropogenic greenhouse gas emitted in the world. The production of synthetic fabrics requires petroleum, and the wood for our furniture may contribute to deforestation, which accounts for another 20 percent of mankind-induced greenhouse gas. Those of us who want to make responsible purchases are now confronted by a slew of products promising to be green. For the most part, this has been more harmful than helpful. Americans who buy a product labeled "green" may be encouraged to use more of it, resulting in more global warming. The rationale: if it's labeled green it can't be harmful to the environment, right? Wrong.

"The Six Sins of Greenwashing," a recent report by the Reading, Pennsylvania, firm TerraChoice Environmental Marketing, examined 1,018 consumer products that make environmental claims. Of those, all but seven made statements that are demonstrably false or that risk misleading consumers. It particularly singled out claims such as "nontoxic," "all natural," and "earth friendly," which are so vague as to be meaningless. The report cited paper products that promote sustainable forestry practices while veiling dirty milling and production practices. TerraChoice calls this the Sin of the Hidden Trade-Off, because it is the truth, but not the whole truth. Then there are those sport-utility vehicles promoted as fuel efficient, but only as measured against other SUVs. These commit the Sin of Relativism. The claims are true, but distract the buyer from more significant disadvantages of the product category as a whole.

The marketing world abounds with sinners simply because it is extremely hard for a company to create truly green products. A number of pioneers in the field are showing how to do this—while making a profit. One emerging movement of sustainability, Cradle to Cradle, is led by green architect William McDonough and his partner Michael Braungart, a chemist and a founding member of Germany's Green Party. Their book, *Cradle to Cradle: Remaking the Way We Make Things*, urges companies to make products designed from the outset with the intention that they will eventually be recycled, either back to the soil, harmlessly, or into some other product. McDonough told me that industry should operate much like a cherry tree that grows and replenishes everything around it. We should create highly productive enterprises that have *positive effects on their* surroundings and make completely healthful products that are either returned to the soil or flow back to industry forever. "It's a life-affirming strategy that celebrates human creativity and the abundance of nature," he says. "The key is not to make industries and systems smaller but to design them to do things that lead to good growth—more niches, health, nourishment, diversity, intelligence, abundance—for this generation of inhabitants on the planet and for generations to come."

McDonough has worked with GE, Google, Herman Miller, Ford, and Nike, among others. Applying the Cradle to Cradle philosophy, Shaw Industries has developed carpeting that can be continually reused, turning old carpet into new. A textile manufacturer in Switzerland, after switching to clean dyes, now exudes wastewater that's clean enough to drink.

No company has made more progress with the principles of Cradle to Cradle than furniture maker Herman Miller. The Michigan company now sells an office chair called the Mirra. The Mirra costs 20 percent less to manufacture than the company's popular Aeron chair, is 96 percent recyclable, and is made of fabric and plastics safe enough to eat. It's been selling faster than the Aeron. Most of its parts are designed to be recycled back into material for new chairs. The manufacturing requires significantly less fossil fuel than that of a traditional chair.

Why doesn't everyone build products this way? It isn't easy. Engineers and chemists at the company had to spend inordinate amounts of time finding safe, affordable materials and designing parts to be recyclable into new chairs. The Mirra chair took more than four years of extensive research and development.

While it might be feasible for a big, powerful company with deep resources to build or sell truly green products, the task is much more daunting for small companies. Paulette Cole, the founder and CEO of ABC Home, a fashion-forward retailer in Manhattan, wants to sell green products. She's making admirable progress but obstacles abound. ABC, with three hundred employees and sales of roughly $80 million a year, offers trendy couches, chairs, fabrics, and decorative items. As a retailer, Cole found that she was at the mercy of her suppliers. At one point Cole traveled to North Carolina to tell her furniture suppliers that she was taking her company in a green direction. She told them that ABC was going to create special labeling and information to educate the consumer, firsthand, about what they're buying. Cole went from showroom to showroom, speaking to the presidents of factories, saying, "Do you know where you're buying the wood? Is this from a responsibly managed forest?"

At first the factory managers would cock their heads and glance at one another, but eventually many of them seemed to understand the need to stop cutting down our old-growth forests, which aggravates global warming. "People would say," recalls Cole, " 'Well, you want to be a charity company.' That's not it at all. We want to be a model for how other companies can be sustainable, and if we're not profitable, they're not going to be inspired to do that." Cole eventually persuaded a number of her suppliers that using sustainable wood for their furniture would not only help reduce greenhouse gas but give their products a competitive edge in a crowded market.

Winning over the furniture makers was just the beginning: going green required revamping the ABC company culture. Cole added a whole new level of management to sort it all out. Inside the company, Cole and her team made sure all the store's packaging was biodegradable, all of its paper was recycled, and all of its printing was soy based. Many of those moves ended up saving ABC money, helping it to boost its profits.

Next, Cole felt the company had to be completely transparent about its products. That meant calling a product green only if it met the exacting standards it set for itself, which assure the wood is from a responsibly managed forest or from salvaged sources instead of old-growth and endangered forest species. ABC's program was developed under the guidance of Rainforest Alliance. Today, about half of ABC's reproduction furniture complies with Rainforest guidelines, and of those pieces, about one in ten earn certification from the Forest Stewardship Council, the gold standard for sustainable forestry practices. The process of vetting the wood can be very tedious and expensive. It means, among other things, keeping track of furniture origins and getting suppliers to fill out forms to verify that the wood was farmed sustainably. In some cases Cole found that the green products cost no more than the rest of her line. But in others, the cost of going green was prohibitive. In Brazil, one manufacturer said his furniture would be 40 percent more expensive if he used certified wood. Cole is now working with that supplier to help it find affordable sources of sustainable wood.

Cole is wrestling with a dilemma faced by many small businesses: can a product be green if it is shipped to the United States from thousands of miles away on greenhouse gas–spewing jets or ships? The ideal would be to buy locally, using furniture made from sustainable wood. Cole says she would like to buy more locally, but woodworking craftsmen are scarce in New York. For the time being the best she can do is to sell sustainable products from overseas.

Although buying locally seems to be the best way to reduce one's carbon footprint, this is not always the case. Researchers from the University of California, Davis, discovered that the distance a product travels from the factory or farm to the consumer is important but so is the way that product is made and transported.[2] The researchers found that strawberries shipped from Chicago to other parts of the country can actually end up emitting less greenhouse gas than those driven by a farmer to his local market. That's because the Chicago berries get shipped in bulk, which consumes less energy per box compared with a farmer carrying his produce in his small truck. The same can be said about furniture. A factory overseas that uses efficient manufacturing techniques and ships by bulk could make a piece that eats up less energy than one that is made locally but has been produced using wasteful practices.

Until she can find more clean sources for her furniture, Cole has decided to plant a tree for each piece of green furniture she sells. Her inspiration came from an old tradition practiced by furniture makers in France who replanted a tree for each one they cut down. But trying to offset the carbon you emit can be fraught with problems. Will the tree ever get planted? Will it die or be cut down before it has had a chance to soak in enough carbon to make a difference? Cole hopes to avoid these problems by paying for trees to be planted by the Greenbelt Movement, a nonprofit in Kenya founded by Nobel Peace Prize Laureate Wangari Matthai. Matthai has so far enabled one hundred thousand African men and women to plant more than 30 million trees, which helps combat global warming and spurs economic and community development. These trees will be tracked by a global positioning system (GPS), the same technology that gives us directions in our cars. The technology allows the Greenbelt Movement to keep watch over Kenya's forests as well as forests elsewhere in Africa. It will help identify areas that are ideal for planting new trees and then monitor their growth over time to ensure they are doing their job sucking up greenhouse gas.

Four years after Cole's trip to North Carolina, more and more suppliers are shipping her furniture made from sustainable forestry practices. The green furniture that ABC features on its second floor sells well. One reason: Cole's marketing campaign attempts to get the customer to look at green products differently. Through advertising, on-floor displays, and trained salespeople ABC tries to persuade the customer that a piece of furniture may look nice, but it won't really look beautiful in a home unless it is contributing significantly to reducing global warming. "This world is still very much the cusp," says Cole. "Every choice that we make in our lives, in terms of integrating green and lifestyles, is about a new way of being and a new age of thinking."

4

High-Rises and
Low-Rises

Creating Green Working and
Living Spaces

We should pursue a strategy of hope, a strategy that allows us to create a world of interdependent natural and human systems powered
by the sun in which safe, healthful materials flow in regenerative cycles, elegantly and equitably deployed for the benefit of all. Doing so
is ultimately an act of love for the future, an act that allows us to take
steps toward not simply loving our own children, but loving all of the
children, of all species, for all time.

—WILLIAM MCDONOUGH

IN THE FALL OF 2006, more than a year after Katrina merci-
lessly pounded New Orleans and left thousands homeless, Bill Mc-
Donough toured the abandoned homes and rubble of the lower
Ninth Ward with Brad Pitt. The Hollywood-heartthrob-turned-
activist, in an earth-color work shirt and jeans, made an odd bedfel-
low with the distinguished-looking McDonough. Pitt was working
with a nonprofit organization called Global Green USA and was
raising money to build 150 low-income green homes in the poor-

est neighborhoods of the crippled city. He hoped to get from Mc-Donough some radical ideas on how to proceed. In place of the dilapidated houses, the two shared a vision of an environmentally sound complex of single-family homes and apartments resting on a site next to the Mississippi River levee. On this sultry day, McDonough, an architect, a designer, an entrepreneur, and one of the world's foremost green thinkers, was discussing with Pitt whether it would be wise to rebuild in an area in harm's way that could be hit with more hurricanes. Perhaps new houses could be built on stilts? McDonough was also discussing with Pitt the intricacies of his Cradle to Cradle philosophy, a sustainable vision of a world where all products and buildings are made of safe materials that can be recycled in endless loops.

The two worried that the effects of global warming would fall disproportionately upon the world's poor. As global warming caused hurricanes to intensify in the Gulf and other coastal regions over the coming years, more and more homes would surely be destroyed. It made no sense, argued McDonough, to build conventional houses that would contribute to global warming, help hurricanes strengthen, and continue a cycle of destruction. The rebuilding of New Orleans, he believed, was an opportunity to show that developers, even in a place as poor as the lower Ninth Ward, could build sustainable housing on a tight budget. A few weeks earlier Pitt had appeared on the *Today* show, telling Ann Curry, "My goal is to see something tangible, to see something built that can become an example, a template . . . a flagship for other people who are facing rebuilding."[1] But what exactly?

McDonough, who had long stressed that the environmental movement had to take into consideration economic equity, believes that green had to be about a lot more than Hollywood celebrities driving a Prius—as Pitt did—or building million-dollar environmentally cool houses in Beverly Hills. Any business needs to balance a triad of concerns—economic growth, environmental health, and social equity. "What if," McDonough likes to say, "these issues were addressed at the beginning of the design process as *triple top line*. That's where the magic begins."

McDonough is referring to a passage in his book *Cradle to Cradle* that explains that any green business needs to balance and honor what he describes as a triangle of Ecology, Economy, and Equity: "In an infinitely interconnected world, triple top line thinkers see rich relationships rather than inherent conflicts. Their goal: to *maximize* value in all areas of the triangle through intelligent design. When designing a housing project, for example, they would ask: How can this project restore more landscape and purify more water? How much social interaction and joy can I create? How do I generate more safety and health? How much prosperity can I grow?"[2]

As they strolled past one ruined house after another deeply engaged in conversation, McDonough laid out the challenge of building green low-income housing on a draconian budget. He knew what Pitt wanted to do would be a tough architectural challenge. Electricity from solar panels costs two to three times the current rate residents pay. The cheapest building materials get shipped on greenhouse gas–belching ships from Brazil and China. Energy-efficient appliances cost more.

McDonough believes that an important element of any sustainable design is to use as much local material and labor as possible. When he was a student at the Yale School of Architecture in the early 1970s, McDonough traveled with a professor and a few classmates to the east bank of the Jordan River Valley. The group was competing in a government-sponsored contest to build new housing for Bedouins who needed somewhere to settle after new political borders had curtailed their nomadic lifestyle. When the team arrived, they encountered a great scarcity of local resources—food, soil, energy, and especially water. But the homes that were already in the valley were of a simple and elegant design, well suited to the locale. They were a model, McDonough said, of "building homes using the right things for the right place."

A competing team had proposed Soviet-style prefabricated housing blocks[3] to be constructed with steel and concrete, much of it imported from distant locales and then assembled on the site. McDonough's team took the opposite approach. They decided to build adobe houses that local people could build using indigenous materials such as clay and straw, horse, camel, or goat hair and, most important, the sun. As McDonough recalls in his book *Cradle to Cradle:* "The materials were ancient, well understood and uniquely suited to the hot dry climate. The structures themselves were designed to optimize temperature flux over the course of the day and year: at night their mass absorbed and stored the coolness of the air, which would keep the interior temperature down during the hot desert days."[4]

This approach promised to create local jobs and reduce the amount of greenhouse gas not only during construction but in daily use. McDonough's team won the contest. He says he learned from the experience to always repeat the question: "What is the right thing for the place?"

Since then, his 46-person architecture firm William McDonough & Partners in Charlottesville, Virginia, has applied this philosophy to buildings it has designed for Herman Miller, the Gap, and Nike. Ford Motor CEO William Ford Jr. hired McDonough to be chief architect for the $2 billion redesign of the River Rouge car factory in Dearborn, Michigan, which is turning this grimy car plant into an environmental showplace. McDonough persuaded the chairman of Gap to put a grass roof on his San Bruno, California, office complex. The grass, argued McDonough, is good for drainage, doesn't need maintenance, and provides UV insulation, and the birds love it, too. Today the roof of the San Bruno building has grass and wildflowers growing on it. The interior, lit by walls of glass and decorated with swaths of indoor plants, in many ways resembles an undulating meadow. McDonough used raised floors through the whole building so he could take the nighttime air, let it flow under the raised floor, and let it cool down the building all night like a tent in Jordan or a hacienda. The place is also 30 percent more energy efficient than state law requires.

McDonough has successfully applied sustainable design in buildings built for big companies with big budgets, but would green work in poor neighborhoods of New Orleans where budgets are tight? Was Brad Pitt jousting at green windmills? Would this project (the first site is currently being prepared for construction) make economic sense? Could it be replicated in other poor and low-income neighborhoods? As these questions whirled through my head, I recalled a recent conversation I had had with a New York developer named Jonathan Rose, which suggested that McDonough was indeed onto something significant.

Green and Affordable

A fiftyish scion of a prominent New York real estate family stretching back to the 1920s, Rose speaks with passion and enthusiasm when you mention "green" and "low-income" in the same breath. For that's what he has been doing for the past two decades—developing housing that's both environmentally friendly and affordable to build. As of 2007, Jonathan Rose Companies had become a fast-growing, profitable firm that owns, designs, or manages over $1 billion of low- and mixed-income properties, schools, performing art centers, and museums nationwide. Among his accomplishments, Rose, in effect, has proven that you don't have to be wealthy to live in a green home.

The significance of Rose's work is that he has demonstrated that a green building, if designed properly, can be built on a tight budget. Sustainable housing doesn't necessarily have to be something only the rich can afford but rather a blueprint that can spread widely. This is crucial since America's homes and buildings generate roughly 40 percent of all its greenhouse gas each year. Yes, it is crucial that utilities increase their use of renewable sources of energy such as wind and solar to help provide heat and hot water and run our appliances, but the nation will never reach its greenhouse gas targets unless the structures that we build over the next twenty-five years are designed to be energy misers. The U.S. Census Bureau expects the U.S. population to grow by 90 million to nearly 400 million by 2050. If the housing we build for them is not energy efficient, it's game over.

James Kunstler, in his book *The Long Emergency*, points out that more than 80 percent of everything built in America was constructed after World War II and most of it with a car culture in mind. Half the U.S. population lives in suburbia, and when you live in a 4,000-square-foot McMansion in the exurbs of Atlanta, you live an energy-intense lifestyle. Heating that huge amount of space is one thing, but just as damaging is the fact that every commute, every shopping trip, and every visit to the doctor requires you to get in a car or an SUV and burn more fossil fuel.

Kunstler argues that global warming and diminishing oil supplies will make us stop building car-centric, sprawling suburbs. "America is in a special predicament," he writes, "due to a set of unfortunate choices we made as a society in the twentieth century. Perhaps the worst was to let our towns and cities rot away and to replace them with suburbia, which had the additional side effect of trashing a lot of the best farmland in America. Suburbia will come to be regarded as the greatest misallocation of resources in the history of the world . . . Before long, the suburbs will fail us in practical terms. We made the ongoing development of housing subdivisions, highway strips, fried-food shacks and shopping malls the basis of our economy, and when we have to stop making more of those things, the bottom will fall out."[5]

Kunstler's vision is overly Malthusian, but he does have a point about the inefficiency of a suburban lifestyle. By Rose's calculation, housing built in the suburbs—whether it is for low-income dwellers or up-and-coming Gen Xers—hogs energy. "A typical suburban single-family house," he says, "when you add in the cars needed to get back and forth to the office or to the grocery store, uses four times the amount of energy as a multifamily house near to mass transit where the parents can take a subway or bus to the office and the kids can walk to school. That's *four* times." And these residents living near mass transit aren't necessarily suffering in this model. Rose's equation allows for them to drive to the seashore—if they wish—for weekend getaways. "If we put people near mass transit and stress high-density housing," Rose says, "we can take future growth and actually use it to reduce energy use. Whereas if we support urban sprawl, we're just digging ourselves deeper and deeper."

Two interesting demographic trends will drive more and more Americans toward high-density urban housing. First, the retirees of the baby boom generation are not moving to Florida or elsewhere in the Sunbelt at the same rate as their parents did. More and more suburban baby boomers are starting to move into the cities because they want to be near museums, concert halls, and theaters. Basically, this generation feels young and lively enough to re-create the lifestyles they enjoyed when they were university students, and to do that many are moving back into the city. Next, the generation now in its twenties and thirties also prefers to live in cities. And finally, a large percentage of future population growth will come through immigration, and many of the nation's new arrivals will end up living in cities where they may already have family connections. That doesn't mean that suburbs will go away, but that cities should grow faster and that any new suburban development should trend toward high-density housing near mass transit.

Rose, who has built or has under construction projects in Albuquerque, Denver, Manhattan, New Haven, Seattle, and the South Bronx, among other places, has already proven his theory that many Americans would enjoy living in high-density urban housing if it is designed smartly. In 2007, Rose completed a mixed-income housing project in Denver called Highlands' Garden

Village. This 26-acre mix includes residential structures, retail stores, offices, and an art school. The town houses, single-family and senior homes, which range in price from $160,000 to $400,000, rest on the site of an abandoned amusement park. The project's energy-efficient housing is near mass transit, and its design encourages walking and biking, and includes an activity center where residents—some of them retired professors—offer classes or put on performances. Rose was shooting for the feel of an old-fashioned town, with a square, sidewalk life, and a place to meet with neighbors. Highlands' Garden Village has a waiting list for tenants, a remarkable achievement in a city that has a 10 percent vacancy rate for rental apartments. Rose's project, on which he made a profit, has won many prizes as a model of western green urbanism, including the Urban Land Institute's 2007 award for excellence.

Rose got his idea for Highlands' from his grandfather and great-uncle, who started the family firm in 1928 based on a simple but very progressive notion for the times—never build more than two blocks away from public transit. When Rose Associates, as his family firm is called, built two office towers in Boston in the 1970s and 1980s, one was directly across from the South Station subway stop, the other a block away. In the 1980s Rose Associates also co-developed the nation's first transit-oriented mall in the country, Pentagon City in Washington, D.C., which has a subway stop adjacent to its basement level. The idea, Rose explains, was that buildings near mass transit would always be in demand. Workers like being able to get to the office without driving their cars, and areas with mass transit tend to be densely developed, making it hard to overbuild and drive rents down. A report called "Emerging Trends in Real Estate 2007," produced by the accounting giant PricewaterhouseCoopers and the Urban Land Institute, pointed to the promise of properties near mass transit: "[L]ocations, especially near mass transit stops, remain attractive to investors and developers. People look for greater convenience and reduced car dependence. Suburban nodes will increasingly look more urban with mid- and high-rise apartments clustering around shopping centers and office cores and in new town centers."

Over the past decades, such a strategy helped build Rose Associates into a powerhouse. As of 2007, the company has under development or management more than 30 million square feet of office towers, commercial retail centers, mixed-use complexes, and high-rise residential buildings throughout the East Coast. The financial success of Rose Associates has allowed the family to be among the leading philanthropists in New York City, as evidenced by the Rose Center for Earth and Space at New York's American Museum of Natural History, and Jazz at Lincoln Center's Frederick P. Rose Hall.

As a young man, however, Rose grew restless working for the family firm and wanted to drive development in a new direction. As an undergraduate at Yale, he had studied urban planning and learned a new, greener way to build than his family's approach. He felt that his family firm was too big and successful to change its business model, so in 1989 he left the management of Rose Associates to other family members and formed Jonathan Rose Companies: "I wanted to do more adventurous things, creative, complex, more working with nonprofits."

When Rose started working on green building projects in the late 1980s, the art was practically unknown. But early in his education, Rose, like the young Al Gore, had learned about the dangers of global warming and felt he should do something about it. What he's done is to create a different model of real estate company and not just because he builds green. Rose figured that to be a successful builder of green low-income communities he'd have to master a full range of skills. Traditional real estate firms splinter into different disciplines. Some build green, others manage property, and still others do urban planning or specialize in working with nonprofits. Rose's firm does all of the above plus more: he has even started a green investment fund to provide capital for green real estate projects. "We asked what does a city need," says Rose. "And we put together a holistic package of green real estate services. You need to finance the projects, design them, build them, manage them, and those are realms that typically don't talk to each other."

HOW EXACTLY DOES ROSE make green housing affordable to the masses? He has capitalized on that hoary nostrum "Less is more." Sitting in his airy Fifth Avenue office on a July morning, Rose, adorned with a bushy salt-and-pepper beard and wire-rim glasses and open-collared white shirt, shows me on his MacBook a black-and-white photograph of two Inuit standing in front of their dome-shaped igloo. "This is the greenest structure I know," he exclaims, "and not just because it's made of ice and then melts back into the earth." This bear of a man who exudes boundless energy and a can-do attitude proceeds at a rapid clip as if we've already wasted too much time when it comes to global warming.

The design of the igloo, he points out, is incredibly sophisticated. The Inuit have figured out how to make the walls just thick enough to capture the heat of the earth and the heat of the people within it so even when it's minus 30 degrees outside it stays between 34 and 60 degrees inside. In other words, every aspect of the design reflects the way they live. What's interesting, for instance, is that the Inuit eat blubber, and it's no coincidence that the igloo's temperature is ideal for storing blubber. The icy skin of the igloo also serves as the frame of the structure, a very efficient use of materials. They've designed their main room as a circular dome and have developed a way of sleeping in a circle to maximize body heat and comfort.

Lesson over. Rose flips to another photo of one of his projects to show how igloos relate to inexpensive green construction. Winrock International in Little Rock, Arkansas, is a nonprofit organization founded by Winthrop Rockefeller whose mission is to help the developing world grow their economies by using sustainable agriculture practices. The foundation had wanted to move to new headquarters, and a local developer had shown them a design of a typical suburban sprawl office building—a rectangular box with a flat roof and tinted windows. But Winrock wanted an environmentally sound building. No problem, said the developer, we'll just add some solar panels and recycled materials. Nothing wrong with that, except that every time you add a new green feature to a building it drives up construction costs.

Taking a page from the Inuit, Rose presented Winrock with a design that uses 55 percent less energy than a conventional building, and offers fresh air and lots of sunlight, at the same cost the developer was charging for a cookie-cutter suburban office building—about $140 a square foot. The difference, says Rose, "is that like the igloo we used the skin and the structure of the building to reflect the surrounding nature and how people work and live."

The 24,000-square-foot rectangular building carries a three-story glass facade that sweeps along a berm overlooking the Arkansas River. Its V-shaped roof makes it look like a waterbird, with wingspan open, about to land softly on the waters of the river. Imagine crossing the elegance of Philip Johnson's glass house in New Canaan, Connecticut, with the soaring feel of the air terminal at Chicago's O'Hare.

Here's where the Inuit come in. Because it rains a lot in Little Rock, Rose, working with the New York City–based architect firm HOK, designed the gull wing–shaped roof to collect the rainwater, which flows into a nearby cistern and is later pumped back into the building for heating and cooling. HOK's architects did computer studies of the sun angles at different times of day to slant the V-shaped roof so that it lets as much light inside the building as possible while keeping the heat out. Significantly, this roof didn't cost any more to build than would a traditional flat roof.

Walk into the interior of the Winrock building and you'll find the same stingy use of materials as inside an igloo. The architects got rid of everything—no hung ceiling, no Sheetrock except on the fire walls around the stairwells. You won't find overhead fluorescent lights either—the building brings in so much daylight workers usually need no lighting. On cloudy days they can just use their desk lamps. (The interior does have a few energy-efficient overhead lights for night events.)

With very few lights generating heat all day—by some estimates 60 percent of the air-conditioning a building requires is used to counteract the heat cast off from its lighting—the building needs much less air-conditioning. In a conventional building you'd have ducts in the ceiling (a big expense), and the air you'd pump out of them would have to be very cold (an even bigger expense) to still provide cooling by the time it mixed with the warm air as it floated down and finally reached the worker at her desk. To make the air-conditioning more efficient, Rose and his team added a twelve-inch raised floor, similar to that used in the Bank of America Tower, which creates a hollow space under the entire floor that acts like a duct system but takes advantage of nature's heating and cooling cycles. Each night, when the outside air cools, it circulates through the hollow layer, chilling the concrete floor, whose thermal mass holds that chill for the next day. Everyone has her own floor vent to control the temperature of her office by regulating the amount of cool air that enters the work space. Because Rose is only cooling the bottom 8 feet of space, it doesn't matter if it is 100 degrees near the ceiling as long as the spot where the Winrock employees sit stays cool.

To cut down on greenhouse gas during the construction, the Winrock project relied heavily on recycled material and on building supplies harvested or extracted from within a five-hundred-mile radius of Little Rock. Rose figures that these local materials represented about 78 percent of the building's $4.2 million construction cost. For its efforts the Winrock headquarters earned the Gold rating from the U.S. Green Building Council (USGBC), the second-highest rating for green buildings. (Platinum is the top.)[6] Says Frank Tugwell, Winrock International's president and CEO, "Our building shows that it doesn't take a lot of money, just good planning and common sense, to build green."

• • •

ROSE HAS APPLIED MANY of the same "less is more" design principles to keep costs down in his low-income projects. "That's the thing about affordable housing," he says. "The organizations funding the project won't pay you extra for being green. You have to work within the parameters and that really drives us to better solutions." Working with the Harlem Congregations for Community Improvement (HCCI) he has built an apartment building for low-income New Yorkers called the David and Joyce Dinkins Gardens, named after the city's first African American mayor and his wife. This eighty-six-unit complex, designed by Dattner Architects, will house teenagers who have grown too old to be in foster care as well as low-income families. In Harlem, some 40 percent of the children who have grown too old to stay with their foster parents end up homeless. HCCI, which owns the building, gave Rose two instructions: make it green and make it affordable.

Working on a tight budget of $170 a square foot—currently high-end commercial building construction costs in Manhattan ring in at $700 to $800 a square foot—Rose needed to take some unorthodox steps. "We try to design buildings that are healthier, happier, greener, lighter, cleaner, brighter, better, and are made simpler, and that's how we're getting there affordably."

Solar power systems are way beyond the $170-a-square-foot budget for Dinkins Gardens, so Rose installed sunshades on this six-story brick building, carefully angled to let in the most light and the least heat. Key is that the building is made out of concrete blocks and precast slabs that have holes through their centers. As with the Winrock building, Rose turns the slabs on their side and puts them under windows as vents so fresh air is always coming in the apartment even though the window is closed. In New York City, kitchens and baths have to be vented by law, which usually means the air goes up through a long pipe and out the roof. Instead, Rose uses a small fan to circulate the air through the slabs and to the outside wall of the apartment.

The advantage? At Dinkins Gardens every apartment is completely sealed off from others with no traditional heating, cooling, and ventilation ducts connecting them—the heat comes in through pipes to a radiator. Old-fashioned vents carry the noise and odors from other apartments, and cockroaches find the vents a convenient way to make the rounds. The Dinkins Gardens apartments, on the other hand, are quiet, clean, and nearly bug free—at least as much as is possible in Manhattan. The air quality is better because the vent system is always circulating fresh air through the apartments. In the winter a radiator warms the air that trickles in through a small vent in the window frame. The thermal mass of the floors absorbs the heat and radiates it back into the apartment. Because Rose eliminated all the ducts, he can save money and make the building more energy efficient than one with a traditional system. A bonus: because of the space saved from having no duct work, Rose gets an extra 1,000 square feet of space, which means he can make the apartments bigger at no extra cost. Plus by putting the boiler on the roof instead of in the basement, he doesn't have to build an $80,000 exhaust vent, and that frees up enough room for another studio apartment—all of which drops the cost per square foot of living space.

One of the tenets of green buildings is to use local labor. The more you can avoid workers traveling back and forth to the work site in their greenhouse gas–belching pickups and SUVs, the better. The foster kids assigned to live in Dinkins Gardens attended a local building trades academy where they learned carpentry, masonry, and electrical work. These youngsters provided some of the labor to build Dinkins Gardens, which now houses the building trades academy in its basement, where they will continue to learn skills and work on other green, low-income housing in the neighborhood.

Dinkins Gardens will consume 20 percent less energy than is required by current national energy standards for construction. Turning the $20 million project green raised construction costs only 1 percent, while yielding a 10 percent return on investment.

A few miles away from Dinkins Gardens, in a blighted section of the South Bronx, Rose is building a mixed-income green complex called Via Verde, whose cascading roofs will be covered with green gardens. This will make the buildings more energy efficient—grass and plants work as great insulators. The facades will be covered with electricity-generating solar panels. (Prices for solar have now dropped enough for small amounts to be applied in low-income housing with the help of government subsidies.)

Rose is only one man in a small but growing field. To make any sort of significant dent in global warming, the green equations he has derived have to spread throughout the construction industry. To help make that happen, Rose has been working with a nonprofit called Enterprise Community Partners—one of the largest financers of low-income housing in the country. Enterprise started a program with the Natural Resources Defense Council (NRDC) called Green Communities, which has raised $555 million to finance low-income green housing and has lobbied around the country for green housing standards. Partly as a result of the efforts of Green Communities, thirty-six states added significant new green policies to their low-income housing tax-credit programs. "Our goal," says Rose, "is that in five years all affordable housing built in the U.S. will be green."

WHILE ROSE HAS PROVEN that green can make sense for new construction, a larger problem looms. In the United States we add 1 percent of our housing stock each year from new construction—and, of course, it's crucial to make that green. The remaining 99 percent of our existing building stock continues to pump greenhouse gas into the atmosphere. When New York City mayor Michael Bloomberg announced his green city initiative, he said that 20 percent of the city's greenhouse gas came from cars and an astonishing 80 percent came from buildings. So if the large cities of the world are to put a dent in greenhouse gas emissions, they will have to figure out how to green existing buildings. "If you can make green buildings in low-income housing," says Rose, "you can make green buildings affordable anywhere."

The most compelling economic argument for turning an existing building green is to weather the higher energy costs that will arise if Congress passes a federal carbon tax, which a growing number of business leaders and politicians believe is all but inevitable. The math is simple. If a carbon tax drives up the cost of heating, cooling, lighting, and traveling to and from a building, the most energy-stingy building will have higher profit margins than structures that squander oil, gas, and electricity.

Rose has a formula for making old buildings green, and to back his notion he's formed the first private equity fund designed to invest solely in green building. Called the Rose Smart Growth Investment Fund, it only buys buildings that are within walking distance of mass transit (shades of Rose's grandfather) and then greens them. As of 2007 the fund has raised $30 million, and the investors are in for the long haul—a forty- or fifty-year hold. "It's so clear to me," says Rose. "A building close to mass transit doesn't cost any more than a building that's not, but ten years from now when energy costs are higher—the one with mass transit will be much more valuable. And it's just amazing to me the rest of the world doesn't see that."

For its first investment, the fund bought in 2006 the fourteen-story Sterling and Vance office buildings in downtown Seattle, which, of course, are near public transportation. Rose spent about $35 a square foot to turn the buildings green. In Seattle's temperate climate, Rose discovered that with the right design elements the buildings didn't need central air-conditioning. On the windows, he simply installed shades and a reflector that bounced daylight in but helped keep heat out, minimizing the need for lighting and reducing glare on computer screens. After he removed the hung ceilings, the new open ceilings reflected more daylight into the offices, again reducing the need for lighting. He installed ceiling fans and pulled out the carpeting, which exposed the thermal mass of the terrazzo floors that retains cool in summer and heat in winter. He replaced the old steam heating system, which had one thermostat for the whole building, with individual controls on each radiator so each worker can adjust the temperature in his space. Before Rose's changes the heat was so uneven and at times excessive that workers flung open their windows in winter. He put thermal glass in all the windows and added weather stripping. So far electrical and heating consumption has dropped 15 percent.

What Rose found was that by greening the buildings he was saving 30 cents a square foot in energy, but was charging higher rents because he could market Sterling and Vance as a green building. In other words, after marketing the building as a hip, green place to work, Rose was able to raise rents from the previous $16 to $18 a square foot to $24 to $26. While some new high-end green office towers have been built in Seattle, the Sterling and Vance buildings basically have no competition in the midmarket. If you're a tenant and want to be in a green building in downtown Seattle, this is your choice.

Will Rose's green approach to building catch on? Rose acknowledges that it won't be easy and will take time. Just try persuading a tightfisted landlord to invest big money in his building up front to get a payoff in energy savings that may be years, even decades, away. What if he sells the building before then? What if energy prices drop? These are certainly valid concerns, but what they fail to take into consideration is that in all likelihood energy prices will keep rising, driven either by dwindling oil supplies or by a federal carbon tax or cap and trade system. Those who start to retrofit their buildings and houses now will not regret it when carbon energy prices increase dramatically. Also, as we saw in chapter 3, programs such as Duke Energy's Save A Watt initiative would allow utilities to supply the capital for energy-saving devices when landlords balk.

Financial incentives are not the sole motivator. "You have to make people want to live a green lifestyle," Rose says. "Society has started to recognize the need to become green and that is rapidly changing every day. So I asked psychologist Daniel Goleman, who wrote the book *Emotional Intelligence*, 'How do we get the culture to change on climate?' First, he said, you have to get people to connect to the problem empathetically. Although you can't prove that Katrina was caused by global warming, it made a lot of people see the suffering it could cause. The more people make the connection between human suffering and climate change, the more it leads to change. But if you don't have a solution, it leads to despair. If you tell people you have to go to 80 percent reductions in greenhouse gas by 2050, it's too big a problem and too far off; it's the next generation's problem. When you say 10 percent by 2010, they say, 'I can do that'; you've got a measurable problem and you can get there. So we should take this momentum that our culture has now, we should lay out solutions people can feel proud about achieving, and that's what builds a movement and then you have continuous improvement. I'd say don't worry about perfection, get to work right now."

Santa Monica Modern

While Rose continues on his quest to increase the nation's stock of affordable green housing, a developer on the West Coast is taking aim at the opposite end of the market—luxury homes. Highland Street runs through the hills of Santa Monica, California, just a few blocks above the Pacific Ocean. Nestled among its rows of 1920s and '30s bungalows with their broad front porches and quaint dormers, stands a very unusual house, one that architects might describe as California modern. To the unschooled eye, the structure seems to be a conglomeration of interconnected cedar, glass, and steel rectangles punctuated with an occasional balcony, bracketed by industrial-style railings. Native, drought-resistant bushes grow on the front lawn and a stone pathway leads to a wooden front door. This four-bedroom, two-story house might seem out of place in such a neighborhood full of vintage homes, yet somehow its warm wood facade and stepped-back stance blend nicely into the streetscape.

Built in the spring of 2006 by a start-up company named LivingHomes and designed by the iconic Southern California architect Ray Kappe, this structure stands as one of the greenest private residences in the country. Most amazingly, it took only one day for a crew with a large crane to assemble the skeleton of this home, a prefab built at a factory in Sante Fe Springs, California. That means the house was produced with 75 percent less construction waste than that from traditional home construction. Most of the elements in the structure derive from recycled materials or are manufactured using sustainable manufacturing processes. Because it is prefab, workers drove fewer trips to the construction site in pollution-making trucks.

LivingHomes founder Steve Glenn both built and lives in the house on Highland Street. He designed it to incorporate a unique blend of materials and innovative environmental systems, making the 2,480-square-foot home 80 percent more energy efficient than a conventional residence of similar size. If every house were as efficient as this one, we would be able to reduce greenhouse gas enough to meet that carbon-reduction target of 80 percent by 2050. Another way to look at it: buildings use 76 percent of the electricity produced by coal plants.[7] If every new building were as efficient as Glenn's, we could practically avoid the need to build any new coal plants.

Working to take advantage of Santa Monica's sunny climate, Glenn ensured that about 70 percent of the home's heating, electricity, and air-conditioning would be produced by on-site solar cells known as photovoltaics. Point these silicon panels at the sun and out comes electricity. Other green features include solar water heating and radiant-heated floors; a native landscape and a rooftop garden to divert storm water and provide insulation; an indoor garden that filters air pollutants and is a prolific generator of oxygen; super-resource-efficient Energy Star appliances from Bosch; LED lights from Permlight that use a fraction of the power of conventional lights; an integrated storm-water management system that includes subsurface irrigation, a 3,500-gallon cistern, and gray water recycling system designed to divert sink and shower water for irrigation.

Glenn launched LivingHomes, an eight-person real estate development firm, in 2005. Two years later a dozen green houses were under contract or under construction. His house on Highland Street was the first he completed and also became the first private residence in the country to achieve the Platinum rating from the USGBC, which certifies buildings for environmental soundness under its LEED program (Leadership in Energy and Environmental Design). Since the LEED program's inception in 2000, 550 buildings in the United States have been certified, but only twenty have been designated Platinum. In Los Angeles County, three public buildings have achieved a Platinum rating: the NRDC's Robert Redford Building in Santa Monica, the Lake View Terrace Branch of the Los Angeles Public Library, and the Audubon Center in northeast Los Angeles.

Other private residences have earned LEED ratings, but no one before Glenn had been able to meet its exacting standards for Platinum. We think LEED will have great brand recognition among home buyers who think about the environment, as it does now in commercial space," notes Glenn. "I want the consumer to have an objective way to distinguish the kind of work we do from others. And frankly it keeps us honest about what we're doing."

Though Glenn has wanted to be a builder since he was a child, he got detoured first into high tech and then into the William J. Clinton Foundation, where he developed an AIDS program in Mozambique. When he started to think about architecture, Glenn observed that most of the housing industry produced the same houses over and over again. "Take your new-home market," he says. "In general builders offer four or five kinds of styles—Tudor, Mediterranean, colonial, ranch, and splits." A business could be built, he reasoned, by targeting home buyers in a more creative and environmentally responsible way. When Glenn launched Liv-ingHomes in 2005, he decided to concentrate on the California modern house—floor-to-ceiling glass, steel beams, and wood walls—that would be among the most ecologically advanced in the world. "I looked at the market and said, 'Wow! The time is right. Consumers are going to want this.' "

But building a Platinum house was not going to be easy. Glenn thought that it would cost about $250 a square foot, but the true number turned out to be closer to $390, or more than $900,000 for the house, not including land. Though houses are expensive in this part of California, and Glenn argues that the price is not out of line for a steel and glass house designed by a renowned archi-tect, this ticket is almost four times the national average.

Part of the cost overrun came about from foundation prob-lems and site conditions that would have held true for any kind of house being built there. Also, Glenn hadn't realized how difficult it would be to find materials to meet the requirements of a Plat-inum LEED house. His staff spent months tracking down materi-als in what turned into a massive research project. Where can we get countertops that have the least impact on the earth? Which parts of the house can be made from materials produced by local suppliers to cut down on the fossil fuel used in delivery? Shipping wood all the way from, say, Brazil would burn too much fossil fuel to allow for a Platinum certification. Which paints and adhesives are made of nontoxic materials? Which solar systems yield the best cost-benefit ratio?

Eventually, Glenn and his team tracked down the greenest products available: a company called Eco-Lumber Co-op, for in-stance, delivered the cedar and other woods for the exterior and interior walls, certifying them to be forest friendly. The insulation, manufactured by US GreenFiber, was made of 100 percent recycled denim jeans. Even the Jacuzzi had to come with a top Energy Star rating.

Glenn had to think green even where it wasn't obvious. One would surmise that stone kitchen counters would be environmentally friendly, but marble from, say, India would have to be shipped halfway around the world, creating a lot of greenhouse gas in the process. Plus, once you quarry rock and rip it from the earth, the landscape can't be restored to its original state. Instead Glenn found countertops that from a distance look like black soapstone but are in fact made of recycled newspapers stuck together with organic glue. Called PaperStone, and made by a company in Hoquiam, Washington, the counters cost about the same as granite ones, will withstand heat up to 350 degrees, and are guaranteed for ten years. When they need to be replaced, they can be returned to the company and made into new countertops. If you use Paper-Stone counters instead of stone in a small kitchen, you'll save 1,233 gallons of water (used in the quarrying and finishing of the stone), and the equivalent in energy to 16 gallons of gasoline.

Glenn designed the house with movable walls, modular millwork, and a structural system that allows for the easy addition and reconfiguration of the space. If the owner wants to remodel, he can do so with much less disruption, waste, and expense than in a traditional renovation. At the end of the home's natural life, it can be easily disassembled for recycling or reuse at another location.

To get his Platinum rating, Glenn had to keep his house beneath 3,000 square feet. This runs counter to the trend in mainstream home building where the industry labels even the biggest houses "green." What this generally means is that a house gets an Energy Star rating. In other words, the insulation, double-paned windows, and appliances meet federal efficiency standards. Typically such a house consumes 15 percent less energy than one that doesn't earn the rating. Yet if you compare two "green" houses, a

3,000-square-foot structure will use 40 percent more energy than a 2,000-square-foot house.[8] For the most part, builders who are slapping "green" labels on their 4,000-square-foot McMansions have simply figured out how to make home owners feel better about buying a big house. After all, doesn't such a huge house eliminate the possibility of living green? In fact, it's the environmental equivalent of driving a Hummer. Whatever energy-saving program or solar array you install, a bigger house uses more resources to build, more energy to run, and more fuel to get to. When it comes to living green, less is truly more. The couple who builds a "green" 4,000-square-foot house in the woods uses far more material and energy than necessary, and, in most cases, the houses are sited so far from town that you have to drive miles to pick up a quart of milk.

When I raised these issues with Glenn he said, "If it's a big home, you have to work harder in the other LEED categories to make an energy-efficient house, and as a developer I totally buy that. These homes are going to be built one way or another, so I might as well build them in a better way. Let's not fight gravity."

Glenn's houses are expensive. The affluent people who buy them probably also own a Prius or a Lexus hybrid. Their motivation is to help fight global warming, not because these purchases necessarily make economic sense. But that may change. While LivingHomes may never be a mass-market builder, it is a pioneer searching for and experimenting with the green building materials and designs that someday could well be applied to less expensive housing. Glenn says, "That's always the role of the small business. We're the pioneers; sometimes we get shot, sometimes we become the settlers and survive. My prediction is that within fifteen years green building goes away as a category; it will just be the way things are built."

On a Clear Day You Can See . . . New Jersey

I'm riding an elevator up to the forty-first floor of what will soon be the new Bank of America Tower on the corner of Sixth Avenue and Forty-second Street in midtown Manhattan. A few minutes earlier, Douglas Durst, whose family owns the building along with Bank of America, had handed me a hard hat and asked whether I had a problem with heights. Now, as we sped up the side of the towering construction site in an open-cage lift, watching the pedestrians and yellow cabs on the street shrink to specks, I began to wish I hadn't spoken so soon. But it was too late to turn back, so after the lift slammed to a halt, I stepped onto the rough concrete surface of the forty-first floor, which was littered with construction debris, and walked reluctantly toward a gaping hole in the side of the building where floor-to-ceiling windows would one day be installed. On this cloudless, crystalline spring day, we looked out over a sweeping panorama that included the Hudson River, the Statue of Liberty, Wall Street's clumped towers, and then beyond the East River to jumbo jets descending in a row as they glided silently to a landing at JFK.

"Not a bad view, hey?" said Durst, who was standing next to me.

That's about as exuberant a statement as you'll ever hear from this New York developer. Wearing a conservative business suit, gray tie, and white hard hat, Durst looks like he'd really rather be planting tomatoes on his five-hundred-acre McEnroe Organic Farm in upstate New York. His modest demeanor, however, belies the fact that he heads one of the most powerful real estate companies in the country and on this day, as he takes me on a tour of the Bank of America Tower construction site, you can tell he is very proud of this particular project. And it's not just because his 1,200-foot skyscraper will be the second tallest in Manhattan after the Empire State Building. More important to Durst: he is building the greenest skyscraper ever built in America. In fact, Durst expects it to be the first skyscraper to earn a much-coveted Platinum LEED rating from the U.S. Green Building Council.

Durst hopes his building will act as a template for the greening of America's buildings, a crucial element in the battle against global warming. As we noted earlier, buildings are the single largest contributor to global warming, accounting for roughly 40 percent of America's CO_2 emissions. Architecture 2030, a Santa Fe, New Mexico, nonprofit think tank that has launched the 2030 challenge, an initiative to make our building stock more energy efficient, calculates that if we can reduce the fossil fuels we use in our existing and new buildings by 50 percent over the next twenty-three years, we won't need to build any new coal plants. Currently the United States has 619 coal plants, with 150 new ones in various stages of development.

Durst calculates that his $1.3 billion skyscraper will meet that target, using 50 percent less water and energy than a conventional skyscraper its size. And the beauty of the math is that the green cost is only 3 to 4 percent more than for traditional construction. Because Durst and his family expect to own the building for the next thirty or forty years, he will more than make up for that extra cost in operating savings. The formula is simple. The construction cost of a building such as Durst's tower accounts for only 10 percent of the total lifetime cost of operating and maintaining it. Any savings in energy and water costs offer Durst and his tenants a huge potential for savings. Bank of America, which will house its giant trading floor in the Tower, will see energy savings, too. As Durst says, "Building green is the same as building smart."

In Europe building owners often have a forty-year horizon when investing in commercial real estate, so almost anything extra spent on energy-saving design and technology will eventually pay off. "In America," says Durst, "more developers are starting to think that way, but not nearly enough."

Almost all the buildings completed in the United States over the past decade were built without a LEED certification. Instead,

American developers typically try to build as cheaply as they can and then flip the building for a quick profit. An extra 3 to 4 percent in costs for greening a building would cut directly into a developer's bottom line. The good news is that many buildings going up today hope to win some kind of LEED ranking. Very few developers, however, are stretching for a Platinum rating, which goes the furthest in terms of cutting back on energy use and would made the biggest dent in global warming.

Durst believes that more developers would be motivated to reach for a Platinum rating if the federal government passed a carbon tax. "It would be a big difference," says Durst in his typically understated manner. If energy costs rose thanks to a carbon tax, tenants would begin to demand more efficient buildings from developers. Those who failed to build them would be at a competitive disadvantage. Who would want to buy a place that generated high energy costs?

Critics argue that the Bank of America Tower may have a green patina, but we shouldn't forget that what Durst is building is in fact a fifty-five-story tower of concrete and steel to house thousands of workers who will consume gargantuan amounts of lighting and air-conditioning. That's hardly a formula for achieving net reductions in greenhouse gases. James Kunstler, in his apocalyptic book *The Long Emergency*, believes that we will run out of oil and not be able to produce enough clean energy to replace it. As a result our major cities will fail utterly to adapt to climate change, making the building of skyscrapers such as the Bank of America Tower sheer folly. The only safe haven—in Kunstler's eyes—will be small rural towns where residents live on locally produced food. (How they will pay for this food remains to be seen.) "In the short term," he writes, "the biggest cities will be places of desperation, disorder, and economic loss. New York City could become largely uninhabitable if the electric grid and the natural gas distribution system malfunction even moderately. Boston, Philadelphia, Baltimore and Washington present similar logistical nightmares, though they contain far fewer high-rise buildings than New York City. All other things equal, I believe every one of these cities will shed large fractions of their populations . . . year after year."

Kunstler may be right, but sound reasons exist to suggest he's not. The advances in biofuels and solar power beginning to emerge from Silicon Valley and elsewhere, coupled with the drive toward greater efficiency, should allow the world to cobble to-gether enough energy to keep our cities humming. That's espe-cially true if we convert our buildings from energy hogs to energy misers along the model of the Bank of America Tower.

What's often overlooked is how much more efficient city sky-scrapers can be than sprawling, suburban office parks. When you calculate the greenhouse gas emitted by workers commuting to and from the office, the extra land needed to house employees in buildings that are only a couple of stories tall, and the heating and cooling inefficiencies of low-rise glass boxes sitting in a sun-baked field, you find that suburban office complexes can generate four times the greenhouse gas per person than their city counterparts. To drive home the point, Durst explains that "the Bank of America Tower sits on two acres. To house the same number of office work-ers in the suburbs, you'd need to use three to four *hundred* acres of land." Some 95 percent of people who work in Manhattan take mass transit. The Bank of America sits between the Sixth and Sev-enth Avenue subway lines, part of arguably the best mass transit system in the world. "This is the type of place," says Durst, "where you want to build high-rises."

Locating new office buildings in cities where there's adequate mass transit is a great start, but it isn't enough to meet that radical target of an 80 percent reduction in greenhouse gases. An in-creased use of clean fuels to heat, cool, and light our buildings should eventually be able to reduce those greenhouse gases enough to meet perhaps half of that target. The rest will have to come from the design of the building itself. The Bank of America Tower shows that even a target this extreme is within reach.

As we continued our tour on the forty-first floor of the tower, Durst stopped and pointed to a rectangular hole in the concrete floor, which turned out to be part of the building's superefficient air-conditioning system. "One of the biggest complaints we get in buildings," he says, "is that you can have two people sitting right next to each other and one is hot and one is cold, but this floor vent alleviates the problem." Durst is obsessed with air-conditioning because, surprisingly, skyscrapers rarely use heat except on the very coldest days of winter. The heat generated by lighting, computers, and people is more than enough. The challenge, says Durst, is to get the heat out.

Like a Rube Goldberg machine, a traditional air-conditioning system in a big building is highly inefficient. You have to cool air to a chilly 55 degrees and blow it through large ceiling ducts, where it exits and then drifts down through a layer of hot air gathered near the ceiling. After the 55-degree air has traveled all that distance and been mixed with the hot air near the ceiling, it finally drifts down to a worker sitting at her desk at a comfortable 62 degrees. A lot of energy has been wasted. Durst explains how in the Bank of America Tower he built a hollow space beneath each floor of the skyscraper that fills with cool air. Each worker has her own vent in the floor, which she can open and close to let in air that's been cooled to only 65 degrees. The beauty of the system is that you are cooling the person not the entire office space. No one cares whether the temperature near the ceiling is 100 degrees if the worker's space is comfortable.

To cut down on the need for air-conditioning even more, Durst has installed special glass embedded with small ceramic heat-reflecting particles called Frits, which keep the interior temperature cooler on a typical sunny day. And to reduce electricity usage for the air-conditioning he does need, Durst installed thirty-seven huge tanks in the basement, which hold 35,000 gallons of ice. A giant ice maker, made by an Englewood, New Jersey, company called CALMAC, fills the tanks at night when electricity rates are cheaper than during the peak hours of use during the day. When electricity rates are highest—such as on a hot August afternoon when everyone is running their air conditioners full blast—Durst's system doesn't even run. It simply uses the cool air from the melting ice. Over the last few years he has been testing a smaller version of this system in one of his other buildings and says, "It's much more efficient than we ever thought."

As efficient as it is, the Bank of America Tower will still need electricity for air-conditioning and lighting. I ask Durst how he can win a Platinum rating if he's buying electricity from a utility such as Con Edison that generates its power from CO_2-spewing plants. Like a chess master, Durst is already a step ahead of me. "We only buy electricity that's generated by wind power." For a small premium, Con Edison offers its clients clean electricity generated by giant wind farms already being built in upstate New York. This is good news for green developers in New York and California, but it doesn't help those erecting buildings in, say, the Southeast, where renewable energy is in short supply.

Interestingly, Durst decided not to install solar panels, which convert sunlight into electricity, on the building. He had draped them on the sides of 4 Times Square, a building he completed in 1999 that sits on the same block as the Bank of America Tower (it's sort of like owning both Boardwalk and Park Place). Durst found the panels were not cost effective. "When we put them on 4 Times Square the payback was twenty-five years, and the life expectancy of the panels was only twenty." As the price of solar panels continues to drop, they could within the next three to five years help buildings such as the Bank of America Tower become completely carbon neutral.

Durst's under-the-floor cooling system saves energy (and costs) in another important way. A big issue for tenants who want to change the layout of their floor is that it's very expensive to move all the ductwork in the ceilings and walls. Tenants won't have that problem with this design. All the electricity, heat, and cooling systems are in the floors; you just move the walls around. "It's very inexpensive to do that," says Durst. Plus, think of the greenhouse gas avoided by having fewer workers traveling to the site to do the renovation job and by eliminating the need to manufacture new metal duct systems and then deliver them in diesel-spewing trucks.

The Bank of America Tower is also designed to minimize what's called sick-building syndrome, where dirty outside air pumped into the stucture combines with fumes from toxic building materials to literally sicken the occupants. The outside air moving through Durst's building gets filtered, taking out 95 percent of the pollution particles, compared with 35 percent for a traditional building. He estimates that the productivity of workers in a green building increases 15 percent because of the cleaner air, more light, and use of nontoxic building materials. "We see lower absenteeism; workers don't mind spending more time in the building," he explains. "Some tenants understand this, and some will never understand this. We tried to explain the increased productivity to one prospective tenant who ran a hedge fund, and he said they made so much money they couldn't be any more productive."

Durst and I ride down the elevator and then descend the stairs to the subbasement of the tower, 85 feet below street level. Gingerly we hop over planks laid down over large puddles. In the distance, a construction worker's boom box plays a U2 song. Groundwater leaches out from the Manhattan schist that holds up the building, and I'm thinking it's just another leaky basement until Durst sets me straight. The water seeping from the stone, plus rainwater that's gathered on the roof, plus the gray water from the building's sinks and showers all flow into a large cistern under the elevator shafts—space that's usually wasted. The water will supply the building's cooling system. He points to the cistern and says, "We'll be saving about ten million gallons of water a year." Which means the building will use half the water of a typical skyscraper and will slice its water bill accordingly.

Many green buildings today opt for what's called a green roof. The idea is to grow grasses and plants on the roof to absorb the rain runoff, provide a home for birds, and insulate the building. While green roofs work for many buildings—the Europeans have been installing them for years—Durst decided to pass. His engineers found that the rainwater would seep through the soil and carry nutrients into the piping of the water-recycling system. Eventually algae would start growing in the pipes, causing a large and expensive maintenance headache.

As I was admiring the large cistern beneath the elevator shafts, I thought to ask Durst how he became an environmentally minded developer of some of the biggest, most expensive buildings in the world. Did he have an epiphany about building green? Did he wake up one morning and decide this was the right thing to do?

He paused in thought for a few moments and then in his typical understated way said, "No."

"What was it then?" I asked.

"It was a long process, starting when I was a child. My grandmother Rose, who was my father's mother, played a very influential role in my life and in the formation of my early beliefs. She was a very early environmentalist. She was involved with Central Park and tried to keep it green when New York Parks Commissioner Robert Moses began to add ballparks, playgrounds, and a zoo. Growing up, we were always taught to leave a place better than we found it. That's what we're trying to do."

The Durst Organization grew into one of New York's oldest and largest family-operated real estate development and ownership firms, with a history that dates back almost ninety years: in fact, in 1913 Douglas's grandfather built the New York Times Building. As copresident with his cousin Jonathan, Douglas Durst represents the third generation of family members at the corporate helm.

The Bank of America Tower is not his first foray into green building. His company's 4 Times Square flagship office tower set new standards for environmental practices when it opened in

1999. Among other green things, the building contains state-of-the-art digital monitoring systems that control high-efficiency gas-fired heating, ventilation, and air-conditioning systems. In 2000 the Natural Resources Defense Council conferred its "Forces for Nature" award on the Durst Organization for the environmentally friendly aspects of 4 Times Square.

Given this kind of success, why aren't more developers building green? Durst will be the first to tell you that it's not easy. The most difficult thing about designing a green building is all the extra planning. "The easiest thing to do is to build a building like the one you built the last time," says Durst. "And to make the same mistakes you made the last time. As our engineers like to say, at least they're our mistakes." From the very beginning of the design process, it takes extra time to understand something like the building's recycled water system to see if it really will work. Durst holds retreats with the engineers, architects, and contractors to just throw out ideas and come up with more suggestions to make the building as efficient as possible.

Durst's team constantly searches for ways to cut energy from the construction phase. All materials must be carried to the site; all the equipment is manufactured. It takes a lot of fossil fuel to make a building like this, and energy costs are rising. That's one major reason the price of construction is going up. The 2.1-million-square-foot Bank of America Tower cost $600 per square foot to build. When Durst finished 1 Times Square, the building next door, in 1999, it cost him $300 per square foot. As of 2007, construction costs in Manhattan had hit $700 to $800.

One of the ideas Durst and his team came up with was to mix the concrete with slag taken from the boilers of nearby steel plants. That keeps the slag, which is rich in carbon, from ever entering the atmosphere and at the same time cuts by half the amount of greenhouse gas created by making the concrete.

Another thing he did was to buy material made locally—a slow, painstaking process—to cut back on the greenhouse gas released by shipping in steel, glass, and piping from overseas locations thousands of miles away. Durst soon realized that sourcing locally was not only an environmental concern but also an efficiency concern: "If you order something from thousands of miles away and it gets lost, it's really lost, and it slows down the job, and you're using resources inefficiently."

As we completed the tour and headed back toward his office on Sixth Avenue, Durst turned to me with a glint in his eye and said, "And that's what green building is really about. It's a smarter way to do things."

5

The Car
You Are Driving
Was Designed by
a Madman

STEVE FAMBRO DIDN'T get into the car business to save the world. He did it to go faster on freeways.

Fambro was driving thirty-six miles a day, during rush hour, to and from his biotech job in La Jolla, California. As traffic slowed to a crawl, motorcycles whizzed past in the carpool lane. He wanted to do the same, and after trying a motorbike and becoming worried about his safety, he decided he wanted to do the same in an enclosed vehicle. He bought a hybrid, but as an engineer he still yearned for a vehicle that got even better fuel economy.

That left electric cars. The selection was discouraging: tiny, boxy vehicles with a short range that took a long time to charge. "Anything you could buy looked as if it was designed in the 1970s," says Fambro.

So he decided to start his own car company. In November 2008 Fambro will begin selling the Aptera. That means "wingless" in Greek, but don't think this car won't fly. It's a sleek two-seat, three-wheel electric vehicle with a top speed of 95 miles per hour, and it comes in two versions: all electric and hybrid. Made of a space-age composite material, the hybrid gets 300 miles per gallon, while the electric goes 100 miles on a single five-hour charge. And it looks great in the carpool lane.

For the first time since the early twentieth century, America is seeing a flowering of entrepreneurship in the auto industry. Today at least fifteen new electric car companies, each working on a wide range of technologies, have launched or plan to launch models. Several of the start-ups are clustered around Silicon Valley, drawing on the brainpower and pocketbooks of high-tech engineers and venture capitalists. These upstarts are not modest. They believe they can do what major automakers have failed to do: bring an electric car to the mass market.

The big automakers, of course, are not going to let these upstarts go without a fight. Toyota, GM, and Honda all have designed prototypes that promise to redefine the automobile. Toyota is working on a plug-in version of its Prius hybrid—just charge it in an electrical outlet in your garage and drive the first thirty or so miles gasoline free. GM has unveiled the Volt, a sleek-looking plug-in hybrid with a range of roughly 640 miles.

800 Million Cars in China?

What's driving this change? One sultry August afternoon I was crawling along Interstate 10 on my way from Santa Monica to downtown L.A., surrounded by hundreds of cars venting greenhouse gas and smog into the air. That day seemed particularly bad, even for L.A., because the cars weren't the only contributors to the smog alert. Depending on the winds, as much as a third of California's air pollution blows in from China.

The Chinese economy is growing at 11 percent a year, and its new, well-heeled middle class is falling in love with the automobile. If the Chinese begin to buy and drive cars at the rate

Americans do, some 800 million cars will clog China's streets and spew greenhouse gases and smog into *our* atmosphere. That's more than all the cars on the road worldwide today. And then factor in that India's rising middle class has its eyes on car ownership, too, as do their counterparts in the Middle East, Africa, and South America.

This is a frightening prospect. Yet the Chinese language character for danger also contains the symbol for opportunity. If the Chinese, Indians, Brazilians, and other citizens of the developing world are to enjoy the benefits of the automobile, the very nature of the vehicle must change. The world needs cars that are affordable yet do not contribute heavily to global warming. The risks of failure and of a poisoned, uninhabitable world are immense but so is the opportunity for innovation. Industry, up to now, has hardly acted as the environment's savior nor have its motives necessarily been to advance the public good at the expense of the bottom line. Nevertheless, we may be about to witness one of the more exciting and potentially profitable experiments in the history of capitalism: the race to build the greenest car of the twenty-first century.

The business world is coming to realize that the entrepreneurs and corporate titans who are the first to build clean, safe cars, made of nontoxic materials and powered by clean fuels, could lead the way in radically transforming our entire economy. If things go well, new businesses will be formed and hundreds of thousands of jobs created. The players in this high stakes competition will need to bet billions on which technologies will prevail. If they do that, if they have the vision to combine the profit motive with global necessity, new fortunes will be made (and old ones lost) in the drive to design the car of the future. As the largest industry in the world, automotive transportation, which sells a unit of its product every two seconds and employs millions of people, is key to the West's economic well-being. GM, Ford, and Chrysler have been shedding tens of thousands of jobs and losing market share. Michigan, the center of the U.S. auto industry, has endured six straight years of job losses with more to come—the longest stretch of employment loss in the state since the Great Depression, according to University of Michigan economists.[1] Ironically, global warming, which will force a radical redesign of the car, may be the best hope for reviving the American auto industry.

A perfect storm has hit the auto industry. Polls show that Americans now believe the vast majority of scientists who say that global warming is real and that cars contribute to it significantly. On 9/11 the country woke to the dangers of dependence upon very unstable parts of the world for its motor fuel. Over half of the oil America uses today is imported from abroad and in many cases from unfriendly regimes—particularly in the Middle East—that support and fund terrorism. No one wants a portion of our gas dollars to be recycled to al Qaeda training camps.

The geopolitics of oil and gas are shifting rapidly and not to our advantage. To power their vehicles, Americans burn roughly 14 million barrels of gasoline a day, or more than one gallon per person. Global demand for oil is expected to rise 25 percent by 2030, according to the U.S. Department of Energy. Yet supplies in many parts of the world are being depleted. Most experts believe that the price trend for oil over the next decade will be up, not down. Production of OECD (Organization for Economic Cooperation and Development) oil from the North Sea, Mexico, and the United States is declining. That puts the geopolitics of oil in the hands of OPEC nations such as Saudi Arabia and Iran. The volatility of gasoline prices that Europe and America have experienced over the past few years can be traced to the aftershocks of the decline in Western oil production. Dr. Peter Wells, an energy consultant for Toyota, expects that the amplitude of the shocks will increase more and more unless the West can produce more oil.

In addition to increasing production in the short term, the West must wean itself from its dependence on oil. That will be a steep challenge. A good way to begin is to increase mass transit in large and small cities and to service suburbs and other outlying areas with light-rail systems. Still, though in the future Americans may drive less and use public transit more, the vast size of the nation suggests that the private car is here to stay.

Why do so many Americans love their cars? Books and articles have been written to probe for an answer. But the bond is so strong that people are willing to drive at 75 miles per hour a two-ton chunk of steel that is involved in the deaths of more than forty thousand Americans every year, that maims many more, and that ruins the environment. For that privilege they pony up an average sticker price of around $28,000. Ever since Horace Greeley urged his generation to "go west, young man," and pioneers, armed with the notion of Manifest Destiny, headed west in their covered wagons, Americans have displayed a restlessness, a desire to wander the open spaces. This tradition carried on in the twentieth century with Jack Kerouac criss-crossing the country and recording his adventures in *On the Road,* and with a drug-crazed Hunter S. Thompson driving his Great Red Shark convertible in *Fear and Loathing in Las Vegas.* And if this summer you were to examine the license plates in the parking lots of Yellowstone National Park, you'd see that Americans are still driving vast distances.

Putting aside the romance, however, most of our driving is fairly local. Even so, Americans may no longer have the choice to give up their cars. According to Kevin Phillips, author of *American Theocracy,* empires, as they grow, invest heavily in their infrastructures and then have a hard time switching to new conditions. As Phillips explains, the Dutch empire of the seventeenth century lost prominence when technology moved from water and wind power to coal. The British empire of the nineteenth century lost sway when coal power gave way to oil. Now America, heavily dependent on oil, remains wedded to the car. We have built rows of suburban houses designed to support an automobile-centric lifestyle. The oil and auto industries have invested hundreds of billions of dollars in factories, oil wells, and gas stations that employ armies of highly trained workers. Such vested interests are powerful and will be slow to change.

The challenge is not to give up the car. It is to create a radically different kind of automobile that is not dependent on oil and that doesn't contribute significantly to global warming. It's a hard challenge, but there are signs that it may be achievable.

The danger is that if the United States doesn't take the lead in the race to build the green car of the future, China, India, Germany, Japan, or some other country will. As a result, the high value jobs and intellectual capital will be created overseas, leaving America a mere consumer of the cars and energy of the twenty-first century. Already Japan's Toyota plans to sell one million hybrids, or 10 percent of its total production, by 2010. Meanwhile Ford and GM have barely left the hybrid starting gate and are laying off tens of thousands of workers as the car market begins to shift away from large and profitable SUVs. In which country will future green jobs be generated?

Transportation now accounts for about 20 percent of the greenhouse gas Americans emit. Worldwide, that figure drops to about 14 percent because the citizens of other nations don't yet own as many cars nor drive as much as Americans do. Princeton professors Robert Socolow and Stephen Pacala, who have studied global warming, estimate that if the industry can build cars that average 60 miles per gallon (mpg) it would help avoid the worst-case global warming scenarios over the next fifty years.

Bill Reinert, U.S. national manager of Toyota's advanced technologies group, points out that automakers know of no inexpensive way to make today's internal combustion engine dramatically more efficient. In fact, an American Society of Mechanical Engineers report concluded that to produce more efficient cars would cost about $250 for every ton of carbon you keep out of the atmosphere. By contrast, paying, say, Brazilian farmers to replant the rain forests costs only $5 to $15 for every ton of carbon reduction. Reinert adds, "If you look at miles per gallon, that's probably the highest hanging fruit; you'd need a ladder to reach it."

Many in the auto industry argue that being forced to build cars that get high mileage would be too expensive and result in the companies losing money and having to lay off more autoworkers. Environmental groups, certain Democratic members of Congress—not including those from Michigan—and some experts see the answer in toughened corporate average fuel economy (CAFE) standards, the federal regulations governing mileage. On the surface this makes sense. The average has basically been flat since the early 1980s. So what's wrong with the new law that forces auto companies to raise the fleet average of cars, light trucks, and SUVs from 25 mpg to 35 mpg by 2020? Well, it will be chancy. In fact, it may lead everyone to believe we're solving global warming when we're not.

Up to now, not many Americans have rushed to buy smaller cars. GM, Ford, and Chrysler already make fuel-efficient cars. GM now has thirty models that get more than 30 mpg on the highway.[2] But American carmakers are not yet doing a good job. In fact, in addition to their cars being less desirable than the Prius, the profit margins on them are thin or nonexistent. Amazingly, Detroit loses money on most small cars it sells.

In the summer of 2007, as the U.S. Senate debated whether to raise CAFE standards, the auto industry fought back, running radio ads in eleven states to try to scare suburbanites into thinking that they would no longer be able to buy SUVs. One spot exhorted: "Why can't they let me make the choice? I'm all for better fuel economy but for me safety is my top concern."

The automakers have a point. Even if they make high-mileage cars, consumers may not buy them and not much will have been accomplished in terms of climate change. Let the consumers choose but also let them pay a price for gasoline that reflects its true costs—damage to health and the environment and the billions spent on keeping the international oil lanes safe. If gas costs $8 a gallon—as it does in many parts of Europe—wedging your body into a car smaller than an SUV suddenly doesn't seem like such a bad idea.

The simplest but most politically controversial way to change Americans' car-buying habits would be to impose a gas tax. In a 2006 New York Times/CBS News poll, 59 percent of respondents nationwide said they would support such a tax if it would result in less fuel consumption and less global warming. That is the position of, for example, Senator Richard Lugar (R-Indiana), who supports a tax credit for ethanol that would effectively create a $45-a-barrel floor on oil.

A gasoline tax of $2 or $3 a gallon may reduce consumption, but it must be designed carefully. Simply tacking a few dollars onto the price of a gallon of gas will hammer both business and consumers. That is why a small but growing number of academics, economists, and experts recommend a different kind of tax: a floor that would kick in only when the price of gas falls below a set price—for example, $4 a gallon. In other words, if, for reasons of supply, the price were to fall to $2 a gallon, the tax would kick in to bring it back to $4. Proceeds from this tariff would be returned to the taxpayer through cuts in other taxes. This approach would reduce fossil fuel consumption and imports. But it would do much more: it would make energy costs more predictable.

Anyone who wants to buy a new car or delivery truck today faces a tough calculation involving lots of guesswork: Will fuel prices remain relatively high, justifying the purchase of a more expensive biodiesel-fueled or hybrid vehicle? Will they fall, making the investment in fuel savings a costly mistake? If gas prices were guaranteed never to fall below $4 a gallon, and if the proceeds of higher energy levies were returned through a cut in the payroll tax, for example, people would have an incentive to drive less and buy more fuel-efficient vehicles.

Assume, for instance, you choose a Ford Escape hybrid over a standard version of an SUV and you drive twelve thousand miles a year. Now assume that you get a tax credit for buying a hybrid and that a federal tax sets a floor of $4 a gallon. Under those hypothetical circumstances, you could recoup the extra $1,218 on the hybrid sticker price in only two and a half years. (If gas dropped to $2 a gallon, the payback would take more than five years.)

Predictable fuel prices would also accclerate development of energy-saving technologies and alternative fuels. Many investors have stayed out of the green game even during times of high gas costs because OPEC tends to slash prices before competing tech- nologies can be developed—as in the 1980s, when gas prices fell 31 percent, to a low of 93 cents a gallon, just as alternative solu- tions such as electric cars and synthetic fuels began gaining mo- mentum. "Lenders in America are worried that the price of oil will come down again, and as a consequence it's hard to get big invest- ments in alternative energy," said Republican senator Pete Domenici of New Mexico. A price floor would benefit scores of entrepreneurs and the investors behind them.

If designed properly, a gas tax can be "revenue neutral": every dollar collected could be refunded by cutting the federal payroll tax. Peter Van Doren, editor of the Cato Institute's *Regulation* magazine, calculates that adding a gas tax of 50 cents a gallon would generate about $68 billion a year in new federal revenues. A worker making $30,000 a year might see his payroll tax cut by a fifth, or roughly $434—enough to offset the higher price of the gas he uses. His employer, who pays half the worker's payroll tax, would enjoy similar savings to help offset his increased fuel costs. Those who cut their energy use most would benefit most from this tax shift.

A well-designed gas tax looks like a good idea, but it has been hard to implement, perhaps because national administrations have been wary of the plan's history. When President Carter proposed a gas tax in 1980, the bill received only thirty-four votes in the House. President Clinton proposed a broad BTU tax in the early 1990s and was laughed off Capitol Hill. As Judi Greenwald, an en- ergy and climate specialist at the Pew Center on Global Climate Change, puts it, "Just about every politician who has ever pushed for a gas tax gets kicked out of office."

The philosophical opposition to a gas tax—that market forces should determine the true price of fuel—falls apart when you consider current government spending, including the billions to defend the flow of oil imports, as well as the public health costs of burning fossil fuels. Such factors constitute at least a $4-a-gallon subsidy on top of the current price of oil, according to the International Center for Technology Assessment.

What's the likelihood of a gas tax passing? Some conservatives like Nobel laureate Gary Becker and N. Gregory Mankiw, George W. Bush's former chief economist, support such a tax. But Arizona Republican senator John McCain told me: "Not while President Bush is still in power."

Whatever the political balance of power, there is little doubt that a gas tax would soon have car buyers clamoring for vehicles that get 60 mpg, thus forcing automakers to speed up their innovations. In the meantime, the auto industry is pushing ahead with the next generation of green cars. Its progress is not as quick as one might like, but it does offer hope.

Today's cars are marvels of engineering and, as Toyota's Reinert has pointed out, are fairly efficient—given what they are. The point is, there must be a better way to move people around. Amory Lovins, head of the Rocky Mountain Institute, an environmental think tank, calculates that every time you fill up your tank, 80 percent of the gasoline's energy is lost, mainly in the engine's heat and exhaust. The remaining energy is used to move your car. But if you weigh about 200 pounds and your car 4,000, only around 1 percent of the energy in every gallon of gas is actually used to move you. Consider the waste: the average American driver burns about 600 gallons of gas a year, and the energy of only six of those gallons moves her to the mall and back.

Teams of engineers and designers at Toyota, GM, and Daimler-Benz are working on radical new designs that promise to replace today's stock with cars that are lighter, that emit less greenhouse gas, and that might soon hit that target of 60 miles per gallon.

Most of these clean cars will be propelled by a hybrid drive system that uses a combustion engine working in conjunction with a powerful battery. Sales of hybrids in the United States rose by 35 percent in 2007. By 2011, car buyers will be able to choose from seventy-five hybrids, up from fourteen in 2007, according to J.D. Power and Associates. U.S. hybrid sales will jump sevenfold to 1.7 million vehicles in 2015—about 10 percent of the total market— from a quarter million in 2006. But a lot will have to happen between now and then to hit those impressive numbers.

Toyota plans to introduce an entire Prius car line in 2010, with various models carrying the Prius insignia. Most likely the line will include a small car, a family car, and a crossover utility vehicle, all eventually powered by high-energy lithium-ion batteries that can be recharged in the home garage. While Toyota has not yet disclosed exact mileage numbers, auto industry observers predict that the next generation of vehicles will get between 60 and 100 miles per gallon. That would be a dramatic improvement over the 2007 Prius, which averages 48 mpg—to say nothing of the average of 25 mpg for American vehicles.

GM, Daimler, and the BMW Group have formed a joint research project called the Global Hybrid Cooperation to develop a next-generation hybrid power system for passenger cars, light-duty trucks, and SUVs. Drawing from this research, Daimler also plans to launch in 2009 a hybrid version of its Citaro city bus, which uses a small diesel engine to charge a lithium ion battery pack located on the roof. The Citaro will use four electric motors—one for each wheel—and will offer 20 to 30 percent lower fuel consumption than conventional diesel engines. We have already seen that in cities like New York, San Francisco, and Seattle hybrid buses have cut down on greenhouse gas emissions, but they cost around $500,000 each, compared with $300,000 for a standard diesel bus. Until the costs come down considerably, we're unlikely to see widespread use of these hybrids.[4]

As of the writing of this book, Toyota is the clear leader in the race to build the green car of the future. In 1997 the Japanese giant launched the Prius, in retrospect a gutsy move, given that oil prices at the time were relatively low. Since the launch, the company has sold 851,000 of this $21,000 model, and in 2007 it sold 181,000 in the United States alone. That, however, is only a sliver of the U.S. market, which moves some 17 million cars a year. Hybrids are expensive and usually don't pay for themselves in gas dollars saved. It's not clear how many more customers will be willing to pay a premium to help save the planet. It seems likely that these cars will have to make economic sense to the consumer to attract a larger audience. At this writing, hybrids command at least a $3,000 premium over traditional models of the same car. *Consumer Reports* in 2007 said that with that kind of premium hybrids in most cases don't yet pay for themselves in gasoline savings without government subsidies. The hybrids can make financial sense for delivery trucks, limos, and taxis because of the high number of miles they are driven each year. New York City mayor Michael Bloomberg ordered the city's taxi fleet to convert to hybrids by 2010. On average a cabdriver may save $4,500 a year in gasoline costs.

Toyota believes that it can cut the cost of its next-generation hybrid system by half or more within a few years. To do that, the company must reduce the cost of the high-powered lithium battery it is developing. Lithium batteries—like the ones used in cell phones and laptops—hold more energy but are more expensive than the nickel metal hydride batteries found in today's Prius. Skeptics point out that battery makers have been promising breakthroughs in cost and performance for years, only to fall short.

Still, it is unlikely that a company as conservative as Toyota would be talking publicly about commercialization of lithium batteries if it did not believe they were close to viability. Toyota's Masatami Takimoto, executive vice president in charge of power train development, told Reuters in the spring of 2007 that Toyota's next-generation lithium-ion battery pack is ready to be used "any time."[5] He made this statement, it should be noted, just before the company delayed the introduction of the battery. If lithium batteries are not designed properly, there is the risk that they can overheat and catch fire. Despite these safety issues, Toyota says it will build plug-in hybrids with lithium batteries before 2010. In the meantime, signs of hope abound. A number of start-ups, such as A123, Altairnano, and EEStor, have been working on promising battery technology. Then in December 2007, ExxonMobil in conjunction with Tonen Chemical of Tokyo, revealed a new generation of lithium car battery that the giant oil company said is affordable and won't catch fire. The battery is now being tested by the independent Sandia National Laboratories in Albuquerque, New Mexico.[6]

The next-generation Prius promises to be revolutionary because it will be a plug-in hybrid. With this technology you could charge the lithium battery in your car every night with enough juice for thirty or forty miles of driving the following day. (Today's Prius can travel only a few miles solely on its nickel metal hydride battery.) That distance would work for most people. According to GM, 78 percent of drivers commute forty miles or less a day.[7]

If you forget to charge your battery or if you exceed forty miles, the gas engine would kick in and the Prius would drive like a regular car. Plug-in hybrids promise to be economical, too. Those thirty to forty all-electric miles will cost only about 3 cents a mile instead of the current 10-cent-a-mile cost of gasoline. (The savings will be even greater if a gas tax is levied.)

The fossil fuel savings would be impressive. Those who drive only short distances each day could conceivably use no gasoline at all. R. James Woolsey, the former CIA head and now a partner with VantagePoint Venture Partners, calculates that plug-in hybrids could conceivably get as much as a thousand miles per gallon of gasoline, if the hybrid alternatively uses gasoline that has a mixture of 85 percent ethanol, known as E85. If the engine is diesel and runs on biofuel, it would be using no gasoline at all.

The creation of a smart electric grid (see page 133) would allow the plug-in hybrid's owner to store electricity in his car's battery when demand is low and prices are cheap and then sell it back to the utility when prices are high—like on a hot summer afternoon. This would help reduce the cost of owning an all-electric car or a plug-in hybrid. In emergencies, the car's battery could also act as a backup power source for your house.

The good news is that a recent study from the U.S. Department of Energy reported that the nation's electricity infrastructure is underused during most of the day and has the capacity to charge tens of millions of electric cars. The existing power system could recharge about three-quarters of all the cars, pickup trucks, and SUVs now on the road because most people would plug in their vehicles at night, when power use is lowest.

And before too long you may be able to pull your plug-in hybrid into a station and fill 'er up—with electricity. Entrepreneur Shai Agassi, a Silicon Valley technologist and a former executive at the software giant SAP, plans to roll out a network of battery-charging stations in the United States, Europe, and the developing world. His company Better Place will sell electricity on a subscription basis and could even lease you the expensive batteries that power your car. This is the way it would work. If you don't want to wait hours for a charge, a driver could pull into a station and swap batteries. (Some entrepreneurs are working on batteries that can recharge in ten minutes.) No carmaker, however, has yet to design a car with removable batteries, but such a system should be technically feasible. The way Agassi sees it, leasing the car owner his battery should lower its overall cost: the driver can spread out the cost of using it over the entire time he drives his car. All batteries eventually lose some of their ability to hold a charge, and when that happens, Agassi can sell the old battery to a utility that will use it to store electricity from wind and solar farms. This will extend the useful life of the battery and thus reduce its overall cost to the driver.[8]

In 2007 Agassi raised $200 million from private venture partners, including the Israel Corporation, a large Israeli transportation and technology holding company; VantagePoint Venture Partners; as well as a group of private investors including Edgar Bronfman Sr., the liquor magnate, and James D. Wolfensohn, former head of the World Bank. The entrepreneur hopes to roll out his electric gas stations by 2010.

S HOULD WE ACCEPT these rosy predictions? It is too early to say. For example, one unanticipated and potentially troublesome aspect of plug-in hybrids is that, because they will be running on battery power most of the time, they will run silent. While that might be a welcome development for people on busy streets, it worries the National Federation of the Blind. That organization points out that partially sighted or nonsighted pedestrians (not to mention children and pets) are at risk of serious injury from the near-silent machines. Car companies will have to design some sort of device that would emit a sound loud enough to warn pedestrians.

And until entrepreneurs such as Agassi build a network of electric gas stations—and this will take time; currently the United States alone has 187,000 gasoline stations—how will people who live, for example, on the sixteenth floor of a Chicago apartment building, with no garage, recharge their car batteries? By stringing an extension cord down the side of the building? More and more people are moving to cities. Many of them drive cars and would be more likely than their country cousins to want small, energy-efficient vehicles.

Even automakers as successful as Honda Motors found hybrids to be rough driving. Honda has sold 200,000 hybrids worldwide. When it launched its space-age-looking hybrid Insight in 1999, it boasted 70 miles per gallon, the highest fuel economy of any vehicle. Yet since that time Toyota hybrids have outsold those of its Japanese rival by a margin of five to one. In fact, in 2007 Honda decided to discontinue its hybrid Accord because it failed to attract buyers. Perhaps that happened because of the Accord's confusing combination of high horsepower, high price, and so-so mileage. Now Honda is trying to play catch-up with a new product, code-named "Global Small Hybrid," a five-passenger, small family car that will be priced around $17,000. The claim is that it will beat the Prius in mileage when it arrives in 2009. Honda's goal is to sell 100,000 units a year in the U.S. market. The company has not yet announced whether it will offer a plug-in version.

It may be that Honda's mistake was to put its hybrid systems inside its already available Civics and Accords. The problem was that drivers could not make a green statement when driving one of these; no one could tell the hybrid models from the regular ones. By contrast, the Prius's unusual styling shouted that the driver was saving the planet. This turned out to be an extremely popular feature with consumers. Hoping to avoid the same mistake, Honda will give its new hybrid a distinct "green" look.

But Honda is hedging. It will put hybrid systems into only its smallest cars, not the rest of its lineup. And it has not given up on the internal combustion engine despite the difficulty and expense of wringing more efficiency from it. Honda has developed a car in Brazil that can burn 100 percent ethanol. And starting in 2010, it will sell cars outfitted with high-mileage "clean diesel" engines that should run as clean as a gas engine—though nowhere near as clean as hybrids or biofueled cars. "In the next fifteen to twenty years," says Honda's Gunnar Lindstrom, "further increase in efficiency of internal combustion engines will be critical."[9] What Lindstrom is getting at is that hybrids—which combine gasoline and electric-powered engines—are sure to grow in popularity.

GM has been taking a different route: it has invested more than $1 billion and hired over a thousand scientists and engineers to design an electric car powered by a hydrogen fuel cell instead of a battery. The appeal of hydrogen is apparent. It is a clean fuel that leaves only water vapor as an exhaust. But hydrogen technology is not likely to develop fast enough to make a difference near term in global warming. Most experts believe that hydrogen will not become commercially viable and widely available for at least fifteen to twenty years.

Hydrogen fuel cells are still enormously expensive. They must drop at least a hundredfold in cost before they become commercially viable. Most important, it takes electricity to make hydrogen, and at this point that means greenhouse gas–emitting coal or natural gas plants. During the hydrogen production process, under present circumstances, you would end up releasing nearly as much carbon as you would from burning gasoline in cars. If hydrogen is to become part of the global warming solution, it must be made from renewable energy such as solar and wind. We do not yet have enough of this kind of power to produce hydrogen in meaningful amounts.

Add another obstacle: hydrogen can't be distributed through our current pipeline and filling station infrastructure. No one has yet provided the capital to retrofit the nation's 187,000 gas stations or its thousands of miles of oil and gas pipelines for hydrogen. Retro-fitting gas stations to charge electric cars or plug in hybrids would be much easier and cheaper.

In 2007, GM tacitly admitted it was de-emphasizing hydrogen technology when it tried to focus the public's attention on the Volt, its own battery-powered hybrid plug-in car. The company unveiled this sleek silver five-passenger sports sedan on January 7, 2007, at the North American International Auto Show in Detroit. It apparently plans to launch the car in 2010. Applying some of the technology that came out of its joint venture with Daimler and BMW, GM designed its E-Flex hybrid system to drive forty miles in pure electric mode before the lithium-ion batteries wear down. When the battery runs out of juice, a small gasoline engine kicks in and recharges the battery. If you drive it until the 12-gallon gas tank is dry and the battery drained, you'll have gone 640 miles at 50 mpg—on one six-hour charge from a home outlet. GM estimates that even after factoring in higher electric bills, the Volt will save drivers some $900 a year in gasoline costs.

This all sounded good until GM executives at the Detroit auto show admitted that the lithium battery technology was not yet ready. Some months later, however, the company announced that it had licensed battery agreements for the Volt with Johnson Controls of Milwaukee and a small company in Watertown, Massachusetts, called A123Systems, one of the numerous start-ups at work on next-generation battery technology. A123 already has experience making lithium batteries for De Walt, Black & Decker's power tool line. The company, spun out of MIT labs, claims that its new car battery will last more than ten years and/or 150,000 miles and will operate over a wide temperature range. David Vieau, president and CEO of A123 Systems, has raised $100 million, including funding from GE Commercial Finance and Procter & Gamble. The money will be used to scale its technology development and manufacturing capacity for plug-in hybrid electric vehicle batteries.

Is the momentum real? Sue Cischke, the senior vice president for sustainability, environment, and safety engineering at Ford, says it is. Cischke believes that the world's transportation system is so large and complex that no one technology or fuel will drive the car of the future.

The evidence of a developing technology is there. The desire of companies to keep their vehicles relevant in the marketplace is also clear. And there are smart and innovative people working in the field both to save the world and to make money. The probability is that plug-in hybrids and all electric vehicles will play a key role. An American family might own a small all-electric for a short, daily commute and a large plug-in hybrid, such as the next-generation Prius or GM's Volt, for longer family trips and vacations. And, in the short run, traditional cars will not disappear—potentially not good news for global warming. But, many entrepreneurs as well as big corporations, as we'll see later, are working on new forms of ethanol and biodiesel that could be burned in conventional cars or in new clean-diesel vehicles. Honda sells an ethanol-burning car in Brazil, where 40 percent of motor fuel comes from sugarcane. As of this writing, some 6 million cars worldwide have the capacity to burn ethanol.

Vinod Khosla, a cofounder of Sun Microsystems who now heads a venture capital firm, has noted that "almost every great new mind has started working on alternative energy. Hundreds of little start-ups are popping up with amazing innovations." Clearly big changes are necessary—as soon as possible. We must travel to Silicon Valley to learn more about this radical technology and a handful of entrepreneurs working on a new kind of car.

Back to the Future: The Electric Car

The red Tesla Roadster whipped off the entrance ramp and onto Route 101 in San Carlos, California, passing cars whose horns blared as they receded in our rearview mirror. Though it felt as if we were driving a powerful Porsche, this peppy two-seater was actually an electric car, powered by 6,831 rechargeable lithium-ion batteries. As we accelerated, the high whining sound of the electric motor was like the noise of a futuristic car in *Blade Runner*. The car soon hit a neck-snapping zero to 60 miles per hour in a little under four seconds—faster, by the way, than the aforementioned Porsche. The Tesla can travel more than 200 miles on a single three-and-a-half-hour charge from a household outlet; it has no transmission and sports only one gear that kicks in when speed reaches 65 mph. The $98,000 Tesla costs just 2 cents a mile to drive. The company says it has about six hundred orders for delivery as soon as it can work out some production snags. Early buyers include California governor Arnold Schwarzenegger and actor George Clooney. This is not your father's electric car.

For the first time since the early twentieth century, the United States is seeing the birth of a new auto industry. During the early days of the automobile, more than four hundred manufacturers tried to compete, but these small shops, each of which produced a few handmade cars, eventually gave way to the Big Three—GM, Ford, and Chrysler. Over the years an entrepreneur would occasionally emerge with a new idea or design to challenge the Big Three, yet all failed. The two most notable examples were Preston Tucker in 1948 with his Tucker Torpedo and John DeLorean with his silver gull-winged sports car in the 1970s.

Today, as we've noted, some fifteen new electric car companies have launched or plan to launch electric or electric hybrid cars. Electric cars are not new. They first hit the streets of New York City in 1897. The Pope Manufacturing Company of Hartford, Connecticut, became the first large-scale American electric automobile manufacturer. Nineteen hundred was the electric automobile's heyday: of the 4,192 cars produced in the United States, 28 percent were powered by electricity, and electric cars represented about one-third of all cars found on the streets of New York City, Boston, and Chicago. At about this time, Thomas Edison joined forces with Henry Ford to develop an electric car that would be as affordable and practical as the Model T. Drivers would recharge their batteries at plug-in sites along trolley lines. The batteries could also be refreshed courtesy of the home windmill. Besides their use as taxis, electric cars were targeted at women drivers because of their clean, quiet, and easy operation. For instance, electrics did not belch thick clouds of black exhaust and did not require the difficult-to-use and sometimes dangerous hand crank to start. That advantage was eliminated in 1913, however, when

Cadillac developed the electric starter, making gas-powered cars easier to use. And the crucial fact that the combustion engine did not need recharging all but killed electric car technology.

The variety of technologies behind today's electric cars is enough to make one's head spin. Most of them still have kinks that may or may not be worked out, but, whatever their motives, the companies behind them are trying. That's the important factor in the race against global warming. It is also what we must bear in mind when evaluating the prospects of their efforts.

At least fifteen car companies are now trying to build electric cars and batteries in the United States alone. Besides Tesla Motors and Aptera, there is Phoenix Motorcars, a company based in Ontario, California, which is building an electric pickup truck with a range of more than 100 miles that can be recharged in ten minutes under certain circumstances. A Danish company that bought what was once Ford's electric car program and opened its U.S. office in Palo Alto will launch the Think City, a tiny electric commuter car, in 2008 in Europe and in 2009 in the United States. Dean Kamen, the American inventor of the Segway scooter, hopes to add his Stirling engine to future generations of the Think City, which he believes will dramatically boost its range and efficiency.

Why do these small, renegade car companies think they can succeed when so many other auto start-ups before them have failed? The entrepreneurs and investors behind these companies point to three factors—an urgent need for a solution to global warming, an abundance of investment capital, and the availability of cheap computing power.

Aᴍᴇʀɪᴄᴀ's ᴄᴀʀs ᴀɴᴅ ᴛʀᴜᴄᴋs emit roughly 20 percent of all the nation's greenhouse gas. Switching some of our cars from the internal combustion engine to electric power over the next fifty years could help meet the environment-saving goal of a 60 mpg fleet average. Less gas burned means less greenhouse gas flowing into the atmosphere. Electric cars—as well as plug-in hybrids—have batteries that must be charged by electricity generated by power plants, most often greenhouse gas–spewing natural gas or coal facilities. When you drive an electric car, all you're doing is transferring the source of greenhouse gas from the tailpipe of the vehicle to the chimney of a coal-fired plant.

And yet, in June 2001, the Argonne National Laboratory released a U.S. Department of Energy–sponsored study that found that driving battery-powered electric vehicles resulted in a 35 percent reduction in greenhouse gases.[10] This reduction was based on electricity generation from the national grid, roughly half of which is derived from coal and roughly 30 percent of which comes from clean sources like nuclear, solar, wind, biomass, and hydroelectric power.

In 2004 an analysis of data from a California Air Resources Board staff report on greenhouse gas emissions from motor vehicles found that the use of electric vehicles resulted in a 67 percent reduction in overall greenhouse gases in California, which uses a high percentage of clean energy to power its grid. Electric vehicles driven by batteries also were dramatically more effective than those using hydrogen fuel cells in reducing greenhouse gas emissions.[11] And the more the grid evolves toward clean energy—wind, solar, hydro—the more electric cars will mitigate the effects of global warming. In California, which gets more of its electricity from clean sources than any other state, electric cars could make a difference. The giant utility PG&E, for instance, serves 15 million customers in northern and central California. On average, more than half of the electricity it delivers comes from sources that emit no CO_2. Other factors are at play as well. Electric cars would help lessen America's dependence on imported oil. And, in dense urban areas, electric cars would cut down on noise and local smog.

Why aren't we all driving electric cars? They have a limited range. Want to drive cross-country? You can't do it unless you stop, on average, every hundred miles or so to recharge. And electric cars are much more expensive than those we now drive. Oh, and there's no dealer network to service them. Yes, GM killed its electric car program in 2003. The documentary *Who Killed the Electric Car?* accused the world's largest automaker of wrenching its fleet of EV1s out of the hands of its passionate owners.[12] Why would they do that? Because of the drawbacks cited above. Today's electric car companies, on the other hand, believe that improvements in technology will bring the price of electric cars down and the distance range up, making the car an attractive choice for consumers.

THE **PLAYERS IN** the nascent electric car industry are taking different routes to market. Tesla Motors is building its $98,000 Roadster for the Hollywood set. The entrepreneur Ian Wright is aiming at the same market with his $100,000 Wrightspeed sports car, whose three-second zero-to-sixty acceleration time ranks it among the fastest production autos in the world. In fact, it is second only to the French-made Bugatti Veyron, a 1,000-horsepower, sixteen-cylinder beast that hits 60 mph half a second faster and goes for $1.25 million. Moving down market, Phoenix is aiming at the business sector, building a $47,500 workday pickup truck. For those looking for a cheap commuter car, Aptera, Tango, Think City and Zenn are all trying to meet that need with small, inexpensive electric vehicles that can be charged to cover enough miles to handle the daily commute to the office.

These companies do not necessarily aim to grow to the size of Toyota or GM. Some will be satisfied if they can become profitable niche players; others hope to sell or license their technology to the big car companies. Says Bill Green, a partner at Vantage-Point, a venture capital firm that has invested in Tesla Motors, "No one argues today that the Tesla will serve anything but a small subset of the market. But it has changed the conversation. People drive it and say 'wow.' We'll look back and we'll see what Tesla is doing with design improvements in body weight and battery technology as a historic and dramatic increase in performance. The big car companies will look at Tesla and say, 'Hey, maybe I can use that technology in my cars.' "

VantagePoint as well as other top venture capital firms such as Draper Fisher Jurvetson and Kleiner Perkins Caufield & Byers are betting big on just that. In 2006 Elon Musk used part of the fortune he made from starting PayPal—the Internet payment system—to help bankroll Tesla Motors. Other investors include Google founders Larry Page and Sergey Brin. Tesla has raised more than $100 million. Kleiner Perkins, along with other investors, has put $7 million into a Cedar Park, Texas, company called EEStor, which has licensed its capacitor technology to Zenn, a Canadian electric car company.

What has these investors excited is that the rules of the car industry are changing. A giant combustion engine pushing 3,500 pounds of steel no longer seems like the best way to transport humans. Radical new car designs using lightweight materials and utilizing new-style power plants are becoming more affordable. It looks like technology—with its computer-controlled battery packs, with power-storage systems that use nanotechnology—may soon become cheap enough to allow upstarts to compete with the Big Three. Stephan Dolezalek, a partner at VantagePoint, believes the cost and performance trajectory of the electric car will follow that of the information technology industry: "I worked at the World Bank in the 1970s and the computer that we used to track currency trading covered an entire floor. It had rows and rows of boxes all needing elaborate cooling. I asked a friend of mine recently to calculate how many personal computers today could give you the same computing power. And he said just a handful." Dolezalek believes that the cost, size, and power of electric car batteries will follow the same dramatic downward curve.

To understand how this new paradigm might work, I met with Steve Fambro, the founder of Aptera, the start-up that is building both a battery-powered and a plug-in hybrid lightweight commuter car. The gas hybrid model with a nickel-zinc battery gets 300 miles per gallon, and the all-electric can go a hundred miles on a charge of 3 to 6 hours when plugged into a household outlet. The three-wheel Aptera accelerates from zero to sixty in a respectable eleven seconds, with a 95 mph top speed. If it launches as planned in late 2008, the Aptera will sell for around $30,000.

This aerodynamic, low-slung commuter car has a composite body made of carbon fiber, fiberglass, and Kevlar that looks like the cockpit of a jet plane yet can hold two passengers and a baby in an infant seat. It weighs only 1,500 pounds compared with the average weight of about 3,500 pounds for today's cars. Because of its composite structure and because it has only three wheels, Aptera is likely to be classified as a motorcycle in most states. It is, however, a bigger car than it looks. One inch shorter than a Toyota Prius, it can still carry a surfboard in the trunk with the passenger seat folded. A solar-assisted air-conditioning system will run on sunny days even when the car is turned off in order to keep the interior cool for the driver's return. Its wheels hang on the ends of protruding axles covered by skirts, leading one auto industry wag to remark that the vehicle looks like "Batman's girlfriend's car."

Before Fambro first got into the car business, he was designing DNA synthesizers at Lumina, a biotech start-up. But he was also a car nut: he had worked as a teenage mechanic in Georgia and later took apart Mustangs for the fun of it. He spent nights and weekends in his garage trying to create a commuter vehicle that would be affordable, lightweight, safe, and fuel efficient. The moment of inspiration came in June 2004. He and a friend had traveled to the Mojave Desert to watch the launch of SpaceShipOne, the vehicle that made the first privately funded human spaceflight and won the $10 million X-Prize. On the long drive back from the Mojave to San Diego, Fambro and his friend marveled that it took only twenty-five people to design, build, and fly both the spaceship and the plane that put it into altitude. Of course, the SpaceShipOne team had access to high-tech tools that enabled the building and design of a rocket for only $25 million—cheap by NASA standards. Could the same tools be applied to the auto industry?

As Fambro recalls, "A light went on and I realized I'm probably not the only person to want such a vehicle. I could sit around and hypothesize whether people would buy it or not, or I could just build it." In January 2006 Fambro left his job at Lumina with some seed money to start his company. He entered a few local business plan competitions and didn't even place. "The judges thought I was crazy to start a car company. They just wanted another hot software company."

Undaunted, Fambro pushed ahead with his plan to turn conventional thinking in the auto industry upside down. In the early twentieth century, Henry Ford sold Model Ts in any color you wanted—as long as it was black. Then in the 1930s, Harley Earl, a GM auto designer, taught the world that style sells. Earl, who became known as Detroit's da Vinci, gave the world the elegant La Salle and much later the Corvette. "All auto designs," Fambro explains, "put styling first and function second. The way cars are designed, half the energy they need is just to push the air out of the way." Fambro asked himself, "What if you changed the styling to make the drag of a car nearly equal to zero?" The result? The Aptera's drag will be a third less than an average car's and less than half of the Prius's, which now has the lowest drag in the industry.

It was cheap technology that allowed Fambro to create such an aerodynamic design on a limited budget. It costs $10,000 a day to test a car's aerodynamics in a wind tunnel. For $50,000 Fambro found some off-the-shelf software—the same NASA uses to test the drag of its space vehicles. The software allows him to make changes in the style of the car and verify very quickly the change's effect on drag. To keep drag as low as possible, for example, the three-wheel car has no side-view mirrors—the driver has 180-degree rear visibility with the help of rear-mounted cameras. "Ten years ago we couldn't do that kind of testing. And five years ago, we couldn't afford it," says Fambro.

His engineers can also use the computer to simulate fifty thousand miles of driving, including over potholes, and to test the stress on the vehicle parts. (The car has also been pushed to its limits on an actual test track.) Because the body of the Aptera is made of lightweight composites, capital costs are lower than those for a typical metal vehicle. It takes as much as $1 billion to set up the facilities for the die stamping, welding, and assembly of a new vehicle. By using composites, Aptera can make parts with a tolerance of 1/1,000 inch very quickly and very cheaply. "I hate to use the term 'new paradigm,' " says Fambro, "but it's an entirely new way of making structural products." He estimates that today's computing power is so fast and so cheap that he can do "with three guys what a big company such as Boeing ten years ago took a few hundred people to do."

Armed with a radical design and a reasonable cost structure, Fambro began to approach investors. In early 2007 he raised $20 million from an anonymous investor and from Bill Gross, the founder of the start-up incubator Idealab. Gross liked Aptera's performance numbers and the minimal impact the product promised to make on the environment. This goal may be achievable because its low-drag design allows the Aptera hybrid to achieve 300 miles per gallon. Fambro would only have to use about 2 gallons of gas a month to make that 36-mile round-trip daily commute to his old biotech firm. Because the three-wheeler probably will be classified as a motorcycle it will be allowed to travel in California's carpool lanes—the wish that got him started in the first place.

Fambro plans to begin marketing his car in the Southwest—in California, Nevada, and Arizona. But there are still large hurdles to overcome. First, he has to make sure that the technology can be produced in large numbers and within budget. Hybrid technology can be very demanding: Toyota, with some of the best auto engineers in the world, took years to work the kinks out of the Prius. Next, Aptera must build a dealer network to sell and service the cars. This takes capital, skilled manpower, and time. (Imagine local mechanics with software degrees.) The good news is that Aptera's electric version of its car—in theory, anyway—should be very easy to maintain. It has no transmission, and its electric motor has only one moving part compared with about four hundred for an internal combustion engine.

And then there's the safety issue. The car weighs only 1,500 pounds (the tiny Toyota Yaris weighs 2,200 pounds), and with its three wheels the Aptera is likely to be rated by insurance companies as a motorcycle—with concomitant high insurance rates. In 2006 Volkswagen was ready to launch a sporty three-wheel car called the GX3 that had no air bags or stability control. They killed the project just before launch because of product-liability worries.[13] Fambro says the Aptera has passed all its stability tests.

Fambro also contends that the Aptera, with its seat belts, air bags, and crumple zones in the nose and doors, will match the safety of a Toyota Yaris. Also, the car has a strong composite body and steel crash frame similar to those used in Formula One racers. In racetrack crashes, you sometimes see a car bounce off the wall, flip over a few times, and then you see the driver unbuckle himself and walk off. But what if the lightweight Aptera gets hit by a speeding eighteen-wheeler? "Well," says Fambro, "I wouldn't want to get hit by an eighteen-wheeler in anything."

Even if Fambro succeeds in building an affordable energy-efficient commuter car, the impact on the market, at least in the short run, will be minimal. He hopes to sell 3,000 to 4,000 cars the first year the Aptera is in production and then ramp up to about 10,000 cars a year soon after that. In comparison, GM alone produces about 300,000 cars *a month*. Fambro would like to prove that cars can be made in a way that could help mitigate global warming. Perhaps the Aptera will be used as part of a light-rail system where the commuter will hop into a small car waiting at the train station that will take him the last few miles to his office. Or maybe it will be the inexpensive second car that a commuter drives to avoid traffic and speed along the carpool lane. Perhaps the Aptera will serve as a model for cars of the future: lightweight, great gas mileage, and loaded with computer controls. Fambro says he plans to build Aptera into a major car company, but like many entrepreneurs he is willing to be flexible: "If a Toyota or Hyundai offered to buy us, we would certainly consider it as would any company."

THE POWER SOURCE of the first Aptera will be a fairly conventional nickel-zinc battery. There are a number of other new battery technologies, however, that could power our cars. One of the most promising is a battery made by a Reno, Nevada, start-up called Altairnano. As its name implies, this company is using nanotechnology to design power plants. Lithium batteries like the ones used in the Tesla have a problem called thermal runaway: they sometimes get very hot and catch fire. Recall the Dell and Sony laptops that burst into flames when their lithium batteries overheated. Tesla uses sophisticated software in its Roadster to regulate the batteries so they don't overheat. Altairnano thinks it has a better idea and is already testing it in a vehicle that is about to go into production.

Ontario, California, is the home of Phoenix Motorcars, another start-up car company. One sunny spring morning, I found myself driving an Altairnano battery-powered two-and-a-half-ton red and black pickup truck through the flat fields of Ontario. Bryon Bliss, the vice president of sales and marketing for Phoenix, was with me, and when I asked him about the high whirring sound coming from under the hood, he laughed. "The electric motor in this truck is so quiet that you're hearing the power steering pump. We didn't anticipate that. You shouldn't be able to hear it in the production models."

Phoenix plans to manufacture 500 of these electric vehicles in

2008 in its Ontario assembly facility. It claims that the 4,800-pound truck can go over a hundred miles on a ten-minute battery charge. The company plans to start selling its electric pickup in 2008 for $47,500, about $10,000 more than the price of a comparable conventional pickup. It will also offer an SUV version for $49,000.

The brains behind Phoenix is Dan Riegert, who founded the company with Dana Muscato in 2001. As a young man he studied chemical engineering and then worked in R&D and manufacturing for twenty years, including a stint developing rocket fuel. In the nineties, Riegert cofounded the Investor Relations Group, a boutique investment bank. He also started a broadband wireless firm. It was during those days that he fell in love with the electric car. In the late 1990s, Riegert, with Muscato, opened an electric car dealership in Ojai, California, at just about the same time that GM announced it was pulling out of its electric car program. Honda and Toyota were also cutting back drastically.

Undaunted, Riegert and Muscato founded Phoenix as an alternative fuel research company that would spin off green products. While Riegert was working in the lab one day, a lithium-ion battery exploded, and he knew he had to switch direction. Aware of Altairnano's battery research, Riegert decided to manufacture electric cars. He managed to raise some seed money from 130 friends and family members, even though many people thought he was crazy to try to start a car company.

"I saw that half the vehicles Americans were buying were light trucks and SUVs," says Riegert, "and that most of those weren't driven more than thirty or so miles a day. And that we don't like to go to the gas pump and fill them up, especially with the price of oil rising. An electric car could easily handle that kind of range, but to appeal to the American market it would have to be midsize and robust. You wouldn't have to feel that you were driving a futuristic bubble car or a glorified golf cart." The market niche that Riegert wants to fill is primarily for service and delivery vehicles. The Phoenix can travel one hundred miles on a charge, and workers at a utility or contracting firm rarely drive their trucks more than that each day. They usually don't need the vehicles at night, when they could be recharged. And these companies, unlike most individuals, have the money to invest in an electric vehicle that would, at least at first, cost more than a gas-powered one.

Would the technology work? On Riegert's first visit to the Altairnano labs, he learned that they had made a crucial change. Lithium batteries, like the ones in Dell laptops, caught fire because the batteries would short-circuit and then overheat, causing fires. The scientists at Altairnano substituted a nanoengineered material, titanate, for the carbon in the battery, which the company says eliminates thermal runaway. This switch, however, reduces the amount of energy Altairnano's battery can hold compared with traditional carbon-based lithium-ion batteries.

What impressed Riegert was that unlike traditional lithium-ion batteries, Altairnano's operated within a broad temperature range from 40 degrees below zero to 150 degrees above. (Traditional lithium batteries don't perform well below freezing or above 100 degrees Fahrenheit.) The Altairnano battery also kept pumping out energy no matter how low the charge. Battery-driven golf carts, for example, often lose power when their charge is low. But Altairnano technicians claimed that their battery would last for 400,000 miles without significant loss of power. The promise: hit the accelerator and you'll always get full power.

Perhaps the most radical claim for these batteries is that they can be recharged in ten minutes compared with three to five hours for lithium. High-voltage lines at special "electric filling stations" would be required to accomplish this. Altairnano says that installing them would be "relatively easy." Utility and car company executives contend that these high-powered pumps can be made safe for drivers to use. The electricity does not flow unless the power cord is attached tightly into the car's receptacle. Yet, anyone installing these lines would still have to cope with the costs of running new cables and with meeting local regulations. At issue are the awesome power levels required. To charge a car battery in ten minutes can require some 250 kilowatts of power—five times as much as the average office building consumes at its peak. It is hard to imagine a small filling station—never mind a home—being able to provide that kind of power.[14]

The jury is still out, but the giant utility PG&E in California is taking a chance. It is buying early models of the Phoenix pickup and also building recharging stations. "If we put a rapid charger halfway there, you could make the three-hour drive from Ontario to Las Vegas," asserts Phoenix's Bliss. "If you want, you can charge your Phoenix in a household outlet, but it will take five or six hours."

Another catch is price. After some production delays—Phoenix Motors originally wanted to build around 6,000 vehicles in 2008 but has cut that number to 500—the company says it is ready to deliver its trucks to big companies such as PG&E. The actor and green activist Ed Begley Jr. has become a Phoenix spokesperson and is likely to be among the first individual owners of the truck. The problem is that the Altairnano batteries alone in those $47,500 trucks that Phoenix will sell cost more than $57,000 each.

What is keeping Phoenix alive despite these terrible numbers? Healthy subsidies from the state of California. First, buyers will get a $5,000 to $10,000 rebate off the $47,500 retail price—making the purchase of a Phoenix very attractive. For about the price of a Chevy Colorado pickup, a customer will be able to buy a low-maintenance electric truck whose fuel costs the equivalent of 30 cents a gallon. Moreover, Phoenix itself will get subsidies from the state for its zero-emission trucks. Under current California law, automakers need to sell a certain number of zero-emission vehicles or ZEVs. Between 2012 and 2017, for instance, they would need to sell in total 75,000 ZEVs. The hitch is that the big car companies don't yet make any of these cars. In order to keep selling cars in the state the big automakers would have to buy credits from carmakers like Phoenix who do. Such credits have never been traded, so no one knows how much they will be worth. Some reports say they could be worth as much as $200,000 per truck,[15] which would make each Phoenix truck profitable the first year. The company argues that the subsidies will allow them to survive long enough to get the truck up to production levels—about twenty thousand vehicles annually—and the price of the $57,000 battery down to a point where the technology would make economic sense. In 2007 Phoenix struggled to raise capital to ramp up production. Investors worried that the state credit could be withdrawn or that the new spate of electric car companies entering the market would drive the price of the credit down to the point where Phoenix would not be able to make any money. The company finally arranged another round of financing and lives on.

While Tesla, Phoenix, Altairnano, and other start-ups work hard to get the cost of their battery technology down, a handful of visionaries are plotting to radically transform the entire U.S. transportation system.

Gridlock

If you want a glimpse of how Americans may be traveling in the not-so-distant future, take a trip to Amsterdam. The Dutch need only walk, hop on a bus, or drive to the nearest light-rail or tram station. There they can board a train for a few euros that will speedily bring them to all parts of the city.

The tram system has been around since 1875, but over the last few years the Amsterdam City Council has undertaken a major building campaign, adding light-rail, new lines, and state-of-the-art cars made by Siemens, the German giant. Better security has cut down on the fare hoppers and drug addicts who earlier made rail travel an unpleasant experience. Commuting times are shorter, and transportation costs cheaper than driving in by car. With gasoline prices rising and global warming threatening, this city with a metropolitan population of 2.2 million has constructed an efficient urban transit system. In the process it has become one of the stingiest emitters of carbon in the world.

Make sense? Of course, but only for Europe, the critics of mass transit have argued ever since Charles Wilson stated at a congressional hearing in the 1950s that "what was good for America was good for General Motors and vice versa." On the Continent, the streets are narrow, the cities dense, and the distances short. Public transportation, it is claimed, won't work in the United States, the home of sprawl. And besides, Americans love their cars.

The urgency of global warming coupled with rapid growth in urban populations may well force Americans to radically rethink their entire transportation system. In the mid-1990s, a prominent architect and city planner named Richard Rogers, who designed France's Pompidou Center and Lloyd's of London, and developed master plans for Berlin and Shanghai, came to the conclusion that population growth would soon make cars and cities incompatible. In 1990 there were 35 urban areas in the world with populations over 5 million. Today there are 54; 38 are in the developing world. And over the next thirty years another 2 billion people will be added to those and other cities. Anyone who has tried to travel through the already traffic-clogged streets of Shanghai or Bangkok knows exactly what Rogers means. And it is not just a matter of wasting time stuck in traffic. Vehicles globally account for about 14 percent of all greenhouse gas emitted (compared with 20 percent in the United States). Increase the number of cars dramatically and global warming worsens, not to mention our health. The Clean Air Task Force, a nonprofit, estimates that fine particles, such as those found in diesel exhaust, shorten the lives of seventy thousand Americans each year.

Calling on his training as an architect, Rogers calculated that a city requires 20 square meters of space to park a single car. As he puts it, "If only one in five Londoners owned a car, then, a city of 10 million (roughly that of London) needs an area about ten times the size of the City of London just to park cars."[16] Something, obviously, has to give.

BUT WHAT WOULD THIS new world look like? To find out, I traveled to Los Angeles, the city built on the car, the city that glorified America's love affair with the automobile in movies as diverse as *American Graffiti* and *The Fast and the Furious*. There I met Bill Reinert, the national manager of Toyota's advanced technologies group and the company's resident futurist. In the 1990s, Reinert helped shape the thinking at the Japanese carmaker that led to the Prius, the top-selling hybrid in the world.

On this afternoon Reinert wears a dark shirt, no tie. His thick brown hair streaked with gray is brushed back, and his rectangular tortoiseshell glasses set off his Southern California tan. He is dashing, Marcello Mastroianni style. Despite his work on the Prius, Reinert can't be pegged as a rigid proponent of conservation. As a young man he worked in a Ford factory, welding chassis. While in the U.S. Navy, he served on a nuclear sub that traversed under the North Pole. Like many Californians, he has had a long-standing love affair with the combustion engine—in his case restoring vintage Ferraris and Porsches in his spare time. Though Reinert drives a Prius to work, he leaves a large carbon footprint, mainly because of his business travel around the world—he's racked up some 2.5 million frequent-flier miles.

His office at Toyota's U.S. headquarters in Torrance looks out over Freeway 405. It's a Thursday afternoon at around 3:30, and the traffic on the twelve-lane highway barely crawls. The city could build more highways, but traffic engineers have found that any new roads they build jam up with heavy traffic about six months after they open. "I worry about L.A.," says Reinert. "Every day I look out my window and see the cars backed up on 405 and I think that the choices we make today are going to last for fifty years. The question is: do our cities continue to adapt to today's idea of personal transportation and build more freeways? Or do the cars we design start to adapt to a new model of urban design? If we're not going to put an electrified rail in L.A.—and this is my future vision for the city—and if we're not looking at charging drivers to enter the city as they do in London, then we're really not looking at a systemic answer."

In Reinert's vision, L.A. and other American cities need to build electrified rail systems similar to the one he himself has enjoyed in Amsterdam. He argues that L.A. is not as spread out as it seems but is, instead, a series of interconnected villages. The idea would be to drive small electric cars from your home to the train station. When you arrive at the neighborhood where you work, a similar car awaits you for the last few miles of your journey. Just wave a wireless key fob at the car and it unlocks the vehicle and charges your account. The result? No horrendous traffic jams, a shorter commute, and less greenhouse gas.

An urban fantasy? Not necessarily. Toyota began to build a system called Crayon in Japan in 1996. The auto giant designed a small two-seat electric vehicle, called the e.com, and matched it with a light-rail train that brought workers to the carmaker's facilities in Toyota City. The e.com is a compact two-seater that resembles the Daimler Smart Car now being sold in the United States. It is powered by nickel-metal hydride batteries, has a range of sixty miles, and a top speed of 62 mph. The car takes more than nine hours to charge when plugged into a household outlet, but recent advances in battery technology could cut that time dramatically. Market research showed that the commuters who used the system loved it.

Crayon, designed to be a demonstration project, turned out to be ahead of its time. In the midnineties—before the wide availability of wireless key fobs, BlackBerries, and cheap computing power—the technology needed to make sure a car waited in the right place for each commuter at the right time either didn't yet exist or was too expensive. Toyota shelved the project a few years after it launched Crayon.

But the idea didn't die with the demise of Crayon. Since then Toyota has been updating the technology of such a system, working with the National Fuel Cell Research Center and the Institute of Transportation Studies, both located at the University of California in Irvine. This new demonstration project is called ZevNet (zero-emission vehicle network). Here you use a handheld device to locate, open, start, and pay for your electric e.com. A GPS satellite system keeps track of the location of each vehicle to make sure cars are available to commuters when they need them. A commuter in L.A. traveling to work in, say, Orange County, some twenty to thirty miles south of the city, would charge his electric car in his garage at night—he could also use it at night to go out on the town—and then would drive it in the morning and plug it in at a parking space at the train station. When he gets off the train, there's another city electric car waiting. The car could be used by the commuter's company during the day. Toyota figures that if the car does five to eight trips a day, it pays for itself, pays for the infrastructure, and pays for the cost of the trip.

Of course, the e.com cars are only as clean as the electricity that powers them. If a greenhouse gas–fired coal plant is providing the juice to recharge your electric car, the benefits begin to diminish. California, however, generates power more cleanly than most other states, with its heavy reliance on hydro, natural gas, nuclear, solar, and wind. In fact, the state has banned its utilities from purchasing electricity generated by coal plants outside its borders.

The e.com car could also help cut greenhouse gas by becoming part of what's called a "smart grid." Today electricity travels over a one-way network from the power plant to your home or business. A smart grid is more like the Internet—it is smart, interactive, and efficient, directing electricity from different sources whenever and wherever it is needed. Electricity demand tends to be highest on hot summer afternoons when air conditioners are running full speed. What if your power company could "buy" the electricity that you had stored overnight in the battery of your e.com car and then use it to power those air conditioners on a sweltering afternoon? While you work in your office and your car is parked in the lot, it could be plugged into a smart-grid outlet that draws the power from the car's battery and credits your utility bill. (The grid would also be smart enough to leave you enough juice in your car to make it back to the train station that day.) Imagine then extending the smart grid into our homes. It could communicate with sensors embedded in washing machines, air conditioners, and other household appliances to allow power to be distributed where and when it is needed most. Hook millions of electric cars and appliances into these smart grids, and the nation could avoid building many of those extra power plants needed to cover those times when electricity demand is highest and make better use of the plants that sit idle during the evening when energy demand is low.

This is not just some pipe dream. Peter Corsell is the founder and CEO of GridPoint, a Washington, D.C., designer of smart-grid systems. Corsell, who served with the U.S. State Department and worked as a political analyst with the Central Intelligence Agency, has raised $88 million in capital, including a large investment by the Goldman Sachs Group, and is working with electric utilities nationwide. At a 2007 Goldman Sachs conference on green energy, Corsell explained the appeal of a smart grid: "If you think about a plug-in hybrid car, it's like a battery on wheels—it will be able to know, like a cell phone, who you are and where you are. If you plug in your hybrid at a not convenient time, we're going to charge you 35 cents a kilowatt-hour for your electricity. But if you plug it in at home at night when demand is low, we'll only charge you 4 cents a kilowatt-hour. I think it's a game-changing play."

Given the scale of the challenge, such systems are probably at least a decade away before they see widespread use. Yet California utility PG&E already has a smart-grid system on its drawing boards and has been in talks with Toyota to develop electric and plug-in hybrid cars that could provide power to the grid during times when electricity demand is at its peak. PG&E is also working with Tesla Motors to develop "smart charging" technology that will allow cars like the Tesla Roadster to be juiced up by remote control, giving utilities the ability to control when the vehicle is charged. Other power companies such as Southern California Edison are working on similar initiatives.

Building such a sophisticated system is expensive, but the nation's grid—as witnessed by the Northeast blackout during the summer of 2003—needs to be replaced anyway, and some utility officials believe that constructing a smart grid would be cheaper than keeping the old grid and building extra power plants to meet growth in demand.

Some Orange County real estate developers are already demonstrating that this kind of lifestyle may not be so far-fetched—even for Californians. The belly of the beast of urban sprawl is to be found in the rows of houses that stretch across Irvine in the heart of Orange County. The city of Irvine is turning the former El Toro Marine Corps Air Station into a new community that will act as an experiment in future lifestyles. At the heart of the project are Orange County Great Park, a 1,347-acre recreation area—almost twice the size of New York City's Central Park—and a 1,000-acre campus called the Lifelong Learning District that have been set aside for educational and research institutions. Surrounding the park will be four communities known as Heritage Fields. In early 2005 a consortium of developers that includes the giant California developer Lennar paid the city approximately $650 million for the right to build on all four parcels of the air base. This 140-acre development of homes and retail businesses has been designed to discourage the use of cars. The old air base runways will be used as roads, but the community encourages the use of low-speed electric vehicles. There is a plan that eventually will connect the community with light-rail transit running through the middle of the village where residents can shop, eat, and go to the movies. In other words, it has been designed *not* to accommodate the existing lifestyle in Southern California.

Reinert argues that there's no reason why a light-rail/electric car system can't connect all the cities in Southern California, from Irvine to L.A., to Torrance, to Pasadena. "We believe there's not a market for a small electric car, but there is a market for a small electric car that's part of a sustainable mobility system. This essentially could present a big business opportunity for Toyota." The carmaker would need to lower the cost of an e.com-like electric car, to secure the intellectual property for running the system, and to work with state and local governments to cover costs of building and operating a light-rail system. He said to think of it as Zipcars on steroids.

Reinert is referring to a Boston start-up named Zipcar that applies technology to let you rent a Cooper Mini, a Prius, or some other car in the city and drop it off at different locations when you're finished. The technology is there, and the company says it's on track to become profitable. If you live in the city and need to use a car for, say, a few hours, you can walk to any number of Zipcar locations, wave your membership card at the door lock, and drive away, paying around $10 per hour. Zipcar now has fifteen locations in cities such as Atlanta, Boston, New York, and San Francisco. In late 2007 it merged with its rival Flexcar, based in Seattle and controlled by America Online founder Steve Case. (Interestingly, some 30 percent of Zipcar's customers have sold their automobiles and use this service exclusively.)

"I'm adamant," says Reinert, "that we launch ZevNet in L.A., and then if you do it in L.A. you can do it anywhere. Why would I want to do it in San Francisco or Portland, where everyone wants to do it anyway? Why not do it here, where it's hard? Then it will be easy everywhere else."

While Reinert is hopeful that his company will, within the next five or ten years, launch such a project, he does concede that Toyota has no immediate plans to do so. Part of the resistance?

Politics. The state of California voted down a light-rail project in the spring of 2007 because Governor Schwarzenegger, with an already ambitious green agenda on his plate, seemingly didn't want to raise taxes to pay for it. Reinert believes that the proceeds of a tax on drivers entering the city of, say, $20 a day could be put toward building a light-rail system.

Light-rail, though, is catching on in other parts of the country. Cities such as Denver, Phoenix, Portland, and Seattle are either building, planning, or expanding light-rail systems. In Denver, which is undertaking perhaps the most ambitious program, light-rail is booming. Of the metro region's 2.4 million residents, about 566,000 live in the city's limits. So far, 61,000 a day have ridden the Southeast line, which links Denver's downtown to its suburbs, since it opened in November 2006, far surpassing expectations. If all goes as planned, the Denver region is expected to build 119 miles of light-rail and commuter rail by 2016. Among the projects are six new lines from Denver to the suburbs, including one to the airport.

In 2003 John Hickenlooper was elected mayor of Denver. A longtime civic activist and owner of a downtown microbrewery, Hickenlooper had never held or sought elected office. He ran on his vision for Denver's future: a vibrant, business-friendly city with more parks and more mass transit. The FasTracks plan qualified for the ballot during Hickenlooper's first year in office. Although it wasn't his idea, Hickenlooper seized on the program and, using his mayoral bully pulpit, began rounding up support from the suburbs, winning the backing of thirty-one different mayors in seven counties—comprising an area the size of Connecticut. Despite opposition from the state's Republican governor and the influential *Rocky Mountain News*, FasTracks won approval, with 58 percent of voters agreeing to a four-tenths of a penny sales tax increase.

Light-rail is expensive. The projected cost of the program has grown from $4.7 billion to $6.5 billion because of rising construction costs. The cost of light-rail systems, however, would be dwarfed by the trillions in damage done to our economy should the worst-case scenarios of climate change play out. And even some proponents of FasTracks concede that rail service may not take a significant number of cars off the road because the population in the region keeps growing faster than the number of rail riders. Hickenlooper, though, believes that the rail will keep enough traffic off the road to keep the region from becoming gridlocked. As the mayor puts it, "You can add more and more traffic to that rail line, and not only does it not slow down, it takes more people."[17]

The rail system is also likely to encourage more growth in the Denver area as developers build housing near commuter rail lines. The mayor sees this more as an opportunity than as a threat. The region will grow anyway, so why not make the most of this trend by building new high-density, ecologically sound, transit-oriented communities near the stations? The city of Denver has drafted new zoning codes for development near future stations, and many of the surrounding cities are doing the same. Boulder wants to transform a 160-acre parcel near its rail and bus stations into what it calls a transit village. In an interview with Global Public Media, Hickenlooper said, "We're really focusing on getting each stop to become a little village. I see a day when people will actually be able to walk right from their home to the light-rail and take a light-rail to work. And more families will be able to be a one-car family, instead of being a two- or even a three-car family. But Americans are funny about their cars; we'll have to see whether it's going to be transferable to our culture."[18]

Americans, however, aren't likely to cut back on driving into the cities unless they have a clear economic incentive to do so. The simplest but most politically controversial way to accomplish this would be to impose a congestion tax. A growing number of the nation's governors and mayors are looking to congestion pricing to encourage Americans to leave their cars at home. Under a proposal by New York City mayor Michael Bloomberg, each truck would have to pay $21 every weekday to enter the central business district between the hours of 6:00 A.M. and 6:00 P.M. (Existing bridge and tunnel tolls for trucks, which can run as much as $6 an axle, would be deducted from the new $21 toll.) Proceeds from the new tolls would go toward improving mass transit. Bloomberg's plan, however, is stalled in the state assembly. Other U.S. municipalities, including Dallas, Miami, Minneapolis, San Diego, and Seattle, are expressing interest in the idea. Groups such as the AARP and the National Supermarkets Association back it. Advocates are studying the results of congestion-pricing programs in London, Singapore, and Stockholm.

Recent studies estimate that traffic jams cost the U.S. economy a whopping $65 billion annually—and the figure is rising. Among the industries hardest hit: trucking, service and repair, wholesale trades, and construction. The Partnership for New York City, a group of two hundred CEOs who support congestion pricing, estimates that gridlock costs New York City $4.6 billion in lost business revenue. The traffic crisis is spreading beyond the largest areas. According to a 2006 report by the libertarian Reason Foundation, traffic in Utah, which has about a third of the population of New York City, will double by 2030.[19] Adam Madetzke, the owner of Salt City Couriers, told *Fortune Small Business* magazine that northbound congestion on Interstate 15— Utah's most clogged highway—has hampered his delivery business: "During rush hour, the heavy traffic drops our profits by 20% to 30%."[20] While it debates congestion pricing, Utah hopes that a new commuter rail system set to open next spring will alleviate the problem.

Congestion pricing treats access to the roadways like any other scarce commodity: when demand is highest, so are prices, just as they are for cell phone service and (in more and more states) electricity. San Diego has been charging commuters a toll on an eight-mile stretch of Interstate 15 since 1998, which allows those who pay to use special lanes during peak hours. The charge varies from 50 cents to $8, depending on demand. Since the toll was imposed, usage of express lanes has nearly doubled, and the number of car pools has gone up more than 70 percent. Denver, Houston, and Minneapolis have similar toll highways.

New technologies, such as video cameras and E-ZPass electronic toll collectors, can make congestion pricing easier to enforce and the fees cheaper to collect. In London, which instituted congestion pricing in 2003, about 5 percent of trips into the central business district over a twelve-hour peak period were eliminated. Trip speed across central London has increased by 19 percent. Businesses in the affected areas say that while they haven't noticed a loss in revenues, they did see a significant change in business patterns. At a garden center in Chelsea, for instance, most of the customers from outside London now drive in on the weekend when tolls are lower.

In the United States, small businesses face not only higher costs from congestion pricing but also the potential for outsized gains, according to an analysis by the Drum Major Institute for Public Policy, a New York City think tank. Unlike CEOs of big corporations, entrepreneurs are usually deeply involved in operations and sales. They don't just have workers caught in traffic— they're often mired in it themselves, losing valuable time and opportunity. Even with a daily fee as high as the $21 proposed in New York, "the extra productivity will more than make up for the charge," the Drum Major report concludes. The Reason Foundation study figures that if rush-hour speed on Atlanta's highways could be raised by just six miles an hour, nearly $5 billion a year would be saved.

Despite opposition, congestion pricing may have legs politically. It's a cheap alternative to building new roads, and it can help cities reduce pollution. That makes it a natural for Democrats, with their base among big-city voters. The Bush administration is on board, too, asking for $130 million in grants to help metro areas plan electronic toll systems for congestion pricing. With the projected growth in the nation's traffic and the billions business loses in delays, it's a political program that all but the most diehard driver is likely to support.

6

Fuel Without
the Fossils

SIR RICHARD BRANSON has circumnavigated the world in a balloon and rappelled down the side of a skyscraper. He is also the founder of the Virgin Group, a 35,000-employee empire that owns airlines, music stores, cable and cell phone companies, and travel bureaus. He realized a few years ago that the airlines' piece of the business required drastic action.

Carbon dioxide emissions from jets are a growing environmental concern. Airlines contribute about 3 percent of the world's greenhouse gas, and with the industry growing every year—Boeing predicts that air travel will double by 2020[1]—that number is expected to rise dramatically. In addition, fuel prices more than doubled from 2000 to 2006, boosting operating costs and making airlines increasingly desperate for a more price-stable alternative.

In 2006, responding to this growing crisis, Branson created Virgin Fuels, a company dedicated to finding a replacement for oil. "I felt that if I contributed 100% of the profits that I made from my airlines and invested them into trying to come up with clean fuels for planes, clean fuels for cars, clean fuels for lorries and buses, it was the right thing to do. I'm not doing it purely as a charity. I'm saying that if we can come up with the right fuels, we'll sell those fuels."[2] By this reckoning, Branson is actually pledging about $3 billion in future profits, a vivid example of putting your money where your mouth is.

As a jetliner cruises at 35,000 feet above the earth, it emits a vapor trail called a contrail. This thin, cirruslike cloud, composed largely of greenhouse gas and water vapor, hangs in the stratosphere. During the day, it reflects some of the sun's rays back into space. But at night, it traps in the atmosphere a lot more of the sun's warmth than it deflects in daylight. Scientists predict that, unless action is taken, jets soon will be the world's largest producer of greenhouse gas. Forecasts for the United Kingdom alone suggest that CO_2 emissions from aviation could account for as much as 25 percent of the nation's total contribution to global warming by 2030.[3] And the CO_2 that planes emit can stay in the atmosphere for one hundred years.[4]

George Monbiot, a columnist for the *Guardian* and author of *Heat: How to Stop the Planet Burning*, has concluded that with current technology, we have no choice but to stop flying if we want to slow global warming. But grounding our fleets would be an economic disaster that would bring to a halt tourism, trade, the airline industry, and Christmas trips to Grandma's house. Like his colleagues, Branson doesn't want to get out of the airline business. Instead he is concentrating on finding a jet fuel that emits less greenhouse gas.

Virgin Atlantic in 2008 flew one of its 747 jumbo jets with some biofuels mixed in its tanks to prove it could be done. But the search for an affordable replacement has just begun. To find the best biofuel for the job, Virgin Fuels has formed a partnership with GE and Boeing to invest in and test substitutes. The airline and its partners have already rejected ethanol. Why? With all the progress and investment in ethanol you'd think it would be a suitable replacement for jet fuel. The trouble is that each gallon of ethanol contains roughly one-third less energy than a gallon of gasoline. To fly a jet its maximum range you'd have to put more ethanol in its tanks; the weight of that extra fuel would necessitate larger wings and engines, which in turn demand still more fuel.

Biodiesel made from soybeans or palm oil doesn't work well either, because at the frigid temperatures in which jets fly, the fuel would turn into sludge—not desirable at 35,000 feet above the earth.

Amyris Biotechnologies, a start-up in Emeryville, California, thinks it has a solution for the aviation industry—as well as for the auto industry. Amyris has raised a total of $90 million from investors including Duff Ackerman & Goodrich and TPG Biotechnology. Venture capitalists Vinod Khosla and John Doerr of Kleiner Perkins have also chipped in funds.

The company is a paradigm for the new green economy, a fresh example of how experts from different disciplines are joining forces to solve global warming. In 2004 UC Berkeley chemical and biological engineering professor Jay Keasling brought together three other specialists with backgrounds in bacteriology, biophysics, and chemical engineering. Originally, the company, backed by a grant from the Bill & Melinda Gates Foundation, was working on a breakthrough process to make more affordable artemisinin, an important antimalarial drug that should be available in the developing world by 2009.

After this breakthrough, the company's focus shifted to biofuels, and it began recruiting talent from ten different industries including, as CEO, John Melo, a former BP executive. In his glass-walled corner office overlooking a quiet courtyard, Melo explained why he moved from one of the world's largest oil companies to a small energy start-up. At BP he had spent years building the company's distribution business into a profitable division and in the process observed that BP itself could save a great deal of money in its operations by using energy more wisely. "That for me was a fundamental breakthrough. Being green didn't mean fewer profits. Being green didn't mean bad for business. It actually was good for business to be green."

Melo also realized the limitations of petroleum. "If you look at the math, we have fifty-five or so years left of oil supply. That's pretty scary if you're sitting there and your core business is oil and gas exploration and production. We spent a lot of time at the corporation thinking, 'So what do we do to go beyond this and how do we get there?' And for me, my second big realization was actually that there's a world beyond big oil."

In the fall of 2006, Melo transferred his experience and knowledge to Amyris. His plan was based on a few essentials: the new fuel must be at least as efficient, convenient, and affordable as fossil fuel. And it must easily fit into a massive distribution system that supplies 243 million cars and trucks and 8,100 commercial jetliners in the United States alone. That, to say the least, is a steep challenge.

To meet those requirements, the Berkeley scientists in the Amyris labs are genetically engineering microorganisms to make jet fuel. The fuel can also be used in diesel- and gasoline-powered cars and trucks. "Amyris is designing better biofuels from designer bugs," said investor John Doerr. "This is a big deal because Amyris's cost-competitive biofuels will work with existing engines without compromising performance and will have a lower carbon footprint."[5]

While working on an inexpensive medicine to treat malaria, scientist Jay Keasling and his team identified more than fifty thousand compounds that could be created with one basic technology. They noted that there were fuels within that family, and these were the molecules they wanted to reproduce. They use a process called synthetic biology, in which you identify the molecules you want among those that nature itself produces. You then design in the laboratory a microbe to produce those molecules.

Keasling and his scientists designed a microorganism that acts like a microscopic factory, constantly fermenting sugar and excreting a hydrocarbon with properties similar to kerosene jet fuel. (Hydrocarbon biofuels are distinct from ethanol, which is alcohol based.) Amyris is putting its first bugs to work on sugarcane. To grow, process, and burn sugarcane releases much less greenhouse gas than fossil fuels and corn ethanol. That is because, unlike corn, sugarcane needs little if any petrochemical fertilizer and its waste can be burned to generate energy to run the refineries.

For example, Brazil's ethanol industry uses the waste from sugarcane to provide the energy to process the cane into ethanol. The only greenhouse gas emitted comes from the diesel in the trucks that move the fuel to market. As a result, Brazilian ethanol emits anywhere from 55 to 90 percent less CO_2 than gasoline. Because Amyris's fuel can also be made from sugarcane, its greenhouse gas emissions are expected to be as low.

Melo hopes to start selling his biofuel by 2010, but first he must buy large amounts of cane. Because only about 2 percent of the available land in Brazil is currently used to grow cane, Melo thinks farmers can grow a lot more without destroying forests or threatening protected spaces. That, of course, remains to be seen. Forests presently are being cleared at so rapid a pace that huge swaths of jungle have been decimated—to the great detriment of the planet's health. There would have to be a massive program of education and compensation to get farmers to keep out of the woods. This would require government cooperation and subsidies that might raise the price and feasibility of the Amyris biofuel.

Then Melo would have to arrange joint ventures with at least thirty or forty Brazilian ethanol refineries—the country has nearly four hundred—to cooperate in the production of bioengineered fuel. That may be a hard sell. Even Melo, at his most enthusiastic, believes his fuel will eventually cost about the same to make as Brazilian ethanol, roughly $25 to $30 a barrel. (Oil, at the start of 2008, was selling for more than $100 a barrel.) Serious financial incentives may be required for the Brazilians to bother with the new technology. But because Amyris's fuel can be used in jets, the Brazilians would be able to expand their markets for fuel.

Brazil would only be the first step. Melo would like to grow and produce his fuel in a band around the globe 15 or 20 degrees on either side of the equator—the best climate for sugarcane. India, Angola, and other countries in the sub-Saharan region would be included.

Though it may take time, Melo thinks his company can help meet the growing global demand for energy. He points out that the Amyris biofuel can be blended in any proportion with gas, diesel, and jet fuel, just the way ethanol is blended with gasoline today. Too many unknown factors are at play to predict precisely how much of the global energy market Amyris could capture, but Melo and his investors think over the next decade they could capture at least 10 percent of the U.S. market. And the potential payoff is enormous. The American wholesale gasoline market is $300 billion a year. If Amyris captured 10 percent of that market through its blends, its revenues would hit $30 billion annually.

Or the company could sell its biofuel to the developing world. This would allow China and India to keep expanding their economies while using less fossil fuel. "It's almost like you end up making China a biodiesel economy, right?" Melo asks. "Eventually you could easily get to a point where the growth in energy demand in the developing world is all covered by renewable fuels. If you could just find a way to keep demand for fossil fuels flat, that would be a great mission."

What about the $100 billion global jet fuel market? Amyris's jet fuel will come to market after its vehicle fuels because it must pass four years of rigorous testing by, among others, Boeing, the Federal Aviation Administration, and the U.S. Air Force. But it may be worth the wait because it would do more than cut down on greenhouse gas. Traditional jet fuel can operate at temperatures as cold as 45 degrees below zero. Amyris has found that its jet fuel will still burn at 60 degrees below zero. This would allow jets to fly higher, and the higher they fly the less fuel they burn. The air force could fly longer military missions, and commercial liners could undertake more over-the-pole flights to Asia, which saves passengers time.

The company faces steep challenges. It has, as of this writing, produced only laboratory amounts of the fuel. Will it perform as well as fossil fuels and be affordable in mass quantities? Some of the regions of the world in which Melo wants to operate are politically unstable. And Brazilian farmers may very well cut down forests to grow cane, negating most of the greenhouse gas savings.

Other firms are working on similar technologies and may beat Amyris to market. Craig Venter, who mapped the human genome, is working on bioengineering gasoline, as is a Silicon Valley start-up called LS 9. Even so, Melo remains undaunted. "We know it works. The only question is, exactly how much will it cost and in what time? I believe by 2011, we'll be a billion-dollar-plus company, and then the upside is really how fast can we go?"

The Next Saudi Arabia

Though more of us may eventually drive all-electric cars, we are much further along with hybrid technology that mates a gasoline or diesel engine with an electric motor. Though hybrids will use less fuel than today's engines now require, we will still need billions of barrels of fuel each year to power them. But we cannot continue to rely on fossil fuels to run our cars or the world will succumb to global warming.

While start-ups such as Amyris work on bioengineered oil, it is ethanol, an alcohol-based fuel made from corn, soybeans, sugarcane, and other organic substances, that is now the organic fuel of choice. GM, Ford, Toyota, Honda, and other manufacturers already produce cars that can use it. Forty percent of Brazil's car and light-truck fuel is ethanol made from sugarcane.

The principle that has been laid out for us goes something like this: fill up your hybrid fuel tank with ethanol, use less gasoline, and advance the environment-saving goal of 60 miles per gallon. All it takes to convert a new car to run on ethanol are some simple modifications, such as adding a stainless-steel gas tank and hardier gaskets. The cost is as little as $100 for every new vehicle that rolls off the assembly line.

Ethanol-powered cars, known as flex-fuel cars because they can also burn gasoline, are in the mainstream. As of this writing, about 1,200 gas stations out of the nation's 187,000 offer E85, a blend of 85 percent ethanol and 15 percent gasoline. Most of these stations are in the Midwest, where corn ethanol is produced. Minnesota has 290 ethanol stations, followed by Illinois with 135. In 2007 racers at the Indianapolis 500 used E100, fuel that is 100 percent ethanol, and David Franchitti's 670-horsepower, orange and black ethanol car won.

Interest in ethanol is burgeoning, but the technology isn't new. A 1927 Indy 500 car ran the race on ethanol. Henry Ford's first car, the quadricycle, built in 1896, was designed to use pure ethanol, as was the original Model T.

Thanks to hefty federal subsidies, America's ethanol industry is booming. Since 1999 the number of U.S. ethanol plants has doubled to 135, with at least 65 more under construction. Though ethanol represented only about 2 percent of America's transportation fuel in 2006, its use is growing so fast that it could be in wide distribution within several years.

In August 2006, Rod Blagojevich, the governor of Illinois, announced a sweeping $1.2 billion plan to replace half of his state's imported oil with ethanol by 2017. He hopes to offer financial incentives to build ethanol plants, adding to the six facilities already operating in Illinois. Other states have similar, if less ambitious, programs. California governor Arnold Schwarzenegger is backing a ballot initiative that would encourage service station owners to offer ethanol at the pump.

Promising? Not if you consider the downside of corn ethanol, in particular. The increased demand for corn for use in fuel drives up the price of food. In 2007 U.S. corn prices doubled, hurting both cattle ranchers and consumers who had to pay more for a box of cornflakes. Around the same time, residents of one Mexican town rioted after the price of their corn tortillas rose as a result of the boom in ethanol products. More telling, the production and use of corn to make ethanol reduces greenhouse gases at best only about 20 percent compared with gasoline. That is helpful, but not helpful enough. If the world adopts corn ethanol as its major fuel, it will succeed in driving food prices up while doing little to combat global warming.

A growing number of forward-looking entrepreneurs, scientists, and corporate titans, including Bill Gates and Richard Branson, are investing hundreds of millions of dollars in companies such as Pacific Ethanol and Virgin Fuels to explore a new, more promising fuel: cellulosic ethanol. This fuel can be made from switchgrass or other prairie grasses and from wood chips. And that's why Branson alone has committed $300 to $400 million over the next few years to cellulosic ethanol production, and thinks he can eventually get a 30 percent return on his money. Royal Dutch Shell and Goldman Sachs have invested in a start-up called Iogen that is building a plant that will turn switchgrass and elephant grass or even wood chips into ethanol in a process that binds the latest in biotech research with the methods that Appalachian residents have used for decades to produce moonshine. (See chapter 7 for the use of algae in converting coal power plant emissions into automobile fuel.)

Transportation fueled by cellulosic ethanol made from plants and wood waste is a natural, closed-loop system. The claim is that it would allow us to drive our cars without in any significant way contributing to global warming or filling the coffers of unfriendly regimes. How will such technology work? The sun, our most bountiful energy source, nourishes the plants, which, while growing, absorb greenhouse gas and turn it into the oxygen we breathe. Then new enzymes developed by the biotech industry turn the biomass into grain alcohol or ethanol that, when we burn it in our cars, produces 80 to 90 percent less greenhouse gas than gasoline. Such a system would go a long way toward combating global warming. It might also create a new energy industry with thousands of jobs to help replace those lost in the oil and coal industries as those begin to shrink.

One of the most persuasive proponents of ethanol's potential is Vinod Khosla, whose passion in life seems to be to invest in companies searching to produce enough ethanol to replace the 385 million gallons of gasoline Americans burn in their cars and trucks each *day*. Khosla studied at Stanford University and then in 1979 with a few colleagues started a small computer firm that became the $15 billion Sun Microsystems. After seventeen years with Sun, Khosla became a partner in the venture firm Kleiner Perkins Caufield & Byers, early investors in Yahoo!, eBay, and Google. Khosla himself is said to be worth an estimated $3 billion.

In 2004 Khosla formed an investment fund called Khosla Ventures dedicated to making cellulosic ethanol a reality. Why would such a wealthy man bother to invest outside of high-tech, the field where he made his fortune? Simply put, he sees green energy as the next great new industry for wealth creation.

Critics of ethanol, many of them in the oil industry, argue that there isn't enough farmland to grow the corn, soybeans, and other crops to meet our nation's fuel needs. They claim that ethanol takes more energy to produce than it yields because its production requires vast amounts of fossil fuels for the tractors and petrochemical fertilizers needed to grow the ethanol crops and for the energy-intensive refining process. Ethanol, they say, would not be economically viable without government handouts. Even leaders of the environmental movement worry that using corn to fuel our cars will drive up food prices. According to Lester Brown, president of the Earth Policy Institute, "The growing myth that corn is a cure-all for our energy woes is leading us toward a potentially dangerous global fight for food." The grain required to fill a 25-gallon SUV gas tank, Brown points out, could feed one person for a year.

But, though he is a soft-spoken man, Khosla loves nothing better than to rebut critics with steely logic. Addressing a roomful of global CEOs, politicians, and scientists during a session of *Fortune* magazine's 2006 Brainstorm Conference in Aspen, Khosla conceded that his critics make some good points—but only if they're talking about ethanol derived from food sources. Ethanol made from corn does generate some greenhouse gas, he says, because the tractors, trucks, and fertilizers needed to grow these crops use fossil fuels. And if the world decides to use vast quantities of these crops for fuel, that could indeed drive up food prices.

However, Khosla feels that the future does not lie in corn or soybean ethanol. In his 2006 State of the Union address, President Bush highlighted cellulosic ethanol, which can be produced from nonfood crops such as switchgrass, elephant grass, and other wild grasses so prevalent in the Midwest. These native crops don't need fertilizer, nor does the soil in which they flourish require tilling by giant machinery. And they certainly don't require elaborate irrigation systems that gulp precious water. Switchgrass (*Panicum virgatum*) belongs to the millet family, and, like other prairie grasses, can grow anywhere in the heartland from Canada to Texas. It thrives in both sandy soil and clay and is tolerant of floods as well as droughts. Because of its deep root system, it helps control erosion by slowing down water runoff and preserving beneficial sediments in the field. Songbirds, game birds, and waterfowl inhabit it.

Cellulosic ethanol can also be made from biowaste like wood chips from sawmills and even from stalks of corn left after the ears are plucked for food. Khosla sums it up: "If you care about energy security and you're a conservative, cellulosic ethanol is the only answer. If you care about farm income and rural employment, it is the only answer. If you care about global warming, it is the answer."

Is there enough America farmland to produce the switchgrass and other plant life needed to fuel our cars and trucks? According to disparate sources on both sides of the fuel debate, the answer is yes. The Natural Resources Defense Council (NRDC), an environmental nonprofit organization with no interest in seeing our soil overfarmed, depleted, and eroded, believes that farmers would need to plant 114 million acres to provide the raw materials for ethanol fuel. On the other hand, under various present federal programs, farmers are now paid *not* to plant 120 million acres. But Khosla believes the NRDC's estimates are too conservative and that it would take only a fraction of those fallow acres to produce the ethanol we need.

Today's croplands yield anywhere from two to six tons of corn, soybeans, or wheat per acre per year. In an experimental project, the University of Illinois is growing miscanthus, the tropical plant known as elephant grass, which, like switchgrass, is a source of cellulosic ethanol. They have reached the point where they can produce elephant grass at seven times the tonnage per acre than corn. A 2005 report by the National Commission on Energy Policy, a bipartisan group of twenty of the nation's leading energy experts from the ranks of industry, government, academia, labor, and consumer organizations, concluded that the United States would need only 30 million acres of farmland to grow enough cellulosic ethanol to replace half its gasoline.

The hope is that cellulosic ethanol will eventually be cheaper than gasoline as technology advances. Some say ethanol eventually can be produced wholesale for as little as 50 cents a gallon. Entrepreneurs are betting that this infant industry will be able to increase production of cellulosic ethanol from the current 400 gallons of motor fuel per acre to 2,000 to 3,000 gallons with modest improvements in techniques. These numbers are speculative, and the side effects and problems that will arise with this new fuel source are unknown. For example, will the use of grasses in cellulosic ethanol diminish the availability of cattle feed and thus, in a roundabout way, also seriously affect food quantities?

Yet critics who say that ethanol will never achieve the economies of scale to replace oil need look no further than Brazil. Brazilians drive 1.3 million flex-fuel cars that can burn either ethanol made from sugarcane or gas or a combination of both. All of Brazil's gas stations sell ethanol, 85 percent of new cars sold can burn it, and it is priced at 20 percent less than gasoline without government subsidies. Like switchgrass and elephant grass, sugarcane is energy efficient. You get eight times more energy from cane than you put into it during production and delivery. And it is sustainable. Cane requires no fertilizer, tilling, or expensive irrigation. It absorbs enough greenhouse gas as it grows to offset most of the CO_2 that is released by driving. Brazil's move to sugarcane ethanol is generating thousands of new jobs. The country has already built 250 mills in its southeastern provinces, and 50 new ones, at $100 million each, are on the way. According to *Fortune* magazine, Brazil no longer needs to import oil, and the $69 billion that would have gone to the Middle East or to Venezuela has stayed in the country and generated jobs in rural areas.

Brazil's climate is perfect for growing sugarcane; ours is not. The way it looks now, if the ethanol industry is to take off in the United States, it will have to rely upon wild grasses and wood waste. Researchers have devised enzymes that convert the cellulose derived from grasses, tree bark, and other fibrous plant material into simple sugars that can then be fermented and distilled into ethanol. Start-ups such as Canada's Iogen and BC International are among the new companies commercializing the process. The new enzymes they are using were developed by small biotech companies, among them Ceres in Thousand Oaks, California, Genencor in Palo Alto, Novozymes in Denmark, and Verenium in Cambridge, Massachusetts. Through their efforts the cost of the enzymes needed to make a gallon of cellulosic ethanol has been cut from $5 several years ago to 20 cents.

So far, the best enzyme, weirdly enough, comes from a hopped-up version of *Trichoderma reesei*, the fungus that causes jungle rot and eats up canvas tents and clothes in the tropics. The technology looks like a cooking exercise: at Iogen's pilot plant in Ottawa, workers take a 1,000-pound bale of straw, shred it, steam it, and then combine it with water, heat, and enzymes in a large sealed cylinder. After a few days the enzymes convert the cellulose in the straw to sugar, which is then fermented and distilled into 200-proof ethanol. The leftover woody matter, lignin, can be dried and pressed into the burnable cakes that Iogen plans to use to power future ethanol plants.

Royal Dutch Shell and Goldman Sachs have invested in Iogen, which annually produces relatively small quantities of ethanol made from straw, barley, wheat, and oats, in a pilot plant in Ottawa. Its planned Idaho plant will be designed to produce 45 million gallons of ethanol a year—about three hours' supply for the United States. It may be a small contribution, but it is an important step in the development of an important biofuel.

Peter Huber, a senior fellow at the Manhattan Institute and coauthor of *The Bottomless Well*, points to a potential downside: people in third world countries will be able to buy cheap enzymes to produce homemade ethanol in their backyards to heat their homes, power their motorbikes, and cook their food. He says, "History has already taught us what a carbohydrate-energy economy does to a rich, green landscape—it levels it." Huber bemoans what 7 billion people in search of wood and plants for ethanol fuel will do to our forests and our grasslands. If people strip the countryside for fuel, we might end up emitting even more carbon into the atmosphere since there would be fewer trees and plants to soak up the CO_2.

The points he makes bear consideration but, if ethanol becomes as cheap and as available as has been predicted, there may be less incentive for rural dwellers to set up, run, and maintain ethanol factories in their backyards.

Vinod Khosla would like to see business ramp up ethanol research and investment and the government provide tax incentives to kick-start this new industry. He and other enthusiasts believe that most Americans could be driving clean-burning cellulosic ethanol cars within the next several years. But to reach that goal, we need political will, capital, and ingenuity. As a nation and a world community, we also must be willing to accept change. We simply can't go on doing what we've always done and thereby destroy our children's world. Khosla likes to quote his favorite inventor, Edwin Land, the creator of the Polaroid camera: "Innovation is the cessation of stupidity."

7

The Carbon-Muncher

The Blooming of Algae

|SAAC BERZIN'S EUREKA MOMENT came one morning while he was trying to figure out how to use algae to increase the oxygen in the atmosphere on board the International Space Station. He was in the basement office of Payload Systems, a Cambridge, Massachussetts, company that develops astronautical gear for NASA. As he watched a culture of green algae voraciously devour its way through a vial of waste, he thought to himself, "Why can't we use algae to get rid of pollutants on Earth?"

The son of an Israeli inventor, Berzin always had a curious mind. He earned a doctorate in chemical engineering from an Israeli university and then came to America to start his postdoctoral work at MIT. Armed with stubborn determination, Berzin has embarked on a journey many of the top scientific minds in his field said was insane—to use algae to take carbon from the exhaust of coal-fired plants and turn it into biofuel.

The best coal plant is the one that's never built. The more we can reduce electricity consumption through conservation, the fewer of these polluting behemoths will be necessary to meet our energy needs. But with the growing thirst for power, more coal plants will be built both in the United States and abroad. America has 619 coal plants and 150 more on the drawing boards. And China is building the equivalent of two new coal plants each *week*. That makes it urgent for industry to find ways to eliminate the CO_2 that comes out of our industrial chimneys.

Around the globe, government and industry are working together to find ways to take greenhouse gas exhaust and bury it underground where it cannot add to global warming. This technology, called carbon sequestration, has been used in the oil and gas industry. Now the challenge is to transfer some version of that technology to coal, cement, and steel plants. The challenges are steep. It is extremely difficult and expensive to capture carbon from existing coal plants. Some experts believe it would be better to replace these old plants with a next-generation coal plant that uses gasification technology that makes it much easier to capture and store carbon. However, doing so will be costly. Burying the carbon is estimated to raise the cost of coal-fired electricity for households in the United States some 50 percent. And where is the economic incentive to do this? Carbon sequestration is a cost, not a business opportunity (except for those manufacturing the equipment to capture the carbon). It simply makes generating electricity and making concrete and steel more expensive. Utilities will have no incentive to purchase these clean coal technologies until the passage of some form of carbon tax or cap and trade system, which would make the cost of *not* sequestering carbon greater.

Even if the sequestration technology worked and made economic sense, the industry would still need to solve some sticky problems. For instance, the polluting coal plants are often not located near the kind of land formations necessary to store CO_2 underground, and in those cases it would have to be piped miles away—an expensive and energy-wasting proposition. If the sequestration isn't handled properly, the CO_2 could escape from underground and suffocate anyone living nearby—the gas crowds out most of the oxygen in the air. In 1986 Nyos, a volcanic crater lake in Cameroon, belched bubbles of CO_2 into the night air, and the gas settled around the lake's shore, where it killed 1,800 people and thousands of animals.[1]

To try to overcome such challenges, the U.S. Department of Energy (DOE) in 2007 awarded funds for the first major carbon sequestration project in the United States—the largest such endeavor in the world to date. Canada, Norway, and Algeria also have experimental carbon storage projects under way. The three DOE projects, which will be located in the Plains states, the Southeast, and the Southwest, will attempt to store large volumes of carbon dioxide in deep saline reservoirs. DOE plans to invest $197 million over ten years, and when you factor in industry's share, the entire investment rises to $318 million.[2] Another DOE project, The FutureGen Alliance, is a consortium of fourteen of the world's largest coal producers and users. The Bush administration has agreed to pay 75 percent of the cost of building experimental plants in Texas and Illinois that cook coal into gas and then separate the CO_2 so it can be pumped underground. So far cost overruns have stalled the project.[3]

Yet, what if there was a simpler way to eliminate carbon *and* make money at the same time? Isaac Berzin believes his algae farms can do just that—suck carbon out of coal plant exhaust and other sources of CO_2. And he is not alone. Some heavy-hitting investors smell money in the pond water. Venture capitalists such as biotech's big backer Craig Venter, Internet investor Bob Metcalfe of Polaris Venture Partners in Boston, and Sandhill Road titan Steve Jurvetson of Draper Fisher Jurvetson have distributed millions of dollars of seed money to more than a dozen green ooze–growing firms, including Aurora Biofuels, Solazyme, and Solix Biofuels.

Doug Henston, a former investment banker and real estate manager, came on board as chief operating officer of Solix Biofuels, a Fort Collins, Colorado, start-up. In 2006 he secured $2 million in funding from Bohemian Investments. Solix, working with Colorado State University engineers to produce biodiesel from oil derived from algae, plans to have its technology on the market over the next two years. The technology is based on twenty years of research from the National Renewable Energy Laboratory's Aquatic Species Program. Henston says the advantage of algae, which grow in plastic bags and feed on carbon from fossil fuel–powered plants, is that they can produce biofuel without competing with the global food supply. Algae production systems do not require soil for growth, use 99 percent less water than conventional agriculture, and can be located on nonagricultural land far from water. The company says that algae can produce more oil in an area the size of a two-car garage than can an entire football field of soybeans.

So far, Berzin's company, which is building two algae farms, seems to hold the lead. He got into the energy game in 2001 after he formed GreenFuel Technologies. He had taken his idea for greenhouse gas–munching algae to MIT, which proposed to patent it and then license it back to him. In exchange, MIT offered Berzin a lab and a salary. Not wanting to hand over his intellectual capital to the university, Berzin quit his job at MIT. The young entrepreneur set out without much money. He and his wife, who was working on a Ph.D. in languages at Harvard, were trying to live on her modest salary. Two friends came to the rescue and invested $200,000 in his fledgling company. For the next two to three years, Berzin kept refining his algae in a lab he set up in the basement of his next-door neighbor.

Berzin points out that algae, an aquatic life-form with no roots, stems, or leaves, are not only the fastest-growing plants on Earth—a colony can double its size in a matter of hours—but also superrich in vegetable oil, which can account for as much as half of their body mass. As important, algae love nothing better than to gobble up vast amounts of carbon dioxide.

As he toiled away in his lab, Berzin envisioned someday building giant bioreactors that would take the greenhouse gas pouring from the chimneys of coal plants, cement factories, and steel mills and channel the smoke through acres and acres of long translucent containers filled with algae and water. The algae would eat the carbon dioxide in the exhaust and turn it into oil that could be harvested each day. The efficiency would be amazing. Algae, after all, synthesize thirty times more vegetable oil per acre than plants like sunflowers or rapeseed. And that vegetable oil, Berzin knew, could be converted to biodiesel to run our cars, trucks, and machinery. The algae, when eating, would also devour as much as 40 percent of the carbon dioxide from our greenhouse gas–spewing factories.

Berzin's idea is paradigm shifting. Imagine a series of bioreactors built next to coal-fired utilities, cement plants, and refineries: they could eliminate a significant portion of the 1 billion tons of carbon dioxide emitted from these sources each year out of the 7 billion tons the world emits. Though these bioreactors would take up 5 million acres of land, most of it would surround dirty industrial facilities where no one wants to live or plant crops anyway. That's an area about the size of two Yellowstone National Parks— on a global scale a tiny fraction of our landmass.

The only problem was, the scientific community said it couldn't be done. In 1978 Jimmy Carter, reacting to the oil crisis, asked the DOE to explore ways to create renewable transportation fuels from pond algae. Scientists with the Aquatic Species Program spent the next eighteen years studying algae in California, Hawaii, and New Mexico and came to the conclusion that you could use algae to produce fuel but it would cost at least $40 a barrel—double the cost of a barrel of oil in 1996, the year the Clinton administration closed down the program. The Aquatic Species experiments had used algae in open ponds to process the greenhouse gas from coal plants into biofuel. The scientists recognized that there were other ways to approach the problem—the governments of Japan, France, and Germany had invested significant R&D dollars on novel closed bioreactor designs for algae production—but noted that their costs were even more prohibitive than those for growing algae in open ponds.

Berzin didn't buy it. "When we looked at the work they did, it turned out a lot of their numbers were wrong. I thought we could make biofuels at a cost competitive to oil." In fact, he believes that he could make algae grow so efficiently that he could beat the price of oil by a lot.

But that left the matter of money. Berzin's start-up funds were almost gone when he met a man who would change the fate of his company. Friends introduced him to Len Blavatnik, an American industrialist who emigrated with his family from Russia in 1978 and got a master's in computer science at Columbia and then an MBA from Harvard in 1989. After earning his business degree, Blavatnik returned to Russia, where he brokered a number of large deals as Russia was privatizing many of its industries in the wake of the fall of the Berlin Wall. His company, Access Industries, now includes investments in industries such as oil, coal, aluminum, telecommunications, media, and real estate. In 2007, according to *Forbes* magazine, Blavatnik was worth $7.2 billion. He apparently spends his time shuttling between homes in New York and London, where he purchased a house in Kensington Palace Gardens for £41 million.

In 2003 Berzin, still playing with vials of algae in his neighbor's basement, described his project to Blavatnik, who offered to write a check for $100,000 on the spot. Berzin, desperate for money, said, "No, no, no, I can't take your money because it's not nearly enough, I need at least $1 million." Blavatnik thought about it for around thirty seconds and said, "OK, that will take a little longer. I'll send my team in here." After his team vetted the project, Blavatnik concluded that Berzin didn't need $1 million—he needed $2 million. (The company has since raised backing from the venture capital firms Draper Fisher Jurvetson in California and Polaris Venture Partners in Massachusetts.)

That seed money let Berzin build a pilot bioreactor on top of an MIT building, which proved, at least on a small scale, that his concept worked. News of the MIT bioreactor was picked up by television, newspapers, and magazines around the world. The scientific operation had been launched, but was it a business? To find out, Berzin added Cary Bullock to GreenFuel's executive team in February 2005. Bullock, an MIT-trained physicist and electrical engineer, had been involved in the energy business since the mid-1970s when he was a principal at a consulting firm called XZenergy that helped large companies cope with the rapid rise in oil prices. He and his partners built up and sold XZenergy. In the early days of GreenFuel, before he was hired, Bullock visited its Cambridge offices to share a sandwich and to bounce ideas around. What he liked about the company was Berzin's vision to tackle global warming head-on. "I've always thought the carbon issue is important," says Bullock. "It fits into the Native American thinking to take only what you need and leave the rest for the next generation. So the sustainable aspect appealed to me."

Yet Bullock realized that nothing was sustainable unless money was made, and after he was asked to join the company as CEO in early 2005, he began turning GreenFuel into a business by cutting deals with utilities to install GreenFuel systems at their coal and natural gas plants. In November 2006, Arizona Public Service Company, the state's largest utility, serving a million customers, announced that it had attached a small GreenFuel system to the exhaust stacks of one of its Redhawk natural gas plants, west of Phoenix. Ray Hobbes, the manager who oversees the project for the utility, says that for every acre of algae grown on the plant site, at least 250 tons of CO_2 can be absorbed—the greatest ever achieved outside of a laboratory.

Arizona Public Service has also become the first utility to produce biodiesel and ethanol on-site using algae. The Arizona utility harvests the algae, which grow as they eat up the CO_2 spilling from the plant's chimney. The utility then turns their starches into ethanol and their lipids into biodiesel. The algae's protein could potentially be converted to high-grade food for livestock. The rest gets returned to the algae farm as nutrients—nothing goes to waste. So far the results are impressive. While each acre of corn produces around 300 gallons of ethanol a year and an acre of soybeans around 60 gallons of biodiesel, each acre of algae, based on Arizona's results, will be able to churn out several thousand gallons of biofuel each year. "At this productivity level, GreenFuel's system is ahead of other biomass production methods," says Professor Otto Pulz, president of the European Society of Microalgal Biotechnology and head of the IGV Institute's Biotechnology Department in Germany.

Ramping up to commercial scale is taking longer than the company hoped. In 2007, Bob Metcalfe, a GreenFuel backer, joined the company as interim CEO, asking Bullock to concentrate on new business development. Metcalfe's pedigree is impressive. This engineer-scientist in the early 1970s co-invented Ethernet, the local-area networking standard. After that he founded and ran 3Com Corporation, the billion-dollar networking company.

For all GreenFuel's success at growing algae, it has run into a serious technical hurdle on the way to mass production. The algae grew so rapidly that the company could not harvest it fast enough. In fact, the algae grew so dense that it blocked sunlight and nutrients, which caused the colony to start dying. GreenFuel had to shut down its greenhouse and is working to redesign the system to prevent this problem. In July 2007, Metcalfe made the case to investors that the setbacks could be reversed successfully and raised $5.5 million to keep the company going.

If it can work through its technological challenges, GreenFuel will next install its technology in the Arizona utility's Four Corners power plant, a massive coal-fired facility near Farmington, Arizona, that spews out tons of carbon each year. This would be the world's first full-scale algae farm. But GreenFuel isn't stopping there. It is also working with the utility NRG, which is located in Princeton, New Jersey, and had sales of $5.9 billion in 2006. The company would like to put a GreenFuel unit in one of its giant 1.4-gigawatt coal power plants in Louisiana. Bullock estimates that it will take about two years from planning to operation before the utility can start capturing large amounts of CO_2.

So how will GreenFuel make money? First, some twenty-three states have passed laws either limiting greenhouse emissions or requiring that a certain percentage of the power generated in the state derive from renewable resources. To meet these new regulations, utilities will pay GreenFuel to take their carbon away.

Next, the company believes it can make a gallon of biodiesel from algae for only $1.40 compared with around $2.40, the average price of a gallon of biofuel in 2007. This fuel can be used in today's cars and trucks. After the oil is extracted for fuel, the algae also generate a mixture of starch and protein that can be used for animal feedstock.

Bullock thinks he can make his biofuel so cheaply because "you're getting a lot of stuff for free that you'd ordinarily have to pay for. You need heat to keep the algae colony growing in a certain temperature range, and we get that free from the waste heat coming from the coal plant. You need carbon dioxide to feed the algae, and we get that for free from the coal plant exhaust. The algae need light to grow and, guess what?—sunlight is free. If you had to duplicate the sun's rays with lamps it would cost a fortune. And I don't need potable water and I don't need expensive land."

Yes, but GreenFuel must find millions of acres on which to build its algae farms. Each GreenFuel unit needs 250 acres of land; some power plants may need as many as sixteen units sprawled over 4,000 acres to capture the maximum amount of CO_2. "Four thousand acres may sound like a lot," says Bullock, "but that's just a normal-size farm in Georgia." Bullock found that many big plants have empty parcels of basically useless land surrounding them, and he has identified enough land around existing power plants to handle 1,700 GreenFuel units. A GreenFuel facility at a large plant will cost a couple hundred million dollars to build. But that price may sound cheap when you consider all the potential sources of revenue.

Is there really a net savings for the environment? After all, the biofuel burned in cars goes back into the atmosphere. Biodiesel burns much cleaner in vehicles, however, and does not release the same toxins as gasoline. Plus each gallon of algae fuel produced means one less gallon of gasoline that has to be burned to meet our driving needs.

In the short term, Bullock thinks GreenFuel can grow to be a business with $100 million in revenues. Beyond the American market, he sees great potential internationally, including licensing the technology to companies in Australia, China, and Europe. (A recent licensing deal to a biofuels firm called DeBeers—no relation to the diamond producer—collapsed as the South African company allegedly couldn't deliver on its promises to investors.) In discussions with executives of Chinese companies, Bullock says that "a major part of the conversation is often about food. They tell us that they are a nation of 1.3 billion and that they have a lot of people to support." He says that investors in China like the idea that one of the by-products of his algae farms is animal feed, always in high demand in such a large nation with limited agricultural land.

Not all is bright in this vision. The commitment of land, money, and effort would be enormous, and it's difficult to estimate the payoff. No one has yet shown that these algae colonies can perform their jobs year after year on a commercial scale. "What worries me most," says Bullock, "is the things we haven't yet discovered, and we might not have an expert who knows how to deal with it." Will the algae colonies get contaminated, will they suddenly stop being highly productive, will someone come up with a better or cheaper technology?

Bullock sounds undaunted: "We have only a few years before investors run out of patience," he says, "We want to show the world what we can really do."

8

Big Sun

O_{N A SULTRY DAY} in the summer of 2005, one of Steven Cohen's deputies flew in from the East Coast to meet secretly with an entrepreneur named Martin Roscheisen in a small, unmarked building tucked away among warehouses on the wrong side of Palo Alto, just off Highway 101. The building was next door to the offices where Larry Page and Sergey Brin had founded Google in 1998. Today, however, the stakes promised to be even larger. Roscheisen, a Ph.D. in engineering from Stanford who had launched three start-ups during the Internet boom—including one that eventually became Yahoo! mail—and sold them for $1.3 billion, was working on a new technology that promised to cut the cost of solar power dramatically. But more on that later.

Cohen was intrigued when his associate reported back on the meetings. So intrigued that he later agreed to join a consortium of investors who put $150 million into Roscheisen's start-up, Nanosolar. What made this move significant was not the size of the investment. As the head of SAC Capital Partners, one of the largest hedge funds in the country with assets of $10 billion, Cohen was accustomed to dealing with much larger numbers than this. The telling fact was that Steven Cohen, one of the shrewdest brains on Wall Street, the man who traded billions daily with the flick of a computer key, who amassed a fortune that would have made the Sun King blush, who owned Picassos and Pollocks, and built a professional hockey rink for his kids in the backyard of his Greenwich, Connecticut, mansion, was investing in a fledgling solar start-up. That was news.

Solar energy has become the darling of both investors and environmentalists. Green advocates note correctly that solar—the conversion of the sun's energy into electricity—emits no greenhouse gas. Investors are flocking to solar, seeing it as one of the fastest-growing industries in the world. Indeed, in 2006, the global industry chalked up $15 billion in sales and grew at a 35 percent rate, and analysts predict it will maintain that breakneck pace for years to come.

SunPower, a California firm that makes solar systems for businesses and homes, expects to generate revenues of more than $1 billion and profits of around $150 million in 2008. Its customers include Wal-Mart, Microsoft, and FedEx. After going public in 2005, the San Jose company watched its stock rise over the next two years some 450 percent, from $18 a share to $82, making it worth nearly $7 billion, a little bigger than Whole Foods Market. And the boom is worldwide. China's first solar billionaire, Dr. Shi Zhengrong, who founded Suntech Power Holdings, is worth $2 billion and his firm $6 billion.[1] Japan's Sharp is the largest producer of solar in the world. About 10 percent of the company's business is solar, yet Katsuhiko Machida, the chairman and CEO, predicts that by 2010 solar power systems will become the largest business line of the company, surpassing sales of its flat-screen televisions. BP Solar, Evergreen Solar, Mitsubishi, Q-Cells, and Sanyo are also investing heavily in solar.

The financial potential of this industry is staggering. Compared with the $1 trillion of the current annual global electricity market, the $15 billion in sales currently generated by the solar industry might be confused with a rounding error. Yet, if solar could capture even 5 percent of the global market over the next decade, its share would be worth roughly $50 billion. Beyond that, solar could capture as much as a 25 percent market share—a remarkable figure but one that many industry players say is not out of the question—and industry sales would rise to $250 billion, at which point this fledgling sector would be generating more sales than General Motors.

In the emerging solar market, dozens of entrepreneurs and big companies are racing to develop the best technology. The choices are dizzying. The biggest and most successful segment of the market so far is photovoltaics (PV), which uses silicon, the building block of computer chips, to turn sunlight directly into electricity. When photons from sunlight pass through PV solar cells—which are typically embedded in the glass panels seen on the roofs of homes and businesses—electrons get knocked into a higher state of energy, creating electricity. Thin film solar, a next-generation PV technology just entering the market and being developed by start-ups such as Nanosolar, involves spreading exotic chemicals over a thin film of foil. When the sun hits, electricity is generated. Entrepreneurs who believe thin film will be cheaper and more versatile than silicon PV envision laying sheets of it on the sides of buildings, on the tops of cars, or even on the backs of cell phones to generate power.

The most common use of silicon PV cells is to generate power on-site to homes and businesses. However, some utilities are installing vast fields of PV solar panels to generate electricity that's fed into the grid. The size of these solar farms offers economies of scale that drive down the price of electricity generated by silicon PV panels. The Juwi Group, based in Bolanden, Germany, is building the world's largest PV power plant. Stretching over an area the size of two hundred soccer fields at a former military base to the east of Leipzig, the Juwi plant will generate 40 megawatts of electricity. That's more than three times larger than any PV plant built to date and enough electricity to service 14,000 homes. Great excitement in the industry also surrounds yet another emerging technology called solar thermal. These massive solar farms deploy thousands of mirrors to concentrate the sun's heat, which then boils liquid and creates steam that powers an electrical generator.

With all this promise, why doesn't the world go 100 percent solar? After all, enough sunlight hits the earth every hour to satisfy the energy needs of everyone on the planet for a year. The answer is simple. The economy runs 24/7, but solar energy systems don't work at night after the sun sets, and they lose efficiency on cloudy days. So far solar has made only minor inroads in power generation. In the United States, solar panels now produce less than 1 percent of the grid's power. Solar is not even close to meeting the equivalent power requirements of one major city. America's utilities generate $330 billion a year of electricity, half from coal plants.[2] The remainder of the power comes from natural gas, nuclear plants, and hydroelectricity.

Solar power by itself, then, will not solve our energy needs. Over the next decade, as noted, solar could provide as much as 5 percent of our electricity. While not a panacea, those kinds of levels of clean power would certainly help put a dent in global warming. Worldwide, electricity generated by fossil fuels accounts for about a quarter of the greenhouse gas emitted each year; in the United States the figure is about a third. If battery technology improves and we are able to store solar power for use when the sun isn't shining, then the sun could provide an even larger percentage of our power. In the meantime, we will still need to pursue other technologies such as wind, wave, clean coal, and nuclear to meet our overall energy needs.

Moreover, solar power still costs roughly two to three times more than electricity generated by coal and other fossil fuels. It's easy to see why. PV technology is based on the same silicon technology used in today's computer chips. The manufacturing process must be conducted in airtight, superclean rooms and is painstaking and expensive. Strong global demand for PV cells has been driving up the price of raw silicon. In fact, more silicon was used for solar cells in 2007 than for computer chips. To get the price down, the industry currently is building more silicon-processing facilities.

Many companies believe they can make solar price-competitive with coal within four or five years, but in the meantime the industry is dependent on substantial local and federal government subsidies. If those subsidies disappear, growth of the solar industry will stall. What's needed in the United States are assurances that the federal 30 percent investment tax credit for solar, which is due to expire at the end of 2008, stays in place long enough to allow solar to become competitive. That day could be hastened by also raising the cost of coal and other fossil fuels through a carbon tax or cap and trade system (see chapter 12).

Where Solar Shines

Europe's generous subsidies for solar have supercharged growth in the industry. The world's largest market for solar power is not temperate California or an area on the sunny shores of the Mediterranean, but cold, cloudy, rainy, snowy Germany. On the outskirts of Munich, solar panels line the autobahn to power nearby homes. Heiner Gärtner, a pig farmer in Buttenwiesen, has placed 10,000 solar panels on his land, enough to supply electricity to 1,500 nearby houses. He received a $5 million bank loan to buy and install the panels because the Federal Republic of Germany guarantees that anyone who produces renewable power will sell it at a profit: Gärtner brings in $600,000 a year, which will allow him to pay off his loan in fifteen years. Germany is so anxious to develop solar power that it pays this farmer two and a half times the going price of electricity to produce it.[3]

Such largesse has given birth to a thriving national solar industry. In 2005, 50 percent of all the PV cells produced in the world were installed in Germany, and the solar industry there has created 170,000 new jobs.[4] The German powerhouse Q-Cells, a world leader in PV solar production based in Bitterfeld-Wolfen, went public in October 2005, and two years later had a market capitalization of roughly $8.5 billion. Sales in 2006 reached $766 million, and in 2007 the company was increasing its sales and earnings about 45 percent a year—not bad for a company that didn't exist less than a decade ago.[5]

Germany has shown the world how government can spur the creation of an important new industry, one that will be crucial in the battle against global warming. The mechanism was simple. In 2004, the German parliament passed a law that mandates that by 2020 20 percent of the country's power must come from renewables such as solar and wind. (Germany is actually ahead of schedule, on track to reach 30 percent by 2020.) The government backed up that law with generous subsidies—the same ones that farmer Gärtner is profiting from. It is deliberately building a solar-based society.

Soon after the bill was passed, Hermann Scheer, one of Germany's leading advocates of renewables and a Social Democratic Party member of parliament, said on the documentary *Nova:* "Our children subsidize fossil fuel, and this is a contradiction that can't happen anymore." His point was that though it looks like we now enjoy cheap fossil fuels, the fact is that we are dumping the real costs—the droughts and floods caused by global warming, air pollution, and world conflicts—on our children and their children. It is not the legacy decent people should leave their offspring.

Scheer and other promoters of clean energy hope that the German government will support the solar industry until it becomes strong enough and its power cheap enough to compete on its own with gas and coal-fired electricity. German consumers do pay for their conversion: electricity prices are among the highest in the world—about twice those in America.

Solar energy gets similar government support in Japan. Its market is the third largest in the world after Germany's and Spain's. In 1994, when the cost of PV was very high, the Japanese government implemented a generous subsidy program. It helped fund five hundred solar installations the first year. By the end of the program in 2005,[6] the number rose to sixty thousand systems. As a result, the price of PV dropped *tenfold.*[7] Together Europe and

Asia have generated hundreds of thousands of new "green collar" jobs. America's solar industry could do the same as more and more workers are needed to install and maintain systems.

Those free market advocates who argue that green technologies should stand on their own from the outset forget that many twentieth-century American industries would not have developed as quickly as they did—if at all—without government largesse. Would the auto industry have prospered if billions of federal dollars had not been invested in our interstate highway system? Would airlines have been feasible if states and cities hadn't built airports? Worldwide, the total subsidy for fossil and nuclear energy is about $500 billion per year, ten times more than what has been spent for renewable energies in the last twenty years.[8] The American oil industry has received—and continues to receive—billions of dollars in subsidies to search for oil and gas. The coal industry also receives subsidies to cover health costs for miners, and the federal government insures the nuclear power industry against accident, which, in the case of a meltdown, could add up to hundreds of billions.

This does not mean that governments should be in the business of picking winners and losers. Governmentally decreed industrial policy usually doesn't work. In the 1980s and '90s the bureaucrats at Japan's Ministry of International Trade and Industry often directed research dollars to computer projects that failed in the marketplace. On the other hand, the freewheeling entrepreneurs of Silicon Valley built powerhouses like Apple, Dell, HP, Sun, and Cisco. When it comes to the energy industry, the free market has failed to price in the true cost of fossil fuels—damage to the environment, the military costs of protecting oil supplies, health problems from bad air quality. By one estimate you would need to tack $3 to $4 to the price of a gallon of gasoline to reflect its true cost to society. The best way to help foster alternative energy is to pass a carbon tax that would raise the price of fossil fuels to reflect their real costs, and then let the best green technologies win.

If the U.S. federal government fails to act, the responsibility to battle global warming will fall to the states. In California Governor Arnold Schwarzenegger has launched a "million solar roofs" initiative, with the state providing $3.2 billion to encourage home owners to install solar systems. Since the initiative, sales of solar systems in California have been booming. And it's no coincidence that, after California, the second-largest solar market in the country is not sunny Arizona or New Mexico, but New Jersey, thanks to generous subsidies in that state. In the absence of a national carbon tax, state subsidies are better than nothing, but they are not ideal. Businesses have to deal with a fragmented market with potentially fifty different sets of subsidies and tax laws. Furthermore, strapped state legislators, in need of raising tax revenues, could eliminate those tax breaks overnight and deal a blow to the solar industry.

Competing with Coal

Though they undoubtedly would welcome more government support, a growing number of big American corporations, venture capitalists, and entrepreneurs claim they can drive the price of PV technology down far enough to make it competitive with coal—the cheapest but most carbon-intensive way to generate electricity. To find out how that might happen, I spoke with Ron Kenedi, who runs Sharp's solar business in the United States. He joined the company in 2001, after the Japanese electronics giant asked him to launch a PV business in America. Sharp, known for its flat-screen TVs, is also the largest PV solar manufacturer in the world, with a 20 percent share of the market—nearly as much generating capacity as the next three largest makers combined. The corporation, which had sales of $26.7 billion in 2007, makes the equipment for large-scale solar power plants spread over acres of desert as well as small rooftop units that generate power for homes and businesses. Some of its solar panels even look like roof tiles that are barely visible from the street. Kenedi thinks his company's future lies in America: "The U.S. market is now growing faster than in Europe. I think it will become the largest in the world. It is bigger— has more sun and more need."

Wearing a black dress shirt with an open collar, the goateed Kenedi, who has an infectious laugh, seems an unlikely corporate power player. In the 1970s, after a stint as a therapist at Ward's Island State Mental Institute in New York City, he moved his family to Grass Valley in northern California, near where Allen Ginsberg and Jerry Brown had homes. There Kenedi took up the kind of back-to-earth life—organic food, straw bale houses, and Birkenstocks—that, he says, "many people are buying now." He ran a general store, and one day a salesman stopped by with some solar panels in the trunk of his car. Kenedi bought them (he later found out that they had been lifted from the trash of Arco Solar) and that was the beginning of what he over the years built into a large mail-order solar business.

In the seventies it seemed as if solar power had a promising future. Though global warming wasn't yet discussed, the oil crisis, gas lines, and strings of bad smog days had raised energy awareness. "The focus," says Kenedi, "was what's going to happen when petroleum starts running out. What about the quality of our air, the building materials? We were looking at life in our own ways, seeing there's got to be a point where gas gets so expensive and the air gets so bad that we had to do something about it." He was right in his analysis, but then the economics turned against him. In the early 1980s oil and natural gas prices collapsed and a nascent solar industry along with it. The economics didn't work, and some scammers who tried to illegally cash in on solar tax credits gave the industry a bad name. "It got so bad," recalls Kenedi, "I used to tell people I was in the energy business, not the solar business."

Kenedi continued to build his Independent Power Company, selling solar systems by mail order to people who lived off the electric power grid and to industries that needed off-grid power to operate traffic signals, oil and gas monitoring, and water pumping in remote areas.

In 2000, the California energy crisis hit and everything changed. In an odd way, Enron gave the solar industry a boost by manipulating the newly deregulated electricity market: the company locked up supplies of electricity in the wholesale market and sold it back to utilities at exorbitant prices. Up to then, most Americans thought of electricity as a God-given right: walk into your home and switch on the light. When electricity prices rose 300 percent in San Diego, many utility customers couldn't afford to pay their bills. Utilities suffered blackouts. Kenedi saw this crisis as an opportunity. "Americans," he says, "need to be affected in their pocketbooks for them to understand the value of solar, and Californians started understanding they are vulnerable."

But pocketbook problems remain: the cost of electricity in California has come down to precrisis levels, and without state subsidies solar remains two to three times more expensive than fossil fuel–based power. Kenedi argues that solar can make economic sense today if you take the long view. He has calculated that each American family on average spends $120,000 over its lifetime for electricity: "That's a lot of money, and at the end of your life, what have you got? Nothing but a bunch of receipts you can hand your kids and say, 'Look how much I spent on electricity.' " He argues that if you had bought a solar system for $30,000, you could leave your children the $90,000 you saved in electricity costs over your lifetime.

Kenedi's formula may work for someone who rolls the cost of a solar system into a new thirty-year mortgage. (Some of today's solar panels can last as long as forty years.) From the first day, the home owner enjoys savings on his electricity bill, and after the mortgage is paid off, he will be generating free electricity from his rooftop.

The trouble is that most home owners are reluctant to invest that kind of money when they are likely to sell their house long before they recoup their investment. Americans, on average, move every seven years and real estate agents, appraisers, and home buyers may not be willing to place a premium on a house with a rooftop solar system.

The solution may lie in plans like Duke Energy's Save A Watt program (see chapter 3) where utilities and other entities with long investing horizons and sufficient capital buy, own, and manage the solar energy systems. Duke's plan is to buy solar panels, install them on your roof, and then bill you each month for the electricity. That's cheaper for Duke than to build new power plants, and the utility would receive a steady income stream over the life of the solar system, no matter who owns the house.

This financing model is already being applied to solar installations on commercial buildings. The roof on the Whole Foods store in Ridgewood, New Jersey, is covered with solar panels that Whole Foods did not pay a cent for. They are owned by a Baltimore start-up, SunEdison. The company acts as a bank, soliciting investors interested in a return from solar energy. SunEdison's investors own the solar panels, and Whole Foods agrees to buy the electricity. MMA Renewable Ventures, a San Francisco start-up, has also been gathering investors who want to take advantage of the federal tax credits that solar power systems generate.

Jennifer McDonnell, a green mission specialist for Whole Foods, explains that the solar panels produce only 15 percent of the energy that the New Jersey store uses, but they function during the day when purchased electricity is most expensive. In New Jersey, during hot summer afternoons when the sun is high and everyone is cranking up the air-conditioning, the price of electricity nearly quadruples. Fortunately, that's the same time of day when solar panels generate the most electricity. During these peak hours solar electricity is cheaper for Whole Foods than power coming from the grid. The other benefit: Whole Foods can lock in the price of electricity for the next twenty years. Since the company believes some sort of carbon tax will eventually drive up the price of electricity, establishing a fixed price seems to be a wise move. By the same token, SunEdison's investors know exactly what their profits will be over the next twenty years. Their solar investment is not unlike a long-term bond held to maturity.[9]

While PV technology is fairly well established, some technological breakthroughs still need to happen before it can grab more than a 5 percent share of the electricity market. Because PV generates electricity only when the sun is shining, its use is now limited. What happens at night or during a string of cloudy days? How useful would PV be in a place like Seattle? To be practical, the panels must be combined with power storage. Battery makers are working on affordable home storage systems that could save up electricity until it is needed. Batteries are still too expensive and lack the power to meet this need, but the technology is on its way. Many of the affordable batteries that car companies are now developing (see chapter 5) could also be deployed as storage systems for power plants and homes.

Technological developments in other fields could help speed these batteries to market. As soon as home owners are able to install low-energy LED lights (see chapter 2), which use up to 80 percent less energy than fluorescent bulbs, the battery storage capacity needed for backup power would shrink dramatically. So would the cost. According to venture capitalist Stephan Dolezalek of VantagePoint Partners, "The beauty is that each new technology enables the next market."

WHO WILL WIN THE RACE? Among big companies, it's hard not to like the chances of Q-Cells of Germany, Sharp of Japan, and SunPower in California. Of this group, Sharp is in the lead. This electronics giant is bigger than the next two largest PV companies combined and is pumping R&D dollars into new technologies.

The company's PV systems are installed on the roofs of homes, warehouses, and stores. In California, Sharp solar systems generate electricity for Google's offices in Mountain View, FedEx's facility in Oakland, and Patagonia's headquarters in Ventura. A recent installation of Sharp's panels is providing electricity to a large frozen and refrigerated food distribution warehouse in West Sacramento owned by Tony's Fine Foods, which delivers fresh and frozen foods to the retail grocery and food services industry. Sharp's PV solar panels, which cover the size of three football fields, generate 1.5 million kilowatt-hours annually, accounting for more than 40 percent of Tony's Fine Foods' energy needs. The panels reduce the company's electric bills by $22,000 per month—more than enough to pay debt service on the equipment after subsidies are figured into the equation.

Sharp believes its solar panels will soon make economic sense even without subsidies. It is constantly improving the efficiency of its cells—its best systems can convert nearly 20 percent of sunlight into electricity. To drive down costs even more Sharp also plans to use solar concentrators that promise to boost dramatically the performance of cells used in giant solar farms in the desert. Much as a child's magnifying glass increases the strength of the sun enough to set a piece of paper on fire, these high-powered, domed magnifying lenses concentrate the amount of sun hitting the solar cell. When combined with a high-efficiency solar cell, Sharp's new system will generate 40 percent more electricity than conventional PV panels, making them nearly competitive with conventional power in parts of the country where rates are high. (Solaria, a California start-up, has a competing concentrator that solar maker Q-Cells is using in some of its systems.)

Sharp executives say that concentrator systems could be installed in giant solar farms along the Mediterranean coast in Europe, North Africa, southern Australia, and the southwestern United States, where sunshine is abundant. These solar concentrators track the sun as it moves through the sky; if they were set up in the deserts of Nevada, Arizona, and New Mexico, they could generate more than 40 percent of all the electricity the United States will need by 2030.[10] Because the first systems will be expensive, Sharp will sell them in Europe and Japan, where government solar subsidies are rich.[11] Though Sharp will not now discuss pricing, as the product improves it should become more attractive to the American market. There is reason to believe that eventually the world's economies will derive a significant portion of their power from a technology that emits virtually no greenhouse gas and comes from a source of free fuel 93 million miles away. And the sun cannot be held hostage by a foreign power.

One of Sharp's biggest competitors is SunPower, the fast-growing San Jose, California, firm that is playing a leading role in America's nascent solar industry. Like Sharp, it makes PV systems for businesses and homes. SunPower is creating new jobs at a fast clip. As of December 2006, the company had over 1,500 full-time employees in manufacturing, research and development, sales and marketing, and administration. Investors are betting SunPower can discover the holy grail of solar: electricity that is competitive with that generated by fossil fuel. So far, the company has played niche markets where the right conditions—lots of sun, high utility rates, and local subsidies—make solar more affordable.

In 2007 SunPower's management boldly stated that it will reduce the cost of an installed solar system by approximately 50 percent within five years—much faster than other experts predict. It will do this by constantly boosting the efficiencies of its cells, coming up with cheaper ways to install the systems on rooftops, and taking advantage of growing economies of scale. A 50 percent drop in cost would make solar—at around 12 cents a kilowatt-hour—still more expensive than electricity generated by coal, which costs around 8 cents, but competitive with higher-cost electricity generated by natural gas. It would also open a market the company says would be worth "hundreds of billions of dollars annually." Thomas Dinwoodie, a SunPower executive and founder of PowerLight, a solar installation company acquired by SunPower in early 2007, says, "I believe that solar one day will be the primary source of energy."

Some Wall Street analysts who are bullish on solar worry that investors are creating a solar bubble that could soon burst. At this writing, it does appear that many solar stock prices have been driven too high, to perhaps unsustainable valuations. Shortages of silicon—the main raw ingredient of PV cells—have pushed up the price, putting a squeeze on margins. If the U.S. government fails to put meaningful curbs on carbon, and local subsidies fade away, solar stocks could plunge, and some of the weaker companies may go out of business. But the parallel to the dot-com failures of several years ago does not hold. Many of those companies were built on clever ideas. They had little or no revenue and no profits. What they did have was a lot of investors greedily watching them. Though one cannot rule out the greed factor—it's what permits these new ventures to function—solar companies at least have real products and real revenues. Under such circumstances, even after a fall, the strongest will eventually bounce back.

At a recent green technology conference in Stockholm, the speaker flashed on the screen a map of North Africa, highlighting a small red square in the corner of Libya. "All we would need is a parcel of land this small to build solar farms and we could generate enough electricity to meet most of Europe's needs." The speaker was Bo Normark, senior vice president of ABB Grid Systems, a division of the $24 billion-a-year Swiss conglomerate that builds oil refineries, power lines, and other utility infrastructures around the globe. Normark was addressing one of the toughest problems in the way of renewable energy: the places where the sun shines most usually aren't those where the most people live. One exception is the high desert areas of the U.S. Southwest, where massive energy demand from the West Coast population could be served over existing transmission lines by the blazing sun in the Mojave Desert.

Today's AC (alternating current) high-voltage lines are best at moving electricity distances of fifty to one hundred miles. Farther than that, they lose power. But even such high-voltage power lines are expensive and difficult to build and situate—no one wants one running through his backyard. ABB, Normark claimed, can now build relatively inexpensive, low-voltage DC (direct current) lines that can carry electricity as far as 1,500 miles with minimal power loss. They can be buried under streets and beside highways safely and relatively cheaply. The vision is a thousand-mile cable stretching from North Africa, across the floor of the Mediterranean, and then underground to wherever power is needed on the European continent.

This promise of an inexpensive way to widely distribute solar energy comes at the start of a global race to build giant solar farms in sunny areas. The farms come in two varieties. Photovoltaic farms use the same technology as those solar rooftop panels found on homes and businesses. Hundreds of PV panels lined up in a sunny region produce electricity for nearby towns and villages. By contrast, solar thermal farms use fields of mirrors to concentrate the sun's heat and create steam that drives an electric turbine.

Solar thermal farms are in a race with photovoltaics to see which will be the first to become cost competitive with fossil fuels without the help of subsidies. It is not yet clear which technology will win, though solar thermal has some distinct advantages. Large-scale solar thermal projects are either under way or on the drawing board in Algeria, Greece, Iran, Mexico, Spain, and the southwestern United States. In Spain a solar thermal plant called Planta Solar 10, the largest of its type in Europe, came online on March 30, 2007. This 11-megawatt plant, owned by the Abengoa Group, provides electricity to more than six hundred homes in Seville province.

Though the excitement over giant solar farms is growing, the technology still presents steep challenges. Michael Peevey, president of the California Public Utilities Commission, argues that even if you could overcome the transmission problems, the technology faces international political issues. If, for instance, you did manage to generate solar power in North Africa or another hard-to-police part of the world, you might be creating a big risk. "It could be quite an exciting place to visit with a small nuclear weapon," says Peevey.[12]

Most important, as with other new technologies, it is more expensive to generate electricity from solar farms than from coal or natural gas. Electricity from Planta Solar 10 costs more than twice what the people in the region paid before. The project is possible only with government subsidies. Seville is a fairly sunny place, but building plants in North Africa, for example, may help drive costs down. It might also have an effect on southern Spain's severe illegal immigration problem. That is, the installation and operation of solar facilities might provide local employment in the very countries whose people are fleeing to Spain to work.

The American Southwest promises to be one of the biggest markets for power from solar farms. In 2006 utilities such as Arizona Public Service, Pacific Gas & Electric, and Southern California Edison contracted for enough new solar thermal energy to equal the capacity of two nuclear plants. That is enough to supply power to a million homes. Many new solar thermal companies, including BrightSource, CSP Technologies, Solargenix-Acciona, Stirling Energy Systems, and Solel, are rising to meet the need. However, each is taking a different approach to turning the sun's heat into power. It is too early to declare which method will work best, but there is little doubt that large solar farms could eventually supply a significant percentage of the world's power at competitive rates. By one count the U.S. Southwest could ultimately produce enough megawatts of solar thermal power to keep eighty coal plants from being built.

Solar power has ancient origins. The Greeks planned their cities so that houses might have access to sunlight during winter. Socrates, who lived in a solar-heated house, observed, "In houses that look toward the south, the sun penetrates the portico in winter." In the fifth century B.C.E., Aeschylus pointed out that only primitives and barbarians "lacked knowledge of houses turned to face the winter sun, dwelling beneath the ground like swarming ants in sunless caves." The Romans added glass or mica to windows in their south-facing rooms to trap more heat, creating what they called a sun furnace.[13]

The Swiss naturalist Horace de Saussure built what was probably the first solar water heater in the 1760s. A small box covered with glass, it was able to heat the water to beyond the boiling point. John Perlin, a solar energy historian, explains how Saussure's solar "hot box" worked in his book *From Space to Earth: The Story of Solar Electricity:*[14] "Sunshine penetrated the glass covers. The black inner lining absorbed the sunlight and converted it into heat. Though clear glass allows the rays of the sun to easily enter through it, it prevents heat from doing the same. As the glass trapped the solar heat in the box, it heated up." Elegantly simple.

In 1878 a dish-shaped mirror was used to focus the sun's rays onto a steam boiler to power a French printing press. At about the same time, a Chilean businessman built a solar distilling operation that converted more than 20,000 liters of saltwater into fresh. It was not until the nineteenth century that the first solar hot-water heaters began to appear on rooftops around America. Borrowing from Saussure's design, entrepreneurs built black metal water tanks to absorb as much heat as possible. By 1900 a third of the homes in Pasadena heated their water with the sun. A 1913 photograph shows the roofs of Los Angeles covered with black boxes, all using the sun to heat water for bathing and dishwashing.

Discoveries of massive amounts of cheap natural gas in the Los Angeles basin in the 1920s and '30s killed the solar industry in California. It wasn't until the rising energy prices of the 1970s that a group of forward-thinking entrepreneurs realized that the sun could be used not just for rooftop water heating but to drive massive turbines that would generate electricity for thousands of homes. It was then that the modern solar industry was born.

One of the most important of these ventures was an Israeli

company called Luz. The company's founder, Arnold Goldman, had long been fascinated with solar energy. In the 1970s, when Goldman lived in California, he created Lexitron, one of the first word-processing programs. After his company went public, Goldman moved his family to Israel to form a spiritual community dedicated to living in harmony with the earth. Though his utopian plans did not come to fruition, they did lead to his finding a primitive solar system he thought could help power his commune: "At the time I saw that solar could provide us with a better way of life, one more in tune with our lives."

When Goldman moved back to America in the 1970s, he built nine solar thermal plants in the Mojave Desert. At the time these represented 90 percent of all the solar capacity not only in the United States but in the world. Luz's fields of parabolic mirrors stretched over two thousand acres to concentrate sunlight much the way a magnifying glass can focus the sun's rays to set a piece of paper on fire. The solar power was used to heat water to drive steam generators and thereby provide enough electricity to power 150,000 homes in Los Angeles. These plants are still in operation today.

Because of the OPEC energy crises of the 1970s, Goldman had no trouble financing his desert power plants. But in the mid-1980s two things happened: Goldman lost a tax break he'd been enjoying, and the price of oil and natural gas dropped, driving Luz out of business and the solar thermal industry along with it.

Not long after 9/11, it became clear that energy prices were again rising and that there was increasing impetus to reduce the carbon emissions responsible for global warming. In 2004 Goldman and other key associates formed BrightSource, a new solar thermal company. Goldman's latest technology promises to generate electricity at about 10 cents per kilowatt-hour, a cost that is competitive with today's gas-fired plants, though more expensive than coal.[15]

BrightSource Energy of Oakland, California, will soon begin

construction of a massive solar power plant in the Mojave Desert, near the California–New Mexico border, where the sun shines reliably 330 to 350 days a year. The Ivanpah Solar Power Complex will be a 400-megawatt behemoth that will provide enough electricity to power 250,000 homes a year. That is what a coal plant now can generate—but without coal's carbon dioxide emissions of over 500,000 tons a year. To put this project in perspective, the Ivanpah facility alone will produce about half of the amount of electricity that is being generated from all the PV rooftop panels in the United States. John Woolard, the company's CEO, believes his solar technology will provide ample electricity at a competitive price by 2010—and sooner than that if Congress passes a carbon tax.

The scale and potential of solar farms is impressive. Picture a 2,400-acre field with nearly 300,000 large rectangular mirrors, all turning with the sun and concentrating their heat on top of a series of 300-foot towers where water will be converted to steam. The tower then will send the steam by pipeline to a generator that produces electricity. Woolard estimates that if he built his plants on just 2 percent of the land in the Mojave, they would provide enough power for all the homes in California.

Goldman had the vision of a giant solar farm in the desert, but to help make it a reality he turned to Woolard. Forty years old, with a sharp gaze and the standard no-tie style, Woolard described the path he took to solar energy. He cofounded, ran, and then sold Silicon Energy, one of the first of the new wave of clean-tech companies. Next, he became an executive-in-residence in VantagePoint Venture Partner's CleanTech Group, where he first met Goldman and the Luz team. Shortly thereafter, he took the corporate equivalent of a sabbatical to spend a year at the famed Lawrence Berkeley National Laboratory of the University of California. There he immersed himself in the study of the energy market. The Lawrence Labs have become a leading incubator for the development of green technology.

Away from the everyday distractions of running a business, Woolard mapped out a fifteen-year view of the energy market and studied various kinds of power technologies from wind, to tide, to photovoltaics. "When I looked at the problem," he recalls, "I realized that if you're going to solve this at scale, you're not going to solve it by installing a few solar panels one roof at a time. What we need is a big solution that has impact."

When Goldman and Woolard first met, the Israeli scientist explained that generating affordable solar electricity on a massive—and therefore meaningful—scale was a lot more complicated than Woolard thought. "It wasn't a ten-thousand-foot mountain," says Woolard. "It was a thirty-thousand-foot mountain." Inspired by the challenge, Woolard joined the company as CEO in 2006.

BrightSource's new Ivanpah plant will cost $300 million for the first stage. To raise that kind of money, Woolard traveled to New York City for a few days in May 2007. There, he found savvy Wall Street investors eager to back his—or, for that matter, just about any—smart, green technology. Yet, on a brilliant spring afternoon in a midtown Manhattan restaurant, Woolard struck a note of caution. "It is a bubble right now. There's way too much money. Everyone wants to do something, but there are very few legitimate, high-quality deals."

What has the titans of Wall Street so excited? The sheer size of the market. Electricity is a $300 billion market in the United States and a $1 trillion market worldwide. Many industry players estimate that solar power will capture 5 percent of the American market, growing from practically nothing to $15 billion over the next decade. "It's a big deal to get there," Woolard says, "but there are obscene amounts of money to be made."

So far Woolard has raised capital from Chevron, Morgan Stanley, VantagePoint, and others to build a pilot plant in Israel that will come online in 2008 and then the full-scale facility in the Mojave that is scheduled to open in 2010. Radically redesigned, BrightSource's new plant will replace the old, expensive parabolic troughs of mirrors with thousands of cheap, flat sun-tracking mirrors that direct heat at the top of 300-foot towers. Inside each tower is a black "heat box" not unlike the one fashioned by Saussure 250 years ago in Switzerland. The sun from the mirrors heats the water in the boxes in the top of the tower to more than 1,000 degrees Fahrenheit, turning it to high-pressure steam that travels to a nearby power plant to turn a generator and create electricity. Because the piping only runs from the towers to the power plant—rather than along the side of every one of the thousands of mirrors as in the old system—the amount of expensive piping is cut dramatically.

Even if this new design works, however, it will only get Goldman and Woolard halfway up that 30,000-foot mountain. All solar projects have the same huge economic flaw. Even if you could generate power at the same price as fossil fuels—as BrightSource's new plant promises to do—unless there are batteries strong and cheap enough to store electricity for days at a time, utility companies will still have to build a coal or natural gas plant to provide backup power when the sun isn't shining. "The irony," says Woolard, "is that with rooftop PV, you don't save building a single power plant."

But BrightSource claims it has a solution. The electric generator used in its solar plant can also burn natural gas. "And on a cloudy day, what happens? You just switch over to natural gas. You don't need a second plant. Your backup plant is built in."

BrightSource has won a contract with PG&E to generate 400 megawatts of solar power by 2010. The company is also negotiating joint ventures in Spain. Hal LaFlash, PG&E's director of renewable energy policy and planning, liked Goldman's experience in the Mojave as well as the promise of cheap electricity from his new design. "The power tower looks like it could be a breakthrough," LaFlash says.[16]

Of course, solar thermal plants work best in warm, dry locations like the Southwest. "It doesn't work that well elsewhere in the country," says Goldman, "because anyplace that gets clouds and rain, even Florida, reduces the effectiveness of the solar farms. Even shadows from vapor trails from planes can curb their production." Those long-distance DC power lines would address that problem, according to Goldman. "There's no reason we can't build thousands of acres of solar farms in the deserts of the Southwest with lines running as far as the Pacific Northwest or the Midwest."

But despite such customer support, Goldman, Woolard, and other solar thermal entrepreneurs worry that an exotic solar technology still being tinkered with in a small lab ultimately will provide a high-tech ultracheap solution. Woolard points to a handful of start-ups with esoteric-sounding names—First Solar, HelioVolt, Miasolé, Nanosolar—that are working on a solar system called thin film, which may provide cheap, ubiquitous solar power. Although such a development might hurt his business, Woolard says philosophically, "Solar will happen. It's the beauty of capitalism. Smart people will come in and figure it out."

VENTURE CAPITALISTS ARE putting their money in solar rather than wind because they see greater opportunity in solar for technological breakthroughs and growth. It's not that wind lacks merit—but from the venture capitalists' point of view, solar has greater investment potential. Wind power will make an important contribution to reducing global warming, but the technology is already quite mature compared to that of solar. Big manufacturers such as Vestas and GE are now at work driving wind prices down through economies of scale. With solar power, investors don't yet know which technologies and companies will dominate the market.

The venture capitalists are busily placing their bets: in 2006 they sunk $2.9 billion into renewable energy, and a healthy percentage of that went into the next generation of solar start-ups that are making thin-film PV, which promises to drive down the costs of solar even further. Traditional PV maker Sharp and start-ups First Solar and SunPower already make thin-film PV, which cuts down on or eliminates the use of expensive silicon. Though less efficient than traditional solar cells, thin film promises to be much cheaper to produce and therefore should before long be able to generate electricity at competitive rates. Depending on the manufacturer, thin-film solar cells are fabricated by depositing thin layers of silicon or other materials such as cadmium telluride on a glass substrate. In Sharp's case this allows a dramatic reduction in the amount of silicon raw material used (approximately one-hundredth the amount used in conventional crystalline solar cells), and also results in shorter production times and lower costs from manufacturing economies of scale. Sharp is planning to build a manufacturing facility in Sakai City, Japan, which could produce enough thin-film solar panels each year to equal the electrical output of a nuclear power plant. This factory, scheduled to open in 2010, will be built close to a next-generation LCD television factory, taking advantage of synergies in the manufacturing process of glass solar modules and glass LCD screens.

One major advantage of thin-film solar cells is that they can be used for many more applications than today's cells. They can be designed to be translucent and used as curtain walls that allow natural light to shine through while generating electricity. As much as half the cost of an installed solar system comes from frames, wiring, and structural supports. (The rest comes from the silicon solar cells that generate the electricity.)[17] The panels often look ugly on housetops, and installers must drill holes into the roof to make them stay put—creating the potential for leaks. Using thin-film technology, Sharp and SunPower have developed solar panels that look like shingles. They blend with existing roof tiles and eliminate the more expensive conventional large rectangular panels that are bolted onto a rooftop. "Solar shingles shine because you can eliminate cost," says Tom Werner, CEO of SunPower.

"Instead of having to install regular shingles, you put in solar shingles. You've eliminated the cost of a regular roof, and you have a solar system." SunPower has already installed these shingles on houses in California.

Werner believes that within five years these thin-film shingles could be a billion-dollar industry. But thin-film panels are hard to mass-produce cost-effectively because it's not easy to spread the PV material over a sheet of glass in a consistent way. Frustrated by thin-film technology, Shell Solar has closed two of its facilities. BP Solar also closed down its thin-film production facilities. The economics simply did not work.

Some small solar companies are taking a different approach, and it involves using flexible foil material rather than glass. The promise of flexible thin film is alluring. Imagine skyscrapers whose sides are covered with strips of thin-film solar that can generate enough electricity to light the building. Or imagine a layer of thin film on the roof of your car that can help run the radio, GPS system, and air-conditioning. Konarka, a start-up in Lowell, Massachusetts, is working on a thin film that can be integrated into the fabric of a jacket. Simply plug your cell phone into your pocket and the energy of the sun will recharge it. The company has already sold thin-film solar tents to the military; soldiers use the power generated to recharge their field equipment. Nathan Lewis, a professor at Caltech, is applying nanotechnology to make a titanium oxide–based thin-film solar that could actually be painted onto the side of a house to generate electricity. "The movement is going to be toward embedding solar; there's no doubt about that," says Ron Pernick, cofounder and principal of Clean Edge, a clean-technology consulting firm. "It's going to disappear into things. Rooftops, your cell phone, the top of your car. The question is, what is it going to take to get there?"

HelioVolt, Miasolé, and Nanosolar are three of the leading U.S. businesses hoping to make flexible thin film a household word. Miasolé uses a combination of the minerals copper, indium, gallium, and selenide, which is known as CIGS. The company, based in Santa Clara, California, is currently building a factory and expects to be in full production by 2008. Its solar cells are roughly one-tenth the weight of silicon cells and don't require the expensive glass panels needed for traditional solar. Miasolé president and CEO Dave Pearce says his solar systems will be both easier to install and less expensive than other products on the market. HelioVolt also uses CIGS and says its manufacturing process is faster, more flexible, and less energy intensive than others. "The speed of the process is our cost advantage," says John Langdon, VP of marketing at HelioVolt. The Austin-based company just finalized a location for its plant and expects to begin shipping products sometime in 2008.

One of the most intriguing thin-film technologies comes from Nanosolar, the Palo Alto start-up. Most thin-film makers must spread or layer different solar materials evenly over a piece of foil. This process can be tricky and time consuming. Combining different chemicals in a uniform way may be doable in a lab, but it's hard to achieve consistently in manufacturing. Any imperfections can dramatically reduce the effectiveness of the product. Nanosolar's breakthrough was to make nano ink, if you will, a concoction with all the materials already mixed. This ink could be easily spread over a thin piece of foil—it is no longer necessary to apply each chemical separately.

In late 2007 CEO Martin Roscheisen shipped Nanosolar's first commercial product from his factory in Silicon Valley. He says that in many markets its price will be competitive with today's electricity. The first Nanosolar systems will be installed at a 1-megawatt solar plant in Germany on a former landfill owned by a waste management company. The plant, being developed by Beck Energy, is expected to initially supply electrical power for about four hundred homes. And his ambitions are anything but humble. "I think Nanosolar can get 25 percent of the electricity market, which is $1 trillion worldwide. We are shooting for a $250 billion market."

Thin-film technology still faces some issues: thin film may

degrade faster than solar systems made from silicon, which can last as long as forty years. Will thin film hold up through years of hot sun, rain, and dust storms? And while it costs less than silicon, it typically doesn't generate as much electricity per square foot of space.

The entrepreneurs behind these thin-film start-ups believe they will overcome these problems. In the meantime, their competitors who make traditional silicon solar systems are working hard to get their costs down to the point where solar will become mainstream. Whichever technology wins—and both may find a place in the market—the potential to create wealth, jobs, and energy independence is enormous. "I'm really optimistic because it scratches a lot of itches," says Sharp's Ron Kenedi. "It's not some wild-eyed idea to create a utopia. It's a proven technology that will create a new industry, will generate jobs, and when it comes to the threat of terrorism, it makes geopolitical sense. Solar is the patriotic power."

9

Strange Bedfellows

The Rebirth of Nuclear Power

STEWART BRAND IS PERHAPS the last person you'd expect to be pushing for a revival of nuclear power. An environmental activist and author of the sixties bible *The Whole Earth Catalog*, Brand helped his readers develop an appreciation for a new, positive, and sustainable culture. Many first learned about the potential of alternative energy sources such as solar, wind, small-hydro, and geothermal through his writings. This West Coast seer popped up as one of Ken Kesey's Merry Pranksters in Tom Wolfe's hippie classic *The Electric Kool-Aid Acid Test*, was one of the first to predict the rise of the personal computer, and has advised a U.S. president, the Pentagon, and multinational corporations. Now in his seventies, Brand, a tall, rangy man who prefers denim to pinstripes, lives on a houseboat in Sausalito. With his cofounder Peter Schwartz, he runs the Global Business Network (GBN) of Emeryville, California, a management consulting firm in the Bay Area that's part of the prestigious Monitor Group.

One of the missions of GBN is to sketch out future scenarios for climate change. Brand was doing just that with a roomful of executives at the 2006 Nuclear Energy Assembly in San Francisco. "It's not that I've seen the light, I've seen the dark," he said, referring to the fear that the global warming crisis is barreling down on us faster than most people predicted. Brand told the audience that the nuclear power industry is now in the best position for a comeback since the 1970s, the last time in America that a contract was signed to build a new nuclear power plant.

Brand understands that nuclear power has its problems—cost overruns and the dangers of accidents, terrorist attacks, and waste disposal. He believes, however, that it has to be part of a comprehensive effort to decarbonize energy production. Brand says we must pursue "Kyoto accords, radical conservation in energy transmission and use, wind energy, solar energy, passive solar, hydroelectric energy, biomass, the whole gamut. But add them all up and it's still only a fraction of enough. The only technology ready to fill the gap and stop the carbon dioxide loading of the atmosphere is nuclear power."[1]

The trick, argued Brand, was for the industry to understand how some environmentalists think. "You have an inconvenient legacy which leads to a bit of a public relations problem," he explained to the audience as he set off the sound of an exploding atomic bomb that roared through the auditorium. "When people look at your cooling towers that's what they see. Hiroshima and Nagasaki were way in the past, but because of the proliferation issue it's still in people's minds." Brand said that the mushroom cloud has been replaced by another icon, the image of planet Earth taken from space. He said the emphasis now has to shift to global warming, a clear and present danger vastly more important than the bomb or terrorism. In the face of so immediate a danger, nuclear power simply can't be taken off the table as an option to be used along with solar, wind, wave, and clean coal.

That an environmentalist with the credentials of Stewart Brand would be urging the nuclear power industry to join forces with the green movement would have been inconceivable only a few years ago. Now the urgency of climate change is forcing these strange bedfellows to work together.

I write this with great hesitation because building scores of nuclear power plants throughout the country is far from an ideal solution. My father, an early antinuke activist, spent a decade organizing resistance to and fighting the construction of the Seabrook nuclear power plant in New Hampshire. His crusade opened my eyes to the potential dangers of nuclear plants: shoddy construction, poorly trained operators, risk of meltdowns, risk of terrorist attack, fuel that remains harmfully radioactive for 10,000 years and must somehow be stored safely. (He lost; the utility won; and the Seabrook plant has been running for years—without incident, so far.)

Yet the logic of nuclear power in the face of global warming seems hard to refute. Except during construction, nuclear plants emit very little greenhouse gas. Unlike solar and wind, they can operate twenty-four hours a day, providing bountiful amounts of electricity whenever it is needed. All this points to a possible nuclear revival. And indeed, more than 20,000 megawatts of nuclear capacity—the equivalent of twenty plants or enough to light up 1.2 million homes—have come online globally since 2000, mostly in the Far East.[2]

At a private equity conference in New York City in 2007, John Rice, General Electric's vice chairman and the man in charge of its nuclear power plant construction business, worked out the math: "The U.S. has 103 aging nuclear plants, and the last one was built in the 1970s. Over the next fifty years, the nation will be retiring about two plants a year. These plants produce about 20 percent of our electricity and demand is supposed to rise by 50 percent by 2030. Where will this power come from? We'll need to build a new plant every six months just to stay even."[3]

That steely logic is creating a strange alliance of longtime nuclear power advocates and former antinuke environmentalists who are reluctantly coming to accept the technology. This partnership is the result of grim realities: the greens can't be concerned about climate change and not support nuclear plants. The pronuke crowd within the Bush administration can't push for nuclear plants and then raise doubts about global warming.

The pronuke faction is already giving ground. As his second term was coming to an end, President Bush finally and reluctantly acknowledged global warming to be a problem and then pushed hard for a nuclear revival. In a *60 Minutes* interview in the spring of 2007, Clay Sell, the deputy secretary of energy and the administration's point man on nuclear power, told correspondent Steve Kroft: "There is a tremendous amount of interest. Two years ago there were exactly zero plants on the drawing boards here in the United States. Today, there are about fifteen companies talking about building over thirty commercial nuclear power reactors. Now, all of those won't get built. But we think there's a significant chance that many of them will be built."

What Sell is counting on is a change of heart among environmentalists. In the 1970s protesters challenged the construction of nuclear power plants at every step, delaying deadlines and driving up costs to the point where no one wanted to finance or build these projects. "I recall one story about a man who is a CEO today of one of our leading companies," Sell told Kroft. "He described the pain associated with beginning what he thought would be a billion-dollar plant in the 1970s, and bringing it online as a $9 billion plant twenty years later. And he made the point that that is not a lesson that will quickly be forgotten in the industry."[4]

In his speech, Brand laid out a road map to help the energy industry gain the confidence of environmentalists. He noted that the industry would not get very far with the most fervent, deeply committed environmentalists. Brand explained that the members of groups such as the Sierra Club and Greenpeace believe that "they're connected with nature, and distrust anything that's unnatural— genetically engineered food, petrochemicals, and nuclear plants."

To UNDERSTAND THE DEEP RESISTANCE to nuclear power in the environmental community, consider the exchange that occurred during a conference at the Aspen Institute in the summer of 2004. In the tent that day were an impressive number of the world's top political and business figures. That year's roster for *Fortune* magazine's annual Brainstorm conference included Google founder Sergey Brin, Carly Fiorina (at the time CEO of HP), Disney president Robert Iger, Her Majesty Queen Noor of Jordan, Paul Wolfowitz, and Bill Bradley.

I was moderating a panel on green business when Stewart Brand's partner at GBN Peter Schwartz—also a proponent of nuclear power—rose to ask a question. A futurist, business strategist, and chairman of GBN, Schwartz made his mark in the 1980s as head of a scenario-planning group at Royal Dutch/Shell Group of Companies in London, which helped the company create alternative perspectives on the future as well as robust strategies for change.

"What do you think of nuclear power?" he asked.

I took the question and lobbed it to Bill McDonough, who had been explaining the ins and outs of his Cradle to Cradle philosophy of sustainability to the audience.

"Don't get me wrong: I love nuclear energy! It's just that I prefer fusion to fission. And it just so happens that there's an enormous fusion reactor safely banked a few million miles from us. It delivers more than we could ever use in just about eight minutes. And it's wireless!"

While McDonough is right to stretch for a world economy powered by solar energy, a lot has changed since he made that comment. The amount of time scientists give us before the effects of global heating become irreversible seems to be shrinking monthly, with many arguing that the United States needs to be all but off fossil fuels by 2050. That's hardly enough time to get solar power costs down and systems installed on a large enough scale to replace the massive coal and oil infrastructure we have built over the past half century.

Still, serious environmentalists such as McDonough have good reason to eschew nuclear power. No one has satisfactorily addressed the nuclear waste problem, and as localities are asked to store more, with increased usage, they will resist. And though there hasn't been a major plant disruption in the United States since Three Mile Island, the Indian Point facility in Buchanan, New York, has frequent "leaks" and can't even get its emergency siren system working properly.

A handful of important leaders of the green movement—including Gaia theorist James Lovelock, Greenpeace cofounder Patrick Moore (who is no longer with the nonprofit), and the recently deceased Friends of the Earth trustee Hugh Montefiore—had been pushing the idea that we need nuclear plants to solve global warming. Even Al Gore is on the fence. His film, *An Inconvenient Truth*, made no mention of nuclear energy as a solution to global warming, but in March 2007 he told a House committee hearing, "I'm not an absolutist in being opposed to nuclear. I think it's likely to play some role." Gore says he would need to see a new generation of reactor that would address the problem of weapons proliferation, and in any case would be only a small part of any solution. Even so, Brand says that "the few prominent environmentalists who have spoken out in its favor have been privately anathematized by other environmentalists."[5]

Although most leaders of the environmental community remain against nuclear power, a few are willing to consider solutions to its problems. Jonathan Lash, the president of the World Resources Institute, and James Gustave Speth, the dean of Yale's School of Forestry and Environmental Studies, have said that it might be worth trying to solve the economic, safety and security, waste storage, and proliferation problems rather than eliminating nuclear power as an option altogether.[6]

Brand argues that the nuclear power industry should work with environmentalists, encouraging them to apply their brainpower toward making nuclear technology a more palatable choice for society. How might that work? The Diablo Canyon nuclear power plant, which sits at the edge of the Pacific in San Luis Obispo, California, generates a tremendous amount of waste heat.

Why not harness it to make hydrogen to power cars and to desalinate ocean water for Los Angeles, taking some pressure off the limited water supply from the Colorado River? That might make it easier to sell the idea of new nuclear plants to local communities. Or the industry could work with environmental attorneys to accelerate the nuclear power plant approval process to get it done in four years as they do in France instead of twelve years, which is typical in the United States. If top environmental lawyers would sign off on more efficient plant approval without sacrificing safety, the green community would be much more likely to accept it.

A large segment of the American public, however, has reason still to deeply distrust nuclear power. The Three Mile Island accident in 1979, though killing no one, raised the specter of what could have happened if things had really gone wrong. Like they did in Chernobyl. In the early hours of April 26, 1986, the explosion of the reactor in Chernobyl, the greatest industrial disaster in the history of humankind, released one hundred times more radiation than the atom bombs dropped over Hiroshima and Nagasaki. The blast contaminated not only parts of the Ukraine, where the plant is located, but also parts of Belarus and Russia.[7] (Other parts of Europe were affected as well, including crops in Germany and Finland.) The *Chernobyl Forum Report 2005*, written by specialists from seven UN organizations including WHO, IAEA, and the World Bank, concluded that the Chernobyl disaster has so far killed 50 people and will eventually claim roughly 4,000 lives. At least 1,800 children and adolescents in the most severely contaminated areas of Belarus have contracted thyroid cancer because of the reactor disaster, and that number could rise to 8,000 in the coming decades.[8] Chernobyl expert Professor Edmund Lengfelder, a German specialist in radiation medicine at the Otto Hug Strahleninstitut in Munich, which has been running a thyroid center in Belarus since 1991, warns of up to 100,000 additional cases of thyroid cancer in all age groups.[9]

Given the track record of the nuclear power industry and the worries of another major accident, the problem of where to store tons of radioactive fuel, and the dangers of a terrorist attack on one of the facilities, is it possible that environmentalists will passively allow scores of new plants to be built? A British scientist named James Lovelock says they have no choice.

The rolling hills of Devon are known for lush pastures, stone farmhouses, and, of course, clotted cream and scones dripping with butter and raspberry jam. In a barn on a Devon farm, Lovelock has built a lab where he does his research on climate change. He is one of this era's most notable polymaths, having earned degrees in chemistry, medicine, and biophysics. He has conducted research projects at Harvard and Yale and has worked with the Jet Propulsion Laboratory in Pasadena on lunar and planetary research. He became a Fellow of the Royal Society and is an Honorary Visiting Fellow of Green College, Oxford University. Lovelock, who has written some two hundred scientific papers on topics ranging from medicine to biology to geophysiology, is also an inventor with more than fifty patents, mostly for instruments that can detect and analyze particles in the environment. One of his inventions, called the electron capture detector, traces the level of pesticide residues in the environment. The data gathered from his machine helped Rachel Carson in the early 1960s to write her groundbreaking book *Silent Spring*. More recently, his invention was used to detect the CFCs in the atmosphere that were destroying the ozone layer.[10]

These days Lovelock's passion is climate change. He has written four books supporting his scientifically controversial Gaia theory. In ancient Greece, Gaia was known as Mother Earth, the goddess who was born from chaos and gave birth to the sea and the sky.[11] Lovelock defines Gaia as an area starting at the earth's crust and extending to the thermosphere at the edge of space. As he explains in his 2006 book *The Revenge of Gaia*, "It is a dynamic physiological system that has kept our planet fit for life for over three billion years. I call Gaia physiological because it appears to have the unconscious goal of regulating the climate and the chemistry at a comfortable state for life."[12] Lovelock believes that the amount of carbon dioxide that man has put into the atmosphere since the dawn of the Industrial Revolution has made Gaia weak and ill and that it may already be too late to prevent dramatic changes in our temperature and atmosphere.

With his shock of white hair, large plastic aviator glasses, and country casual dress, Lovelock seems a typical rural retiree. But he has the fiery demeanor of a man bent on changing the world and frustrated by the lack of urgency in addressing climate change. In a recent interview with the BBC, Lovelock explained, "What we're doing is changing the earth faster than we ever had in human history. We have about a half century left . . . before we're committed to a warming that will melt Greenland and part of Antarctica, which would be quite devastating."[13]

Lovelock rankles many environmentalists by arguing that sustainable development from solar, wind, or biofuel will not develop fast enough or provide enough clean energy over the next fifty years if we're even going to have a chance to mitigate the damage we're doing to Gaia. "To expect sustainable development or a trust in business as usual to be viable policies is like expecting a lung cancer victim to be cured by stopping smoking; both measures deny the existence of Earth's disease, the fever brought on by a plague of people."[14]

That leaves Lovelock, who is a member of a group called Environmentalists for Nuclear Energy, to the ineluctable conclusion that "nuclear is the only source of energy that will satisfy our demands and yet not be a hazard to Gaia and interfere with its capacity to sustain a comfortable climate and atmospheric condition."[15] When pressed about the potential dangers of nuclear power, he argues that compared to other sources of power it is quite safe. Whereas thousands of miners die every year in the coal industry, no one was killed at Three Mile Island, and only about fifty people, most of them firefighters, died as a result of the explosion at Chernobyl. As for seemingly safer forms of energy such as hydroelectric power, Lovelock points out that if China's new Yangtze River dam ruptured or was destroyed by terrorists, some 1 million people living downstream would drown. In the building of the dam, 1 million local residents have been displaced from their homes, and there is evidence of landslides, silting, and other environmental damage.

What about the thousands of cancer victims of Chernobyl? Lovelock doesn't believe the numbers will be nearly as high as reports suggest. And besides, "even if nuclear power were more dangerous than burning coal, which it isn't, the dangers from continuing to burn coal are so infinitely greater that we're not talking about deaths of thousands but deaths of billions. Something must be done soon if we are to avoid this threshold and not condemn our descendants to a miserable world."[16]

Environmentalists rightly point out that no one yet knows how to safely store atomic waste, which remains dangerous for 10,000 years. David Whitford, a *Fortune* writer, recently drove seven thousand miles around the country visiting nuclear power facilities. He reported that when he visited the Yucca Mountain atomic waste storage project in Nevada, on which the federal government has so far spent $9 billion since work began in 1983, he was struck by how little progress has been made. Construction has been stalled for the last decade. Yucca Mountain, with its planned 1,000-foot-deep tunnels, is meant to hold 77,000 tons of waste. The United States has already generated 55,000 tons, which is now sitting in storage tanks at power plants around the country.[17] The government hopes Yucca Mountain will begin accepting deliveries in 2017. If the nuclear power industry grows as fast and as large as its advocates envision, the nation will have to build three facilities the size of Yucca Mountain every decade for the next fifty years to handle all the spent radioactive fuel.[18]

Obstacles remain, however, to building even a single storage facility. More water than engineers had predicted is seeping into the storage area at Yucca Mountain, complicating construction. Environmentalists have joined with local governments and are suing to shut down the site. Concerns range from the radioactive waste being shipped by trucks past population centers to the fuel leaching out of the storage facility into the air and groundwater.

Jim Rogers, the CEO of Duke Energy, which recently applied to build a new nuclear power facility in South Carolina, believes that the industry will eventually invest in facilities to recycle nuclear fuel, which would mean that "we could easily store all our waste in a single facility the size of Yucca Mountain." However, Rogers admits that there is still political opposition to overcome. Senate Majority Leader Harry Reid of Nevada told Rogers he doesn't want to store nuclear waste in his state, and he wants to shut down its coal plants. Rogers responded, "Well, which part of the Las Vegas strip are you going to shut down?" Reid made no reply.

Stewart Brand and others advocate using temporary (hundred-year) storage sites to give the government time to figure out the complexities of Yucca Mountain. The idea is to let future generations solve the storage problem. That's not a wonderful legacy to leave our great-grandchildren.

Yet, even if the storage problem can be solved, will American industry put up the capital to build the plants? Ernie Moniz, who heads up MIT's climate program and who served as deputy secretary of energy during the Clinton administration, told me in his Cambridge office that the United States would need to triple its number of nuclear power plants from 103 to 300, at a cost of $5 billion each, to make a meaningful dent in global warming.[19] When you include all the cradle-to-grave costs, such as disassembling the plants and storing the spent fuel, that represents, he calculates, a $2 trillion investment over the next fifty years. Rather than wait for a next-generation technology, Moniz believes we should start building what are called generation III light-water reactors. They are based on designs developed in the 1990s and have since been improved by features such as passive safety. The reactor shuts itself down in the event of an accident. The first generation III reactor was built in Japan in 1996 and has thus far been accident free.

Some in the industry point to a next-generation design called a pebble-bed reactor that they argue is cheaper and safer than current plants. South Africa is scheduled to begin construction of a 110-megawatt demonstration pebble-bed plant, to be completed by 2011. Critics say that because these plants don't have a containment vessel, they will be vulnerable to terrorist attacks; furthermore, imperfections in the pebble-shaped fuel pellets could cause accidents. Germany abandoned a pebble-bed test plant in 1986, declaring the technology unsafe.[20] Even if the industry could overcome these hurdles, it is not clear that these plants could be deployed fast enough to make a meaningful reduction in global warming.

The utility industry, of course, will only pony up $2 trillion in new capital for nuclear power plants if it thinks that such power can be competitive with fossil fuels and renewables and that it can get a decent return on its investment. Currently, electricity generated by nuclear power, Moniz estimates, is about 60 percent more expensive than coal and about 15 percent more expensive than natural gas. His calculations include all costs of the life span of a plant, including decommissioning the facility and making it radiation safe after its useful life is over. Moniz believes that if we can streamline the approval process and standardize construction, operation, and maintenance, the cost of nuclear power could drop by 25 percent, making it more attractive than gas and much closer to coal. Of course, if the U.S. government passes a carbon tax, Moniz reckons it could raise the cost of coal, making it as much as a third more expensive than nuclear power.

The model that America could emulate is France. The French have fully embraced nuclear power and enjoy some of the cleanest air in Europe. The government has built fifty-eight nuclear plants in a country the size of Texas, which today generate 78 percent of its electricity. (The European Union gets 35 percent of its electricity from nuclear.)[21] AREVA, the French government monopoly, controls every step of its nuclear industry from uranium mining to plant design and construction to radioactive waste disposal. Because it decided long ago to standardize its plant design, AREVA has been able to keep costs somewhat under control. The country produces so much nuclear power that it sells its excess to Germany, Italy, and even London. AREVA chairwoman Anne Lauvergeon, an engineer and onetime political aide to former French president François Mitterrand, points out that the nuclear power industry employs 150,000 people, and as a key exporter of electricity and power equipment, adds to the French economy. She may be the most powerful businesswoman in France, where everyone knows her as "Atomic Anne."

Nonetheless, nuclear power plants are huge capital-intensive projects and to get costs down would not be an easy task. The industry lost a lot of credibility in the early days when it claimed that nuclear power would be "too cheap to meter." Of course, cost overruns eventually reached into the billions. As an ominous sign of the future, an advanced (generation III+) nuclear power plant being built by France's AREVA in Olkiluoto, Finland, has run into serious construction delays and cost overruns.

And what investor would want to put his capital at risk in a business where one accident could bring the entire industry to a standstill? The U.S. government will provide insurance for new nuclear plants, basically agreeing to pay for all the costs incurred by a major accident. Even so, owners and builders worry that a public backlash from another Three Mile Island–style incident could bring construction to a grinding halt.

Sadly, whatever the risks and costs and legitimate safety concerns, if we are to stop global warming, many experts believe, we apparently have little choice but to start building nuclear power plants.

10

A Mighty Wind

But, Please, NIMBY

EVERYONE KNOWS that Warren Buffett is one of the world's savviest investors. As head of the holding company Berkshire Hathaway, the Oracle of Omaha has amassed a fortune of around $52 billion, making him as of 2007 the third-richest person on the planet behind Carlos Slim and Bill Gates. What most don't realize, however, is that Buffett is also one of the world's biggest investors in wind power. Berkshire Hathaway owns 87.4 percent of MidAmerican Energy Holdings, an Iowa-based power company with annual sales of $10.3 billion and the largest owner among rate-regulated utilities of wind power farms in the United States.

MidAmerican operates 1,000 megawatts of wind power in Iowa, enough to supply nearly 300,000 homes, making the state third in the nation in wind energy generation, behind Texas and California. The clean energy that MidAmerican generates is equivalent to removing more than 682,000, or 43 percent, of Iowa's registered vehicles from the road. The farmers who allow turbines to be installed on their land receive annual royalties—a new cash crop.[1]

Currently, Iowa gets 85 percent of its power from coal, 9 percent from nuclear, and the rest from wind and other sources. Wind can play a vital role in reducing the need for greenhouse gas–spewing coal plants. Iowa has a vast wind energy potential—nine times larger than that of California,[2] and five times that of Germany, the world leader in installed wind power capacity. Buffett sees the potential, too. He has said that Berkshire will look to acquire energy assets around the world, and that "there is no limit to the money we have to spend."[3]

Buffett's not the only one opening his wallet. The wind business is growing at hurricane speed. Worldwide, 15,200 megawatts of new wind generating capacity—the equivalent of about a half dozen nuclear power plants—were installed in 2006, with about $19.5 billion invested, an increase of 32 percent over the previous year. The United States led the way, installing more wind capacity than any other country, with Germany second and India third. Total wind investment in America reached a record $3.7 billion that year.

The reason for the growth: wind has become the most affordable source of renewable energy and is now competitive with fossil fuel power in many areas of the United States. A federal tax credit—due to expire in 2008—as well as local subsidies have helped trigger the boom, but even without them, wind would still, in many instances, be cost-competitive with natural gas, although more expensive than coal.

Though wind provides less than 1 percent of all electricity in America, experts think that number could rise to 20 percent by 2030. The European Commission estimates that wind power will be able to meet 12 percent of the EU's electricity needs by 2020, up from 3.3 percent today.[4] The official German objective for wind power is even more ambitious. Germany expects wind to meet 20 percent of its need for electricity in 2020 compared with 4 percent today.[5] And Denmark, the world champ of wind power, already generates 20 percent of its electricity from the breeze racing across the North Sea.[6]

There is big money to be made from such growth rates. Among companies that build wind turbines, in 2006 GE was the market leader with nearly a 50 percent share followed by Germany's Siemens (23 percent) and Denmark's Vestas (19 percent). Together, these three control more than 90 percent of the wind turbine market. Demand is so brisk for these $2 million to $3 million turbines that GE has orders booked into 2009. The company has increased production fivefold since buying bankrupt Enron Wind in 2002.[7] High demand and rising commodity prices are pushing up the price of wind turbines—but so far not enough to prevent them from remaining price-competitive with fossil fuels.

The manufacturing boom is creating jobs. In 2006 alone, leading wind turbine manufacturers opened facilities in Iowa, Minnesota, Texas, and Pennsylvania. New contracts for wind energy components such as towers and gearboxes create jobs across the country, even in states that do not have a large wind resource. Rust Belt communities that have been losing manufacturing jobs now see economic opportunity in the high demand for wind turbines. Acciona Energía of Spain announced that it would build a new wind turbine manufacturing facility in West Branch, Iowa. Vestas plans to open a facility in Colorado, the company's first-ever in the United States. Farmers also benefit year-round from turbines in their fields, earning income that may help them stay on the land. FPL, formerly Florida Power & Light, now generates more than a quarter of its electricity from wind and is one of the largest builders of wind farms in the country.

The Voices of Tug Hill

Despite this promise, wind faces some tough obstacles, among them resistance from people living near these gargantuan towers. Tug Hill is a region running along the ridges of upstate New York, tucked between the east end of Lake Ontario and the Adirondack

Mountains. Twenty-three square miles of land are scattered with red dairy barns, fields rich with deer and wild turkey, general stores, schools—and 195 windmills. This is the site of the largest windmill farm east of the Mississippi, the Maple Ridge complex, owned by Horizon Inc. and PPM Energy. Each tower is 260 feet tall with three 130-foot blades that rotate at a steady 14 miles per hour. Each is anchored in a concrete block 8 feet deep and 50 feet in diameter. The wind farm generates enough electricity for 146,000 homes.

People in Tug Hill were happy to see the windmills when they were first installed. The utility would pay local taxes, and those farmers who agreed to allow windmills on their land received as much as $7,000 a year. During construction local restaurants and bars were bustling with welders, masons, and heavy-equipment operators. The small-business owners in the town liked the extra revenue.

Then one day it started. The steady whoosh . . . whoosh . . . whoosh . . . whoosh . . . whoosh . . . of the mammoth blades as the winds sweeping down from Canada drove them for hours on end. People who lived within earshot but received no money from the utility began to complain. They couldn't sleep. Their nerves were shot.

The Voices of Tug Hill, a half-hour documentary, turned up on YouTube. It showed Rick, a young man in a black baseball cap and black parka, standing in the barn of his family's dairy farm beside a red tractor. As he tells it, his dad got money to put windmills on his land but now regretted the decision. "He never dreamed it would make this much noise," Rick complains.[8] A hunter in the film describes how the local fields used to be full of deer and wild turkey, but since the towers were erected, the fowl have disappeared and the deer population seems to have been cut in half. Some local merchants now worry that with the drop-off in the game population, fewer hunters will travel to their region.

Wind turbines make a low-frequency thumping noise every

time one of the blades passes the tower. The thumping is especially noticeable at night when there's little background noise. Wind power is more plentiful in Europe, and governments there are trying to deal with this problem. France's Academy of Medicine recommends that wind turbines be built at least a mile away from any home: "People living near the towers sometimes complain of functional disturbances similar to those observed in syndromes of chronic sound trauma. Studies conducted in the neighborhoods of airports have clearly demonstrated that chronic invasive sound involves neurobiological reactions associated with an increased frequency of hypertension and cardiovascular illness. Unfortunately, no such study has been done near wind turbines. But the sounds emitted by the blades being low frequency, which therefore travel easily and vary according to the wind, constitute a permanent risk for the people exposed to them."[9]

Such health concerns would certainly limit the amount of land available for large-scale wind farms. It might also affect people like Michael Mercurio, who, in the fall of 2006, installed in his Long Beach Island, New Jersey, backyard a $15,000 40-foot-high windmill with 12-foot rotor blades. The windmill, combined with rooftop solar panels, reduced Mercurio's annual utility costs of more than $4,000 to $114.

Mercurio, who runs a windmill installation company, was pleased, but his neighbors were not. Annoyed by the noise of the turbine as well as the strobelike shadows the blades throw on their property, his neighbors have gone to court to make Mercurio take the tower down, arguing that it violates a local ordinance that limits the height of towers. A handmade sign on Mercurio's front lawn reads, "Wind power makes America strong," and he recently told the *New York Times:* "People always say, 'Not in my backyard, not in my backyard.' I want to flip it around. It should start in my backyard."[10]

There's not only concern with noise but also the danger to birds. The blade tips of the turbine can reach speeds six or seven times faster than the wind. Thus far, windows, cars, and cats kill far more birds than wind turbines, but the Fish and Wildlife Service has noted that bats and an unusual number of raptors—hawks, owls, eagles—fall victim to blades.[11] One theory is that while small birds have peripheral vision to help them spot predators, raptors see straight ahead to better home in on their prey. That may be the reason predators are more likely to run into a spinning blade. The Fish and Wildlife Service recommends that wind turbines not be permitted near wetlands, mountain ridges, or shorelines where birds tend to concentrate.

The hope is that the wind industry will eventually accommodate itself to local residents and to wildlife. In the meantime, most wind farms are being built close to existing grids where they can provide power to nearby towns and cities. That limits the extent to which they will help us provide renewable power. But there is a larger and simpler question: what happens when the wind isn't blowing? Utilities claim that a typical 1.5-megawatt windmill will provide power to 750 homes. Well, that's true—on paper. To reach that capacity, the wind would have to blow hard twenty-four hours a day, 365 days a year. In real-world conditions, a wind turbine generates power on average about 30 percent of the time—so drop those 750 homes to 250. Take Arkansas, for example. By one calculation, to provide 11 percent of its power needs in 2020, the state would have to build 3,516 windmills stretching over the equivalent of 494 square miles. That is an area about 1 percent of the entire state.[12] It is not clear that so many windy and unpopulated ridges and hilltops are to be found there.

The dilemma facing the industry is this: the best place to put a giant windmill is far from the people who need its power. How do you get it to them? One way would be to better integrate the power grid: if wind stops blowing at one wind farm, switch to the power from another in a different part of the country where the wind is blowing. In Europe, engineers who manage the grid can juggle the variability of wind power so that it can serve customer needs. In Denmark, northern Germany, and parts of Spain, wind is supplying 20 to 40 percent of electric loads without sacrificing reliability.[13]

One way to approach this problem harks back to the days of Thomas Edison: long-distance DC power lines. The windiest spots in America are in the Dakotas and Texas. By one estimate South Dakota has enough wind to generate electricity to power the entire United States. Could these vast resources of wind be harnessed to provide clean, affordable electricity to most of the nation? To do it, many more transmission lines would be required. As we saw in chapter 8, the most efficient transmission would use the DC power lines that can carry electricity for distances of 1,500 miles. Such power lines are already in use, including Path 65, a system that runs for 841 miles along the West Coast carrying enough power from the Bonneville hydroelectric dams of the Pacific Northwest to serve 2 to 3 million households in Los Angeles.[14]

In Europe, a consortium of Norwegian companies have begun the installation of high-voltage DC lines between Scandinavia, the Netherlands, and Germany. Called the NorNed HVDC cable link, this 360-mile-long cable will connect hydropower generated in Norway to the grid in the Netherlands.[15] According to Jürgen Schmid, the head of ISET, Germany's alternative-energy institute at the University of Kassel, DC grids could allow wind to supply at least 30 percent of the power needed in Europe.[16]

But because wind does not blow constantly, backup power sources would be required. In the Pacific Northwest and Northeast of the United States, where hydropower is plentiful, a utility could "store" power by not releasing water when the windmills are running strong and then release it when the gusts disappear. Excess wind power could even be used to pump more water from a river into the reservoir, in effect making the dam a storage battery.

But in the Southeast and the Southwest the wind dies down on hot summer afternoons, just when most air conditioners are turned on. The power backup would probably be plants run on oil or coal. Such installations can't be turned on and off at will but have to be kept running on a standby level—meaning they are emitting greenhouse gas all the time the windmills generate "clean power." Chapter 5 examines recent breakthroughs in battery technology that would allow power to be stored. Until such technology is in widespread use, wind is not likely to provide more than 10 to 20 percent of our energy under the most optimistic scenarios.

Tilting at Windmills?

If wind poses NIMBY problems, especially in the densely populated Northeast, why not build the giant turbines offshore? The wind blows longer and harder offshore than on land, and turbines would be far from where people live. Jim Gordon, an entrepreneurial pioneer, plans to install one of the world's largest wind farms on a 25-square-mile site in Nantucket Sound. He projects that when it is installed, his Cape Wind project would provide about 1 percent of New England's electricity. One hundred thirty wind turbines, each over 440 feet tall with 182-foot-long blades, would be erected. They would be connected to a ten-story service platform that would hold 40,000 gallons of oil and 10,000 gallons of diesel fuel. As one local protester blogged. "Imagine 130 rotating football fields!"

From the day the project was announced, resistance began to build against it. Senator Ted Kennedy, who owns a vacation house in Hyannisport on Cape Cod, and media celebrities such as Walter Cronkite, who has a house on Martha's Vineyard, opposed the project, saying that the huge towers just a few miles offshore would spoil the beautiful view that makes the area so desirable. At this writing, a well-financed campaign to kill the project was still in place as Cape Wind continued its fight to win government approval. A final decision on the project from the federal government is expected in late 2008.

Bill Koch, a resident of Nantucket, opposed Cape Wind for different reasons. In 2002 Jim Gordon asked Koch to invest in Cape Wind. At first this avid sailor—Koch won the America's Cup in 1992—and hard-minded businessman liked the deal. Using the analytical skills he developed while earning his Ph.D. in chemical engineering from MIT, he saw that Cape Wind could provide electricity at a reasonable cost to residents of the area. But the harder he looked at the risks the more skeptical he became. If the political climate changed and federal and state subsidies were abolished— something that had already happened to the wind industry more than once—then the return on investment didn't look nearly as attractive. Koch also knew that to measure the deal's true economic return you'd have to add in the cost of a new transmission line to bring the wind power to the Cape, as well as the hefty expenses from demolishing the turbines after they became obsolete. If Cape Wind got stuck bearing some of these costs, the return wouldn't be worth the risk. Koch passed on the opportunity to invest.

Koch wrote an editorial in the *Wall Street Journal* in the spring of 2006 titled "Tilting at Windmills," which argued that the numbers had grown even worse since he'd first looked at the deal four years earlier. He posited that for Cape Wind to earn a 20 percent return, it would have to sell its electricity for 18 cents a kilowatt-hour, roughly twice what Cape residents were currently paying. In fact, if Cape Wind sold electricity at the going rate and lost its hefty subsidies, the project would lose money. David G. Tuerck, executive director of the Beacon Hill Institute, also studied the business model: "What we found was quite remarkable. Cape Wind stands to receive subsidies worth $731 million, or 77 percent of the cost of installing the project and 48 percent of the revenues it would generate."[17] Koch calculated that Cape Wind's project would mean the price of electricity would rise by $1,300 more per year for a typical family.

What had happened to the numbers since the project was conceived? The boom in global business, especially in fast-growing economies such as China and India, drove up the price of steel and other construction materials. Many of the components of wind turbines are made in Europe, and a weak dollar also pushed up the costs. For offshore towers, the price tag has jumped even more. These units require steel that can withstand not only a harsh, corrosive maritime environment but hurricanes as well.

Jim Gordon disagrees with these estimates. He cites a study by La Capra Associates, a consultancy focusing on the electricity industry, of the regional energy market for 2005–2009. La Capra found that the addition of Cape Wind electricity would exert a downward pressure on wholesale electricity market prices, leading to a savings of approximately $25 million per year for the New England electricity market. The study, however, was finished before the run-up in material and construction costs, and it also assumes that the subsidies for wind would be renewed. A single offshore wind farm has yet to be built in the United States.

The momentum for offshore wind power seems to be going in the wrong direction. In August 2007, the Long Island Power Authority (LIPA) canceled a long-standing plan for a wind farm off of Jones Beach. LIPA chairman Kevin Law said that while he was still committed to renewable energy, an independent study showed that power generated by natural gas would be much cheaper. In fact, construction costs for the offshore wind farm had soared from the $356 million first estimated in 2004 to $811 million, more than double what LIPA thought the project would cost.

Several of Europe's offshore wind projects have also stalled over cost overruns and technical problems. Vestas, which produces both land and offshore wind turbines, is redesigning one of its offshore turbines because it would not hold up under harsh maritime conditions. On the other hand, the Irish company Airtricity has erected offshore windmills that provide power to homes in Ireland. Furthermore, the company wants to build a "Supergrid" that could bring electricity over long-distance power lines from planned offshore wind farms in the North Atlantic and the Irish, North, and Baltic Seas—two thousand wind turbines in total. The power could then be delivered to customers throughout northern Europe.

But offshore wind power in Europe is still roughly twice as expensive as onshore wind. As the English newspaper *Independent* concluded, "Offshore wind is floundering and larger projects needed more government support. Wind and other renewables will only take off when they can compete in the marketplace without subsidy and that day has not yet come."[18]

Over lunch at a Cambridge coffee shop, Stephen Connors, the director of MIT's AGREA program, which studies alternative energy, explained the main problem with offshore wind turbines: all those already built in Europe and planned in the United States are in shallow waters in sight of land. That means they are located in shipping channels and in places day sailors use. "There are not enough of these shallow spots on the East Coast for wind to be a major factor in solving the global warming problem," he said. Even if you were able to utilize all the shallow offshore waters from Delaware to Maine, that would still provide only a small percentage of all power. And you'd still have NIMBY—not on my horizon problems.

Connors believes that deep-water wind turbines would work better. He points to the cutting-edge work of Paul Sclavounos, an MIT professor of mechanical engineering and naval architecture. In 2004 Sclavounos and his colleagues teamed up with wind turbine experts from the National Renewable Energy Laboratory (NREL) to design giant floating wind turbines that can be tethered to the ocean floor in waters as deep as 600 feet and as far as hundreds of miles offshore. Sclavounos cites the oil companies' thirty years of experience with floating oil and gas rigs.

Though it would work on the same principle, a waterborne windmill's platform would look different from an oil rig's, which

typically sits on four floating cylinders. The much smaller windmill platform would top a floater, a single slender cylinder. Rigid
steel tethers would be anchored in the seafloor so that even in severe storms the floater and the wind tower—nearly the height of
the Washington Monument—would not capsize. "These oil rigs
are built to withstand waves two to three times as high as anything
they're ever likely to encounter," notes Sclavounos. "Very few oil
rigs have been lost in severe storms."[19]

Sclavounos argues that these giant turbines would be as much
as a third cheaper than the offshore windmills being built today.
Because winds blow harder out at sea, the turbine itself can be
larger, thus yielding more energy per wind tower. It would not be
more expensive to do this since the cost depends more on the
number of turbines than on their size. Sclavounos envisions his
deep-water wind farms employing giant 5-megawatt turbines,
compared with 1.5 MW for onshore units and 3.5 MW for conventional offshore setups. Because of the strong winds far out at
sea, the floating turbines should produce up to twice as much electricity per year as wind turbines now in operation.

This doesn't seem to be pie-in-the-sky thinking. In March
2006 GE announced a $27 million partnership with the U.S. De-
partment of Energy to develop 5- to 7-megawatt turbines by 2009,
supplanting the company's current 3.6-megawatt turbines. Each of
these giant energy factories, with rotors 140 meters in diameter,
would produce enough electricity to power up to 1,750 homes.

One of the highest costs of traditional offshore wind farms is
installing the giant pillars that support the blades and turbines.
After the towers are set in the ocean floor, as much as 20 feet of
crushed stone gravel must be piled around each one to prevent serious erosion. Sclavounos claims that with his design, the entire
rig, including the float and pillar, can be assembled on land, floated
out to sea by tugboat, and then dropped in place. Once on-site, the
platform is hooked to previously installed tethers. Water is
pumped out of the cylinders until the entire assembly lifts up in

the water, pulling the tethers taut. The design is said to reduce dramatically the amount of time needed for construction under heavy winds, high waves, and other harsh and dangerous maritime conditions.

Floating turbines have another possible advantage. If Sclavounos decided to put his four-hundred-turbine farm off the coast of Massachusetts but some years later found that New York City needed more power and was willing to pay a premium for it, he could simply unhook his windmills from their tethers and tow them south.

A Norwegian company has its own design for a deep-water wind turbine and has raised $26 million to build a prototype. Sway, founded in 2001 and based in Bergen, Norway, puts its wind turbine atop a floating elongated pole shooting 270 feet above the ocean's surface and nearly 300 feet below it to act as ballast. This floating tower is then anchored to the seabed by a tension leg and suction anchor allowing the entire windmill, including the tower, to rotate with the wind direction and survive 90-foot waves.

The company says that its design will be cost-competitive and produce as much as 30 percent more power than today's offshore wind turbines. Sway, which says its first full-scale turbine will be installed sometime after 2010, also claims that building deep-sea wind farms on only 0.5 percent of Norwegian waters would produce 100 percent of the nation's total electricity consumption.

Many details remain to be worked out. Walt Musial, a senior engineer and an offshore energy expert at the National Renewable Energy Laboratory, cautioned against expecting too much too quickly. "It's very difficult to do things at sea," Musial told a blogger from LiveScience. "It's the right way to go, but it's not going to work the first time. It's not going to be economical." Musial emphasized that new and expensive technologies must be developed before floating wind farms are technically feasible and competitively priced.[20]

As scientists and engineers figure out how to tap the heavy offshore winds, a different band of entrepreneurs believes the best way to harness the energy of the sea is to dive below it.

AT THE BOTTOM OF New York City's East River, beside the old tires and the unlucky wiseguys, sit six 20-foot propellers that turn slowly with the incoming and outgoing tide. The turbines generate enough electricity to support the Gristedes supermarket on nearby Roosevelt Island. Verdant Power hopes eventually to install enough turbines to power five thousand homes in New York.

Verdant is one of dozens of start-ups hoping to harness the energy in the world's tides and waves. Oceans cover over 70 percent of the earth. They store tremendous amounts of energy generated by their moon-driven tides and wind-powered waves. Researchers at Oregon State University say that only 0.2 percent of the ocean's untapped wave energy could power the entire world. This figure may seem incredible, but water is a very dense medium, about a thousand times thicker than air, and capable of transmitting immense energy when in motion. According to a recent report from the Electric Power Research Institute (EPRI), tapping into 20 percent of the wave power off the shores of the United States has the potential to supply as much as 7 percent of the nation's electricity, the same amount generated today by hydropower. EPRI estimates that five states have good tidal flows and perhaps as many as eight states have good waves. Canada, where in areas like the Bay of Fundy tide power is much more abundant, could also provide North America with meaningful amounts of clean electricity.

Yet wave and tidal power remains the dark horse of the renewable energy boom. For decades, scientists and engineers have tried to channel the waves and tides into electricity with little success. Part of the problem is a scarcity of R&D funding. Start-ups can't raise federal or private funds without proving their design feasible, and it's difficult to prove feasibility without the R&D money. The harsh conditions at sea and the power of the tides have made commercial projects expensive and complex. Entrepreneurs are finding that containing and converting this potent power to electricity is far from simple or cost-effective. After a few weeks of operation, the powerful tides of the East River damaged Verdant's turbines, seriously setting back the project.

But ocean energy advocates remain undeterred. Prototypes of wave and tide machines, with various technological designs, are being tested throughout the world. These technologies include wave generators and free-floating power buoys that use waves for energy. Turbines like those built by Verdant Power try to take advantage of the potential energy in tides and rivers. Europe, Australia, and other parts of the world are further along in ocean power projects than the United States, mostly because of active support from their governments. Off the west coast of Scotland, Wavegen, a company in Inverness, uses ocean waves to pull and push air through a turbine in what is called an "oscillating water column." Another Scottish company, Ocean Power Delivery, in partnership with EnerSys of Reading, Pennsylvania, has developed Pelamis, a snakelike floating device moored off the shore of Portugal that generates power as the waves knock the sections to and fro, moving hydraulic pistons that drive turbines. In the first leg of the project, the snake will provide electricity to three thousand homes. The Australian company Energetech is installing a pilot wave energy project off the Australian coast.

One promising U.S. company is Ocean Power Technologies of Pennington, New Jersey. That is probably because in this instance the company received a $12 million contract from the U.S. Navy to install its electricity-generating buoys in the waters off Hawaii to power a Marine base there. The company is also undertaking demonstration projects for Lockheed Martin and is working on projects in France, Scotland, and Spain. In its most ambitious project to date, Ocean Power has set its eyes on the wave-rich Oregon coast. Waves arrive there with immense power, having traveled across thousands of miles of open water with few barrier islands, reefs, or other obstructions to slow them down.

Ocean Power founder George Taylor, a former surfer who grew up in Australia, plans to put his first 30-acre wave power farm off the shore of Reedsport on Oregon's central coast. When completed in 2008, this installation is projected to provide enough power for two thousand homes, but the ultimate goal is enough electricity for fifty thousand. Each buoy will be 30 feet wide, weigh 50 tons, and house a massive float that moves up and down like a piston as a wave passes. The piston's motion drives a generator near the top of the buoy that creates an electric current without emitting greenhouse gas. This current then can be carried ashore by undersea cables and fed into the power grid. Sophisticated computer controls adjust for variations in the size of the waves.

Unlike towering offshore windmills, these buoys, which project only 9 feet above the ocean's surface, can barely be seen from shore. After testing the buoys, the navy concluded that there was no danger that birds or marine mammals might become entangled in the mooring lines or that electrical currents would disrupt sea life. They did find that the undersea cables and anchors provided a place for coral to grow and attracted fish, much like an artificial reef.

This leaves the question of cost. Taylor expects his Oregon buoys eventually to generate electricity at rates competitive with cheap power produced by coal. But that is yet to be seen. Installing and maintaining buoys in a hard ocean environment can be costly, as is laying the underwater cables needed to hook the wave power into the grid. Ocean Power is a public company—in an IPO in 2003 it raised $40 million—but it has been losing money. Nevertheless, it believes it will be able to make the price of wave power competitive with fossil fuels before its capital runs out.

While entrepreneurs work to harness the power of the oceans, another vast source of potential energy sits untapped: the heat below the earth's surface.

The beauty of geothermal is that it generates power twenty-four hours a day, compared with solar, which stops working after the sun sets, and wind power, whose turbines stop when the breezes abate. Holes are drilled into the earth, pipes inserted, and hot water or steam rushes to the surface where it drives a generator and produces electricity. A 2006 report by MIT and the Department of Energy concluded that geothermal could provide the United States alone with the equivalent energy of 100 nuclear power plants by 2050, or about 20 percent of the nation's current electricity, and do it while emitting only trace amounts of greenhouse gas. Professor Jefferson Tester, the study's lead author, believes that geothermal energy potential in the uppermost 6 miles of the earth's crust amounts to 50,000 times the energy of all known oil and gas resources in the world.[21]

For the most part, American investors have been cool to the idea of geothermal power, the art of turning the warmth miles beneath the planet's surface into energy. For decades, a handful of plants in Alaska, California, Hawaii, Nevada, and Utah have been tapping hot underground water or steam, turning it into electricity. Today, geothermal produces less than 1 percent of the nation's electricity—about enough to power 1.7 million households.[22] California, with some forty small plants, produces an impressive 5 percent of all its electrical power from the earth's heat. America is the world leader in geothermal power, yet only a handful of new geothermal plants, all of them small scale, are currently being built in this country.[23] This lack of enthusiasm among big money investors is curious considering that geothermal shows much long-term promise. Why are they so gun shy?

Trouble is, no one has yet to prove that geothermal can be scaled economically, and that risk has kept most American investors at bay. The geothermal plants operating today are located in spots where the hot water or steam is very close to the surface and easy to access—think California geysers such as Old Faithful.

Steam and hot water reservoirs, however, are just a small part of the geothermal reserves. For geothermal to provide the vast amounts of energy envisioned by MIT, the plants would have to be spread throughout the country in spots where the heat of the earth is much deeper and thus harder to access. The challenge, as the authors of the MIT report see it, is to develop a next-generation technology that can drive pipes two miles or more beneath the earth's surface and tap into water heated to as much as 400 degrees Fahrenheit by hot granite rock.

To do this, a new technique called dry rock geothermal is being tested at a number of sites around the world, and early results suggest that mining geothermal waters deep below the earth's surface may be feasible. Currently, two companies in Europe and nine in Australia are pursuing new geothermal technologies, and a few have received government backing for R&D. U.S. funding for research in this area is negligible. MIT believes that $300 to $400 million in U.S. government–sponsored R&D, combined with $500 to $600 million in private funds, could within a ten- to fifteen-year period produce commercial scale, demonstration plants nation-wide. This would amount to less than the cost of a single new-generation, clean-coal power plant.

In the meantime, the Australian company Geodynamics seems the furthest along in trying to build the world's first commercial, dry rock geothermal plant. (A private project in Landau, Germany, is also said to be getting impressive results, but little information is available.) So far Geodynamics has sunk more than $100 million into its Habenero project. The publicly traded company, which has a market capitalization of $380 million, is drilling holes into the hot, dry rocks some 3 miles beneath the surface of the barren lands of South Australia. Since 2003, Geodynamics has been drilling wells into the granite, and then breaking up or fracturing the hot rock with hydraulic pressure by pumping water down the wells. The idea is that these cracks or breaks in the hot, dry rock will allow water to seep through and become heated. A power plant on the surface would draw hot water out of this well, convert its energy into electricity, then pump the cooled water down a second well, establishing a flow of water through the underground reservoir.

As you might guess, drilling more than 2 miles beneath the surface through granite is no easy feat. At one point the Habenero project ground to a halt after a series of problems, including a drill malfunction, which left a length of pipe stuck in the hole. And questions remain. Will the underground reservoirs supply enough hot water to generate commercial amounts of power? Can these superdeep holes be drilled economically? Will the drilling trigger earthquakes?

Despite many delays and difficulties,[24] Geodynamics CEO Adrian Williams emphasizes that the drilling problems have been overcome and that his company "has completed the pioneering stage." In 2008, the company will drill another series of wells, which Williams claims will make possible the world's first commercial deep geothermal plant. The plant could be operating as early as 2010.

Risky, dry-rock geothermal certainly seems worth exploring. Johan Hedstrom, a securities analyst who covers the industry for Bell Potter Securities, believes that dry-rock geothermal plants could generate electricity at rates competitive with fossil fuels and "well below other alternatives such as wind, biomass and solar." And the beauty of geothermal is that the fuel is local, free, gets produced twenty-four hours a day, and, most important, generates little or no greenhouse gas.

11

Arnie and Mike

Grassroots Green

CALIFORNIA GOVERNOR Arnold Schwarzenegger is a Republican who likes to drive gas-guzzling Hummers, travel in his private jet, live in big houses, and smoke cigars. He's not whom you'd think of as your typical environmentalist. In fact, when he first ran for governor, protesters followed him with signs disparaging his un-green lifestyle.

In a Nixon-goes-to-China way, this Republican governor has the credibility to make wind, solar, and other renewable technologies mainstream in his state, and California is already far in the lead on this issue. In the absence of any meaningful leadership from the Bush administration, the battle against global warming has fallen into the hands of our states and cities. Schwarzenegger, for instance, sponsored a law to cut greenhouse gas emissions by 25 percent by the year 2020—essentially rolling such gas emissions back to their 1990 level. By 2050, that level is projected to fall another 80 percent.

The governor ordered a 10 percent cut in the carbon content of transportation fuels. He mandated subsidies to help Californians install solar collectors on 1 million roofs. He has proposed a market-driven cap and trade system for carbon under which businesses could buy and sell the right to release CO_2 while keeping overall emissions low. A coalition of more than one hundred major business groups in California have pledged their support.

Schwarzenegger has even tried to make his own lifestyle more acceptable to the protesters. His Hummers run on biodiesel and hydrogen fuel. Solar panels have been installed on the governor's residence. And Schwarzenegger even seems to be trying to turn his hobbies green. In 2007 he appeared on the TV show *Pimp My Ride* and helped transform a 1965 Impala into a lowrider with an 800-horsepower engine that goes from zero to sixty in three seconds. But this muscle car runs on biofuels, which means, says Schwarzenegger, that it emits 50 percent less greenhouse gas and goes twice as far as it would burning gasoline. "Now, that's what I call cool," says the governor. "You see, now we cut down on the greenhouse emissions. So we don't have to really go and take away the muscle cars. We don't have to take away the Hummers or the SUVs or anything like this, because that's a formula for failure. Instead, what we have to do is make those cars more environmentally muscular."

Any member of the Sierra Club may wonder why Schwarzenegger or anyone else would need to go from zero to sixty in three seconds. After all, driving a powerful car that fast emits a lot more greenhouse gas than driving the same distance in a Prius. But Schwarzenegger counters that it really is all about winning political acceptance. He admits that the standards that California sets will not by themselves solve global warming problems. But if it were a nation, California, with its 36 million citizens, would be the sixth-largest economy in the world and the twelfth-biggest emitter of greenhouse gas. When California speaks, the rest of America listens, and Schwarzenegger is giving everyone an earful on climate change.

Addressing a packed audience at Georgetown University on April 11, 2007, an animated Schwarzenegger explained that he and other politicians must push the environmental movement to a tipping point: "Bodybuilding, you know, is another passion of mine, and it used to have a very sketchy image . . . so that some people that worked out seriously and pumped weights didn't admit they were bodybuilding. . . . In the old days some of the very famous Hollywood actors, like Kirk Douglas, Clint Eastwood, Charles Bronson—and the list goes on and on—all worked out with weights. But they never admitted it publicly because they didn't want to be associated with the gymnasiums that were like dungeons and that had fanatics and that had weird people training in there.

"That is the kind of an image that it had. We consciously changed that. . . . We came up with a book called *Pumping Iron*. And the movie *Pumping Iron* and that changed the image of bodybuilding dramatically. . . . It became more and more hip and more and more attractive. And then, all of a sudden, everyone wanted to exercise. . . . It became sexy, attractive."

What does that have to do with the green movement? Schwarzenegger believes that "environmentalists were no fun. They were like Prohibitionists at the fraternity party." The key, he believes, is to get people to see environmentalism as positive, dynamic, and capable of bringing about major change. He urges that we encourage entrepreneurs and the high-tech brainpower of Silicon Valley to figure out how we can cruise the streets in biodiesel muscle cars without adding to global warming. Schwarzenegger says, "The smokestacks belching pollution are powering our Jacuzzis and our big screen TVs, and in my case, powering my private airplanes. So it is too bad, of course, that we can't all live as simple lives as the Buddhist monks in Tibet. But you know something? That's not going to happen."

The governor is betting that California's radical environmental laws can show the rest of the nation how to go green without repeating the mistakes made during the energy crisis of the 1970s, when President Jimmy Carter urged Americans to turn down the thermostat and put on a cardigan. He believes that California will be the place where the green revolution will occur first.

The governor's green campaign has already had an impact on

voters. A Field poll released in the spring of 2007 showed that 81 percent of state voters said global warming was a very serious or somewhat serious problem, and only 21 percent felt the federal government was doing a good job addressing it. It is easy to understand why Californians have become serious about global warming. A 2007 report by a newly formed state climate commission found that if greenhouse gas emissions are not cut, global warming is expected to raise temperatures between 8 and 10.4 degrees Fahrenheit in California and diminish the Sierra snowpack—a major source of drinking water—by 90 percent over the next century. Warming could also raise the sea level 4 to 33 inches, causing coastal erosion and sending saltwater surging into Sacramento Delta water supplies. Such effects would be economically disastrous to agricultural production. They would increase the risk of forest fires and produce a surge in utility costs for cooling. Climate warming could also cause large numbers of heat-related deaths, increase the incidence of certain diseases, and lead to a higher number of bad ozone days.

Many business leaders do not share Schwarzenegger's vision. They warn that his green policies will increase costs and force them to scale back their California operations. They say that voters should be told that greenhouse gas regulations will increase the price of everything from electricity to gasoline to food.

The truth is that even those who most fervently push for measures to control climate change admit that the transition to a carbon-free economy will not be free. A 2006 MIT study of the coal industry estimated that building and installing the technology to wring the CO_2 from the exhaust of a coal-fired plant and bury it safely in the ground would raise the price of electricity as much as 50 percent. Among those hit hardest would be consumers and businesses in Kentucky and West Virginia that depend heavily on coal. Some economists and utility executives believe that the damage from such price increases could be offset by residents and businesses buying more-efficient refrigerators and air conditioners and by switching to energy-miser fluorescent lightbulbs. But people don't switch their behavior—or their appliances—overnight and there's sure to be economic hardship, especially for low- and middle-income Americans.

Schwarzenegger dismisses the criticism, arguing that the new jobs and wealth created by going green will more than offset any higher costs to society. He cites two studies to back his claims. Ned Helme, president of the Center for Clean Air Policy, an environmental think tank based in Washington, D.C., estimated that California could meet its 2010 emissions-reduction goals at no cost to consumers and that they might save money if the 2020 goals were met. The study described a number of cost-effective ways to cut emissions, including capturing methane from landfills and manure and using it to generate energy, and switching freight transport from diesel trucks to rail.

The second study, by the University of California at Berkeley, analyzed eight policies the state could undertake to reach half of the 2020 target. Achieving that goal would result in an additional twenty thousand jobs and increase the state's economy by $60 billion. The logic is simple: spend less on energy through conservation and develop cheaper alternative power. The result? More money in the pockets of consumers who will then spend more and thus create new jobs.

"We can save money now by addressing climate change," said Alex Farrell, an assistant professor in the energy resources group at UC Berkeley who co-led the study with W. Michael Hanemann, an economist who directs the Climate Change Center at UC Berkeley.[1] "By acting now, California can gain a competitive advantage by becoming a leader in new technologies that will be used worldwide."

The New 80/20 Rule

Three thousand miles from the California governor's mansion is the Milstein Hall of Ocean Life at the American Museum of Natural

History in New York City. It is Earth Day 2007, and beneath the 94-foot, 21,000-pound model of a blue whale that hangs from the ceiling, New York City mayor Michael Bloomberg—whom Schwarzenegger calls his "soul mate"—is, to the beat of African drums, about to mount the podium. The five hundred dignitaries, business executives, city planners, and environmentalists in the audience applaud when the billionaire mayor announces "the broadest scale attack on the causes of global warming that any city has ever undertaken."

His new program, called PlaNYC, contains 127 initiatives aimed at making New York City "greener" and "greater" by 2030. PlaNYC calls for cutting carbon emissions from buildings, planting green beltways throughout the city and green roofs on its buildings, mandating hybrid taxis, and, most controversial, charging motorists to enter Manhattan during the workday.

Behind Bloomberg's initiative are some stark and pressing facts. Some 8.2 million people live in New York City—and more are coming, probably a million more by 2030. That kind of growth could paralyze the city, stretching the infrastructure beyond its limits. As Bloomberg paints the picture: "Parks, bursting at their seams. Streets, choked with traffic. Trains, packed beyond capacity. Dirtier air, more polluted water. And climate change that is real and worrisome. As a coastal city, we're on the leading edge of one of the most dramatic effects of global warming: rising sea levels and intensifying storms."

These are big problems and to solve them the mayor is thinking big. He plans to create what he calls the first environmentally sustainable twenty-first-century city. Bloomberg, a no-nonsense political Independent, runs the city like a CEO. This is hardly surprising for a man who, after leaving Salomon Brothers in 1981 built a media empire. According to an April 2007 article in *Fortune* magazine, Bloomberg News reported 2006 sales of $4.7 billion, operating profits of $1.5 billion, and a news staff 2,300 strong.[2] Bloomberg himself is worth $5.5 billion and leads a life with a fairly immodest carbon footprint. He lives in a five-story town house on Manhattan's Upper East Side, weekends on his farm in North Salem, Westchester County, New York, and has homes in Bermuda, London, and Vail. To his credit, he does regularly take the subway to work at City Hall—though his car and driver deliver him to the most convenient station.

Using the same intense drive that enabled him to build one of America's premier media companies, he has slowly but steadily been building a political consensus for change. He has formed a Sustainability Advisory Board composed of leaders from the private, public, and nonprofit sectors. In early 2007—through the use of eleven town hall meetings, more than fifty presentations to over 150 advocacy groups, as well as an interactive Web site— Bloomberg reached out to New Yorkers to help figure out the best ways to achieve the goals of PlaNYC.

Bloomberg's overall goal: to cut 30 percent of the greenhouse gas the city emits by 2030, enough to make significant headway against global warming. On an individual basis, New Yorkers already generate less CO_2 than most other Americans. Of those who work in Manhattan, only 5 percent commute by car; the rest walk or ride some sort of mass transit. Living in a high-rise apartment building and working in an office tower devour much less energy than residing in a private home and commuting and shopping by car.

A study the Bloomberg administration released in 2007 found that 20 percent of the CO_2 New York City generated came from vehicles and 80 percent came from buildings. New Yorkers still breathe high levels of the dirty air that may contribute to deadly heart and lung disease. Diesel exhaust from idling trucks and smoke-belching power plants—especially in low-income communities—has helped create a health crisis. (In parts of the Bronx, Brooklyn, and Harlem, children are hospitalized for asthma at nearly four times the national average, triggered at least in part by bad air quality.) To meet his 2030 goals Bloomberg wants to cut soot and CO_2 by requiring the use of higher grades of fuel oil to heat homes, schools, and places of business. The city will provide investments and incentives to encourage owners of heavy-duty diesel trucks and buses to switch to cleaner fuels such as biodiesel. Bloomberg has pushed through an agreement that all the city's new taxis by 2009 will need to meet high-mileage standards, which in most cases means hybrids. Not only does this cut down on greenhouse gas—hybrids are most fuel efficient in stop-and-go traffic—but it makes good business sense. A New York City cabdriver can save as much as $4,500 a year in fuel costs by switching to a hybrid.

As part of PlaNYC, Bloomberg will toughen energy standards for construction, which, as we have seen, will result in projects like the Durst Organization's Bank of America Tower, which emits half the carbon of a traditional high-rise. While he's at it, the mayor says he will plant over 1 million trees in the city, which not only suck up greenhouse gas but should make his plan easier to sell politically. Who doesn't want trees in his neighborhood? "I think it's safe to say," says the mayor, "I've never been accused of being a tree-hugger before but facts are facts. And the fact is—people like trees in their neighborhoods, and they're good for our health. So why wouldn't we plant more of them?"[3] The mayor's plan also calls for more rooftop gardens—which should also help him sell his agenda. In fact, many Manhattan buildings have already started planting them, and new buildings feature them.

But Bloomberg's most controversial measure—and one that suggests just how hard it will be to get Americans to adapt to a carbon-free lifestyle—is to tax cars entering Manhattan during business hours. In December 2006, Bloomberg had joined me and several colleagues for lunch in a Time Inc. dining room. Pointing down to the clogged Christmas holiday traffic on Sixth Avenue, I asked the mayor whether he would consider a program like London's to charge cars coming into Manhattan. "I know, I know," he answered. "All my aides keep saying is London, London, London. You know, I own a town house in London and I haven't been there in six years. Maybe I should go check it out. Politically, though, it's a tough sell." Five months later, Bloomberg had a traffic plan on the table that caused—as he had predicted at the luncheon that day—a political firestorm.

Keep as many cars as possible out of Manhattan, Bloomberg's thinking goes, and you'll cut down on greenhouse gas, make the air cleaner, and boost business while you're at it. "As the city continues to grow, the costs of congestion—to our health, to our environment, and to our economy—are only going to get worse," he says. "The question is not whether we want to pay but how do we want to pay. With an increased asthma rate? With more greenhouse gases? Wasted time? Lost business? And higher prices? Or, do we charge a modest fee to encourage more people to take mass transit?"

Congestion pricing isn't new. Besides London, Singapore and Stockholm also charge drivers who enter the center of those cities, and it has greatly reduced traffic. Taking a taxi across central London today is a much quicker trip than it was before Mayor Ken Livingstone started charging £8 for most cars to enter a zone in central London. The air is cleaner, and London officials calculate that the program is keeping significant amounts of carbon out of the atmosphere each year.

In Bloomberg's proposed plan, any car entering south of Eighty-sixth Street in Manhattan from 6:00 A.M. to 6:00 P.M. on weekdays would pay $8 and any truck $21. Drivers can deduct bridge or tunnel tolls they pay for entering the city. (Cars starting and travelling within the zone will pay $4; taxis are exempt.) As in London, thousands of cameras installed at intersections will record license plates of vehicles entering the zone to make sure drivers pay.

How does the business community feel about the plan? Some small-business owners don't think the added cost will be a big deal. Thomas Nathan is co-owner of Techline Studio, a Manhattan custom cabinetry and office furniture business. Nathan's warehouse is in New Jersey, and his fleet of trucks regularly drives into Manhattan to make deliveries and handle installations. "We'll just tack the

$21 toll onto the delivery charge," says Nathan. "Most of our customers won't care or notice. And we may even get more jobs done each day because my installers will spend less time stuck in traffic." Other companies worry. Will suburban shoppers drive to local stores rather than into the city? In London most shoppers simply changed their patterns, driving into the city to shop on weekends when the toll wasn't in effect.

Much of the resistance to congestion pricing comes from the city's outer boroughs and suburbs. Thousands of residents of Queens, Brooklyn, and the suburbs of Long Island, Westchester, and Connecticut commute to Manhattan daily. Some residents of Queens even drive through the middle of Manhattan each day on their way to jobs in New Jersey. Many people who live in Queens have to take a bus and then the subway to get to work in Manhattan. Some live a far walk from the nearest public transportation. If you've ever seen the long rush-hour bus lines at the last Jamaica subway stations, you know why these workers choose to drive. Bloomberg says he plans to invest the $300 million a year collected from the fees to improve mass transit in the outer boroughs.

Republican legislators, who oppose the plan and whose power base is in the outer boroughs and suburbs, raise some legitimate points about the possible unintended consequences of the plan. They fear, as only one example, that neighborhoods just outside the zone will become giant parking lots for commuters who would drive in and then hop on a bus or subway. Supporters say that neighborhood parking permits for residents only would address that particular problem.

Of course, that's a relatively small side effect of the plan. Perhaps the most frightening impact on people in the boroughs is financial. Some Brooklyn commuters, for example, drive their cars into Manhattan because they need them during the day, perhaps to make deliveries. Just because they own a car does not mean they are rich. Eight dollars a day comes to an outlay of $40 for a workweek, more than $150 a month. That is a big hunk of cash and would require a big and, perhaps, overwhelming adjustment in how people do business.

Such problems have been faced and dealt with in London—though not to everyone's satisfaction. Will Bloomberg get his way in New York? In the summer of 2007 the New York State Assembly voted to form a commission to study the proposal—which in political-speak means Albany is in no rush to upset suburban commuters. As this book went to press, however, the state assembly had blocked Bloomberg's plan.

What politicians such as Schwarzenegger and Bloomberg are doing on the grassroots level is surely helpful, but not enough. What's needed is not only a national but also an international framework to battle global warming, and a handful of leaders in business and in Washington are working on just that.

12

The High Cost of
Doing Nothing

THE BUSINESS COMMUNITY has been making solid progress on global warming, but most economists believe that it won't be able to create clean technologies fast enough without government help. Is the American public ready for strong action from Washington? The national zeitgeist seems to be changing. After Katrina hit New Orleans and the Gulf Coast in the summer of 2005, pictures of what a warming world might look like flashed across television screens and the Internet. The storm killed an estimated 1,836 people, destroying or damaging hundreds of thousands of homes and "laying waste to 90,000 square miles, an area the size of the United Kingdom," according to a U.S. Senate committee report.[1] Although scientists and meteorologists cannot prove that global warming caused the storm, they did raise the possibility that global warming was a factor in the ferocity of Katrina and the unusually high number of other storms that season.

Then in 2006 Al Gore launched his documentary *An Inconvenient Truth*, a film that with charts and graphs presented the scientific evidence for climate change and dramatically portrayed its dire consequences, from drowning polar bears to category 5 hurricanes. The fact that a PowerPoint presentation could win an Academy Award suggested that global warming had penetrated the consciousness of Americans. A perfect storm was brewing: the devastation of Katrina, the scorching heat wave in the summer of 2006, and the impact of Gore's *An Inconvenient Truth*. Finally, the country seemed to be hearing the message that the Natural Resources Defense Council, the Environmental Defense Fund, the Sierra Club, and other environmental groups had been hammering away at for a decade or more—global warming is an issue that must be dealt with now.

A 2007 *New York Times* poll found 52 percent of Americans rating global warming as "very serious," while 63 percent agreed that "protecting the environment is so important that . . . continuing environmental improvements must be made regardless of cost." A Zogby International poll found that three of every four Americans were "more convinced today that global warming is a reality than they were two years ago." One surprising finding of the poll was how widely the specter of global warming has spread across political lines. While 87 percent of Democrats believe in global warming, 56 percent of Republicans now concur, an astonishingly high number considering that even some powerful Republican senators still consider themselves global warming doubters. Senator James Inhofe (R-OK) said in 2003: "Man-made global warming is the greatest hoax ever perpetrated on the American people."[2]

Many Republicans have moved into the global warming camp because of a switch in thinking among influential members of the religious community. In 2002 a bumper-sticker campaign called "What Would Jesus Drive?" was launched in an attempt to get Christians to hand over the keys of their SUVs and trade them for fuel misers such as the Prius and the Honda Civic. To launch the campaign, Rev. Dr. Bob Edgar, general secretary of the National Council of Churches, presented auto executives with a letter signed by over a hundred major religious leaders that called for fuel economy improvements across the fleet. The campaign was picked up by news organizations all over the world.

Global warming also became a concern of members of the

Evangelical Environmental Network, a Bible-based orthodox Christian organization. It believes that the human behavior that causes climate change and resource destruction is not consistent with Bible teachings. The group charter states that "it fulfills the Great Commandments to love God and love what God loves."

The movement to save the earth has grown exponentially and now includes liberal environmentalists, far-right Christians, and the majority of all Americans. Even some conservative politicians who once dismissed global warming have joined in. Newt Gingrich, the Georgia Republican Speaker of the House in the late 1990s, argues in his book *A Contract with the Earth* that climate change has become too important to ignore and that America's dependency on imported oil threatens its security. He sees global warming as an opportunity to unleash America's technological genius and create huge, new green industries through what he calls entrepreneurial environmentalism.

Joining the fray is a group of influential players, many with military or CIA backgrounds, who believe that America should wean itself from fossil fuels not necessarily to stem global warming but for reasons of national security. They have launched Securing America's Future Energy (SAFE), an organization whose mission is to reduce America's dependence on fossil fuels. Among the group's members are John Lehman, former Secretary of the Navy; General P. X. Kelley, former commandant of the U.S. Marine Corps; and Michael Ryan, former chief of staff of the U.S. Air Force. These Washington insiders have been joined by top leaders of the business community, including Fred Smith of FedEx and Herb Kelleher of Southwest Airlines.

Their concern is the political and economic disruption that could occur should America experience another energy crisis. On June 23, 2005, nine SAFE members conducted a mock cabinet meeting in Washington, D.C. The idea was to simulate a seven-month oil crisis due to a war or terrorist strike in the Middle East. In this exercise, the mock cabinet advised a president of the effects of an oil crisis and outlined his options. The results were not encouraging. When a hypothetical 4 percent of oil was taken out of the world market, the price rose to $150 a barrel—$5.74 a gallon at the pump, or $130 to fill an SUV. The U.S. economy lost 2 million jobs, suffered a 28 percent decline in the S&P stock index, and a recession was triggered.

As SAFE founder Robbie Diamond writes, "In an age characterized by instability throughout much of the oil-producing world, a supply crisis cannot be reasonably dismissed as a low-probability event. On the contrary, hostile state actors and terrorist organizations clearly intend to use oil as a potent strategic weapon to attack the United States. The threat is made ever more serious by rapidly rising global consumption."[3]

SAFE, despite its military-industrial pedigree, now oddly finds itself aligned with the environmental movement. In a 2007 letter to House Speaker Nancy Pelosi, the group asked that an energy bill under consideration be strengthened to include tough provisions on energy efficiency, higher standards for automobile mileage, and more support for alternative fuels. Most tellingly, the letter asked Pelosi to "strengthen diplomatic and military arrangements to protect global oil flows." Where SAFE differs from environmentalists is that it is willing to increase production of domestic oil and gas in the name of national security—among other measures, to open the Outer Continental Shelf to offshore drilling. Even so, the group's strong position on efficiency and alternative fuels makes it an effective force in the battle to reduce global warming.

It seems clear that to be effective we must understand not only the dangers of global warming but also the opportunities a green economy presents. Michael Shellenberger, coauthor of *Break Through*, argues that constantly scaring people with global warming horror stories will turn them off. What we need instead is a dialogue on how we can achieve positive change. "Martin Luther King," he says, "didn't give an 'I have a nightmare' speech but an 'I have a dream' speech."[4]

Though Americans say they care about global warming, will

they be willing to make the necessary sacrifices? In a New York Times/CBS News poll conducted before the 2007 Iowa caucuses, only 3 percent of the state's Democrats and 2 percent of the state's Republicans picked the environment as the issue they most wanted the presidential candidates to discuss. It will be an uphill battle to persuade Americans to make sacrifices for the good of future generations. These sacrifices will involve conserving energy as well as supporting a tax on fossil fuels, which most experts believe is the best way to speed the development of solar, wind, wave, and other green technology.

It seems unquestionable that the first step is to increase federal investment in green R&D. The National Renewable Energy Laboratory is working on technology such as "four-junction" solar cells that could generate more than twice the electricity of today's photovoltaic solar cells. But to get the price of these cells down, much more work is needed. Despite recent administration pledges to wean the country from its addiction to oil, the federal government spends only about $800 million a year on green R&D—approximately what we spend in Iraq every four *days*.[5]

One significant change would take place immediately if government agencies, including the military, were instructed to buy green products and use clean energy: if federal office buildings and military bases converted to solar and wind power and used hybrid and electric cars, a considerable amount of money would be funneled into a new green economy. We could thereby stimulate the production of solar panels, wind turbines, and clean cars. As a result, prices of renewables in the entire economy would drop, making them more cost-competitive with fossil fuels. The 2003 Oberstar-Norton amendment empowers the General Services Administration for five years to equip new and existing federal buildings with solar systems. It allocated the pitifully small amount of $50 million a year to pay for them. And though some military bases have gone solar, they have done so only on a volunteer basis.

• • •

THE MOST CONTROVERSIAL and important issue facing world leaders is the carbon tax. Without such a tax, the destruction of the earth's atmosphere will keep accelerating. The free market has failed to reflect the true cost of greenhouse gas, including damage from droughts, floods, and severe storms. Burning carbon in much of the world is free, so why would industry ever use cleaner technologies that cost more? So far the debate has centered around two approaches to limit the use of fossil fuels: a carbon tax and a carbon cap and trade system—another form of tax. A carbon tax is straightforward: using the existing tax structure, the federal government would place a levy on all forms of carbon, including coal, oil, oil shale, natural gas, and tar sands, at the source; that is, where the fuels are extracted from the earth or at the ports where they enter the United States. The energy industry would pass along the costs of this tax to the consumer. However, to balance the burden on taxpayers, payroll taxes could be cut to help offset the higher costs of fuel. Money would flow back into the American economy rather than into the Russian, Venezuelan, Saudi, and Iranian treasuries.

Many economists have crafted tax formulas, and Congress has a number of proposals before it. At this writing, it is not clear which of these, if any, will become law. One of the smartest proposals, America's Energy Security Trust Fund Act, was crafted by Representative John Larson (D-CT) and based on work by Tufts University economics professor Gilbert Metcalf. America emitted 6 billion tons of carbon dioxide in 2005, according to the Energy Information Administration. The Trust Fund Act would put a tax of $15 per ton on carbon dioxide emissions. This would result in an increase of 13 cents per gallon of gasoline, a 14.1 percent increase in electricity and natural gas prices, and a 10.9 percent increase in home-heating costs. Revenues thus raised would go into America's Energy Security Trust Fund. One-sixth of the fund, up to $10 billion, would be invested to develop clean-energy technology. Half would be used to offer relief to industries under pressure from technological changes. The remainder would be returned to the public by offsetting payroll taxes. Metcalf estimates that the bill would reduce carbon emissions by about 12 percent and raise over $80 billion in revenue to be redistributed to the public. A typical worker would save $560 in payroll taxes, which would help offset the higher prices paid for gasoline, home heating oil, and other forms of energy.

Will we be able to implement any proposal that relies on substantial tax increases that may have a regressive impact on our population? Will lawmakers indeed spend these carbon revenues to stop global warming and return them to taxpayers through payroll tax reductions? No one really knows, but the world's leading scientists and environmentalists see a carbon tax as our best shot at winning the battle against global warming.

In this country, however, the political momentum appears to be behind a cap and trade system. In 2006 CEOs from Alcoa, Duke Energy, Du Pont, Caterpillar, PG&E, GE, and others joined together to create the United States Climate Action Partnership (USCAP) to lobby for a cap and trade system. Senators John McCain, Joe Lieberman, Barack Obama, and Hillary Clinton, among others, support some form of cap and trade.

Yet cap and trade seems a circuitous way to battle global warming, especially when compared to a direct tax on carbon. In a cap and trade system, the government sets an overall limit—squeezed lower and lower each year—on the total amount of carbon dioxide that can be pumped into the atmosphere. Washington then either allocates or auctions to energy producers only enough permits to emit a set proportionate amount of carbon. It is left to industry to find ways to meet those targets. If Congress decides that it wants to cut all carbon by 15 percent below 2005 levels by 2020, as proposed by Senators Joe Lieberman and John Warner, industry must figure out how to achieve those reduced levels of greenhouse gas. A trading market—most likely run by Wall Street firms—would allow companies that use less than their carbon emission allocation to sell their excess permits to companies that need them to comply with the law. The trading market would set a price for a ton of carbon emissions based on the supply and demand of the permits.

The reason a growing number of politicians and big business CEOs like cap and trade is that it is an invisible tax and therefore has a better chance of passing in Congress than a straightforward carbon tax. But, obviously, carbon cap and trade is a tax, albeit an indirect one. Prices of oil, gas, and coal undoubtedly would rise under such a system, though it will be hard to figure out exactly who would be affected, by how much, and when. The free market element of cap and trade is what most appeals to its supporters in Congress and in the financial community—let the market decide how much carbon reduction should cost and who the winners and losers will be. We should not forget that many would grow rich under such a system, and many in Congress would get credit for making them so. Wall Street operators would receive their cut for managing a carbon market, a cut potentially worth billions in trading fees.

The system also appeals to the business community because, with the current absence of national leadership, the states are stepping in to pass their own carbon laws. This creates a patchwork of shifting, complex state and local regulations that make it difficult for business to predictably operate. What executive would want to deal with different regulations in all fifty states as well as scores of cities?

To date, twenty-seven states have passed laws either regulating greenhouse gas emissions or mandating that a percentage of the power generated within their borders be produced by solar, wind, or other renewables. California mandated that the businesses and utilities operating in the state reduce greenhouse gas. Nine Midwestern governors have signed an agreement to reduce carbon emissions and set up a trading system to meet reduction targets. Even cities are getting into the act, with New York's mayor Michael Bloomberg unrolling a "green city" program in the spring of 2007 (see chapter 11).

The concept of cap and trade is not a new one. In 1990, in an effort to stem the growing threat of acid rain, Congress passed the Clean Air Act amendments. These rules established a cap and trade system that *The Economist* would later call "the greatest green success story of the past decade."[6] According to the Environmental Defense Fund, within five years industry had cut emissions 30 percent more than the law required.

The program created a market in which the right to emit sulfur dioxide could be bought and sold. The government issued allowances worth 1 ton of SO_2 each to 110 power plants in the Northeast, the Mid Atlantic, and the Midwest. The plants, monitored by the Environmental Protection Agency, could emit as much sulfur dioxide as the permits in their possession allowed. If they exceeded their allocation, they could purchase allowances from plants that did not need them. Simply put, the dirtier the plant, the more it would cost to operate. A clean plant, however, could actually increase its revenue through selling its allowances. As a result, many plants began to voluntarily install technologies that limited their SO_2 emissions.

But harnessing SO_2 is much easier than harnessing carbon. The Chicago Climate Exchange is the world's first legally binding gas emissions allowance trading system. A growing group of companies, including Du Pont, Dow Corning, Ford, and Bayer, as well as numerous city governments, have signed on, but this system is voluntary and has yet to reduce national CO_2 levels enough to be meaningful.

The details of implementing such a plan are complex. How many permits should the government issue? Should they be free or auctioned off to industry? Who will check for compliance? What will be the penalties for noncompliance? Will elected officials want to hand out exemptions to special interests? The EU now uses cap and trade as a way to reduce CO_2 in keeping with the Kyoto Protocol, the international treaty that sets limits on greenhouse gas emissions. When the EU launched its carbon trading system in 2005, it issued too many carbon permits and their price fell dramatically. The system has failed to deliver a uniform and predictable cost of carbon and therefore has done little to reduce carbon emission and encourage the use of alternative fuels. Supporters of the European cap and trade system argue that they have learned their lesson, and that the next issuance of permits will create an efficient market that will help meet the region's carbon reduction goals.

Maybe, but cap and trade systems are bureaucratically cumbersome and are open to manipulation and political influence. Lewis Hay III, CEO of FPL Group, one of the nation's largest utilities, favors a carbon tax over a cap and trade system. He believes that cap and trade would result in a "giant food fight over these [carbon] allowances," invite fraud such as that which has marred similar programs in Europe, and result in volatile carbon pricing. According to Hay, "we think the big winners in a trading scheme will all be the investment bankers." Rex Tillerson, CEO of ExxonMobil, concurs. "It's all about moving the money around," he said.[7]

To get a taste of how far Washington is from tackling global warming, consider what happened in early 2007: Republican senator Jim Bunning of Kentucky rose to support the little-noticed bill, S 155, saying, "For too long America has ignored its energy security. Many of us can remember the energy crisis of the 1970s. We were held ransom by a monopolistic oil cartel and forced to endure shortages, gas lines, and high prices." The fine print of this bill proposed a massive federal package of loan guarantees ($10 billion for construction of new plants), tax credits, and subsidies for an obscure technology called coal-to-liquid, or CTL, which turns coal into a liquid form that can be used to fill the gas tanks of our cars, trucks, and planes. This technology is not new. During World War II, Nazi Germany produced liquefied coal to run its panzer tanks. In the 1970s Jimmy Carter's ill-fated syn-fuels project pushed liquid coal. Today South Africa, which developed the technology during its oil-scarce days of the apartheid embargo, gets 30 percent of its fuel from liquid coal.

Senator Bunning glossed over in his speech the fact that liquid coal emits twice as much greenhouse gas as does a gallon of gasoline. Is it just coincidence that Kentucky, Bunning's home state, is the third-largest coal producer in the country? Or that the bill's cosponsors, Republican senator Mike Enzi of Wyoming and Democrat Barack Obama of Illinois, also represent major players in the coal industry? We will not reduce greenhouse gas if our legislators support a technology that will double the amount of greenhouse gas already billowing into our atmosphere. Not all the news was bad. On June 19, 2007, the Senate ended up voting down a bill that contained a provision to subsidize coal-to-gasoline production. At about the same time, a Senate committee approved $10 billion in additional tax breaks for companies that generate electricity from renewables such as solar, wind, and methane from landfills.[8] And Senator Obama has since altered his position, saying that he will not support the development of any coal-to-liquid fuels unless they emit at least 20 percent less life-cycle carbon than conventional fuels.

This seesawing is indicative of where, up to now, America has stood on energy legislation. A band of green-minded members of Congress who wanted to tackle global warming were up against a powerful coalition with backing from an administration that believed energy needs should be met primarily through gas and coal. At this writing, the national political scene is in flux, and it remains to be seen whether more effective legislation will be passed and sustained.

More than global warming is at stake. If America does not have a coherent energy policy, will we ever become a leader in green technology? Without regulation that puts a price on carbon, U.S. business has less incentive to invest in green technology. The country could fall by the wayside and become a purchaser of green tech from countries that grow rich from designing and building everything from hybrids to solar panels, from windmills to clean coal plants. After all, like pollution itself, green technology knows no geographic or political boundaries. A German or Japanese or Chinese solar panel will generate the same amount of electricity from the sun whether it is installed in America or in Africa or in India. In the long run, millions of new jobs and the future prosperity of the United States are at stake.

The effects of global warming are also not confined by borders. It will do little good if America agrees to cut back on CO_2, while China, India, and the rest of the developing world constantly increase their levels of heat-trapping gases. International cooperation is crucial. No country in the world market should be allowed to gain a competitive advantage by burning cheap fossil fuels. If, say, the United States fails to put a price on carbon, what is there to stop European companies, who face stiff energy prices, from moving their operations to America? EU businesses would then put pressure on their political leaders to gut carbon regulations in Europe to level the playing field, and an important weapon in fighting global warming would be lost.

America is out of step with most of the developed world on the issue of climate change. The Kyoto Protocol, the international treaty to reduce carbon, expires in 2012. The European Union, Japan, and Canada believe that without a strong new framework, the chances of reducing carbon emissions by 80 percent by 2050 will be slim or impossible. The United States refused to ratify the first Kyoto treaty, arguing that developing countries such as China and India should be subject to it as well. As Prime Minister Tony Blair declared, even if England's economy were to shut down completely for two years, the *increase* in China's greenhouse gas emissions over that period alone would negate any savings in global CO_2 emissions.[9]

The rub is that China is unlikely to agree to any international treaty that would hamper its economic growth. Beijing's position is that in the twentieth century the West polluted at will as it grew its economies and became rich. One only need conjure images of a pollution-choked Pittsburgh or Detroit in the 1960s to grasp this argument. Now it is China's and India's turn. Why should these nations adopt expensive clean-coal technology or invest in solar panels that cost three times more than old technologies like dirty coal and hydro? The money, China's leaders believe, would be better used to rebuild infrastructure, grow food, and sustain business and job growth.

China, India, and the rest of the developing world are likely to produce most of the increase in greenhouse gas emissions between now and 2050. European leaders are calling for a new plan that would put binding limits on overall global CO_2 emissions. At the same time, it would provide ways for developing economies to grow while minimizing greenhouse gas emissions.

The first way to implement this goal is to set a price on carbon in the developed world. This would give industry a larger incentive to drive down the price of clean energy sources to the point where it would make economic sense for developing countries to buy wind or solar or biofuels. China and India would choose these over current coal technology because they would be not only cleaner but also cheaper.

The second way to encourage burgeoning economies is to implement a strong international clean-development mechanism. Under such a plan, companies in rich countries could earn credits to pollute by installing greenhouse gas–saving technology in developing countries. For example, an American company that has already become relatively efficient in its operations but still needs to cut its greenhouse gas emissions might pay to install solar systems or clean-coal technology in China. In exchange, the American company would get credits for the CO_2 it saved in China. It would be in compliance with international regulations yet able to continue with business as usual.

This exchange would help cut back on Chinese pollution, but it might be a tough political sell. American companies would be seen giving away valuable technology to China at a time when American jobs are being threatened by cheap Chinese imports. And how would such a system be enforced? Who would measure whether carbon had actually been reduced at a Chinese company? On a visit to China, Treasury Secretary Henry Paulson toured a chemical plant 150 miles from Shanghai. The company, he said, measured its pollution by placing two camels and a cow in a field. When they fell over, management would shut down the plant.

But, with proper oversight and regulation, international carbon swapping ought to work and it could lower the *overall* amount of carbon emitted annually throughout the world. Such a cooperative and closely monitored system, for example, could channel capital from Germany, Japan, or the United States to Ethiopia, which is eager to tap into clean technology but doesn't have the money to do it. Meles Zenawi, prime minister of the Federal Democratic Republic of Ethiopia, believes that a carbon market is the only "realistic way" Africa could grow in a carbon-neutral manner.[10] He points out that his region could generate enough hydroelectricity to power the entire African continent, and that locally produced sugarcane could provide biofuels for transportation, but "we have to have access to carbon trade as a matter of right. We did not pollute and we're being punished for what you did."

South America could also benefit. Money flowing in from carbon credits could help reduce deforestation, which accounts for 20 percent of man-induced CO_2 worldwide. That's more greenhouse gas than transportation emits and is second only to fossil fuel–generated electricity and heat. In Brazil, vast swaths of rain forest have fallen to road development, cattle ranching, soy farming, and clear-cut logging (including the decimation of mahogany trees). An estimated 3 percent of the forest was gone in 1980. Now 20 percent is gone. By some estimates, the Amazon will have lost a quarter of its original size by the year 2020.[11] Under an international trade system, a corporation could earn carbon credits by paying a Brazilian not to cut down forests or to farm them sustainably. The money from the credits could support initiatives such as one put in place by Eduardo Braga, governor of the Amazonas state in Brazil. He has cut deforestation of the rain forest in his region by 41 percent over four years. Under Braga, the government pays two thousand farmers not to cut down trees. The money helps provide well-paying jobs for those who might otherwise turn to illegal logging. The state also encourages loggers to create "certified" forests, in which trees are cut in rotation to protect species. And it urges farmers to pursue alternative uses of the land, from jute production to exotic fish farms. The state offers credit, tech support, logistical support, and tax breaks for products from the rain forest. Says Braga, "Before, we used to give people a chain saw; now we give them a new economic model that doesn't deforest and they have a better condition of life."[12]

A growing number of environmentalists want forest conservation to be part of the next international climate agreement. The World Bank hopes to lead in setting global initiatives to reduce deforestation. The bank is asking the G8 group of industrialized countries to give political and financial backing to a pilot project to reduce emissions from deforestation in five tropical countries.[13] Dense tropical forest is often cleared in Latin America to create pastures worth as little as $300 a hectare, while releasing large amounts of CO_2. Some deforestation in Africa and Asia is equally unproductive. These forests may be worth five times more if left to stand and provide carbon-storage services than if cleared and burned. If developing countries could tap this value, they could also stimulate more productive agriculture in degraded areas, while preserving the environmental services of forests.

At this writing, America remained at a deadly standoff with the rest of the world in its reluctance to participate in international initiatives. At a meeting of 187 nations in Bali in late 2007 to discuss a new framework for the Kyoto Protocol, the U.S. delegates were booed and hissed for their obstructionism. In the final hours, the United States agreed to a two-year timetable to craft a new agreement—although it's still not clear how hard America will push for change. With the threat to Earth increasing daily, the United States—the world's largest polluter—should take the lead in aggressively combating global warming. Time is running out.

At the Crossroad

THE NEWS ABOUT GLOBAL WARMING keeps getting worse. The earth is warming faster than most scientists previously predicted. We can look forward to an increasing number of extreme weather events, including melting ice sheets that could lead to a rapid rise in sea levels, crop failures from drought or torrential rains, even the extinction of large numbers of species.

And while this is going on, we are increasing, not reducing, the amount of greenhouse gas we emit into the atmosphere. China now builds the equivalent of two coal plants a week. The United States has 150 such plants on the drawing boards. And ExxonMobil and Chevron are planning to tap into Alberta tar sands, which will emit significantly more CO_2 than oil. In 2006 the world belched out 8.4 gigatons of carbon from burning fossil fuels, almost identical to the UN's worst-case predictions for that year.[1]

Nor are we making progress in weaning ourselves from oil. Worldwide demand remains strong. China and the United States are importing record levels of crude, and the price in early 2008 remained more than $100 a barrel, thus far an all-time high. The threat that a terrorist attack could disrupt world oil supplies remains high. While it is true that we Americans have become more energy efficient than we were, we are still consuming more than ever—mainly because so many of us are living in bigger homes and driving bigger, more powerful cars.

Record numbers of companies now claim to use green manufacturing to produce green products. Actually, their activities could be characterized as greenwash. Gluing an earth-friendly label on a bottle of water or advertising an eco-friendly SUV lulls us into thinking the problem of climate change is being solved. It is not.

The time has come to stop playing at being green and begin the revolution. The only way to solve the problem is to move quickly beyond hype to real environmental benefit and a real return on investment. In this book, we have seen entrepreneurs and corporate innovators searching for workable solutions to global warming. There has been some heartening progress. Private industry seems, to a certain degree, to be working with environmentalists to pinpoint areas that may be productive and to ensure that their technology does not create more environmental hazards. Venture money continues to flow into fledgling solar, wave, biofuel, and electric car companies. Big companies such as GE, Du Pont, Duke Energy, and Sharp are boosting their green R&D budgets and are searching for innovative solutions to our energy crisis.

Scientists say that America and Europe must take most of the carbon out of the air by midcentury. In the United States, strides made in energy efficiency—smart grids, LED lighting, better building designs—should get the nation roughly halfway to that goal. The rest must come from improvements in our power plants and cars. Solar, wind and wave, hydro, and geothermal technologies should be able to contribute significantly, perhaps supplying as much as 25 percent of our electricity if battery technology can be developed to store power on cloudy or windless days. Nuclear power, which exudes no greenhouse gas and currently provides the United States with 20 percent of its power, will, for better and worse, play a role. New nuclear plants will have to be built as those now in use age and are taken off-line.

Coal now supplies half our electricity. There is no question about it. It must be cleaned up. Carbon sequestration technologies will eventually become affordable and new approaches, such as using algae to eat the carbon in coal exhaust, may become commercially viable. These technologies have worked in pilot projects. Now the pattern must be scaled up and the costs scaled down if such innovations are to have a timely effect on the earth.

Advances in the automobile industry would help us reach our midcentury carbon goal. The technology now exists to get 60 miles per gallon or more. The most likely scenario will be small electric cars for daily commutes and plug-in hybrids for longer trips. The battery technology to drive these vehicles is in reach, but the costs must be brought down to where this power source becomes affordable.

We should not forget that industry is pursuing green tech to make money. A lot of people are going to get very rich from these enterprises. We now see the birth of the companies that will be the stock market stars of tomorrow. It is much like being present in Silicon Valley in the 1960s and 1970s and watching the struggles of start-ups named HP, Intel, Microsoft, and Apple.

Some of these green companies will fall by the wayside because their technology fails or is impractical or too expensive. Corn ethanol, heavily dependent on government subsidies, produces at best only minor overall reductions in greenhouse gases and puts a strain on the food supply. A company that sells a $57,000 car battery has a long way to go before gaining consumer acceptance and cannot count on continued taxpayer support. Companies betting on hydrogen seem to be overlooking the daunting challenge of an entirely new delivery system than the oil trucks, gas stations, pipelines, and refineries that deliver our present fuels.

Industries that do not adapt to these profound changes will have trouble surviving. Workers in their plants will be out of jobs. Big oil and big coal companies that resist change may become the buggy whip makers of tomorrow. Those who do adapt can be at the forefront of a new industry that produces jobs and prosperity. Consider that Duke Energy, one of the largest coal producers in the United States, is investing in a "smart power grid" that promises to cut electricity use while boosting profits. Toyota is betting its future on clean hybrid technology.

The free market will come up with potential solutions, but will it be in time? Perhaps, if global warming and its disastrous consequences were not yet so prevalent, we would do best, as we have done in the past, to let Yankee ingenuity solve the problem and come up with a Green Revolution that would parallel the Industrial Revolution. But we don't have the leisure to test that proposition. Without government support, the private sector will fail to make sufficient progress. Increased federal R&D investment will speed the pace of innovation as would some form of carbon tax. Without such assistance we are unlikely to meet the aggressive and essential targets to reduce heat-trapping gases by midcentury. We should bear in mind that the Internet was born in federal labs.

O N MAY 25, 1961, President John F. Kennedy addressed a joint session of Congress: "I believe this nation should commit itself to achieving the goal, before this decade is out, of landing a man on the moon and returning him safely to earth." Eight years later, ahead of schedule, Neil Armstrong became the first man to walk on the moon. President Kennedy had asked the nation to put its vast resources and brainpower behind the Apollo project, and America responded to the challenge.

Now the nation needs the equivalent of another Apollo moon shot to tackle global warming. But this time the challenge is even more daunting. Strong political leadership is required. The most powerful people in government must urge Americans to conserve energy and accept the benefits and inconveniences of what is probably our best hope: a tax on carbon. We need new federal tax incentives to reduce dependency on fossil fuels and thereby make green technology affordable.

We should take a fresh look at the next Kyoto agreement. Such a global framework for reducing greenhouse gases can never equally please all the nations of the world. It is quite possible that China and other fast-growing and polluting countries may not join the protocol, but the United States has to take a leadership role in conforming to global restrictions and setting goals. Otherwise, we will all go under, with each nation, each locality, stubbornly clutching to its positions.

There is another way to look at it. Rather than a threat, global warming might be seen as an opportunity to unleash America's technological genius and create huge, new green industries through a fresh wave of government and entrepreneurial environmentalism. It is also an opportunity for one generation to transcend its own wasteful lifestyle and leave behind not devastation but a clean and prosperous world.

Notes

All quotations are from interviews conducted by the author
unless otherwise referenced.

Introduction: Plotters

1. Mark Townsend and Paul Harris, "Now the Pentagon Tells Bush: Climate Change Will Destroy Us," *Observer*, February 22, 2004.
2. Carbon is the biggest contributor to global warming, but there are five other greenhouse gases: methane, nitrous oxide, sulfur hexafluoride, perfluorocarbons, and hydrofluorocarbons.
3. Elisabeth Rosenthal, "U.N. Chief Seeks More Climate Change Leadership," *New York Times*, November 18, 2007.
4. Speech by John Doerr at the TED conference, March 2007.
5. Global investment in renewable energy. http://www.ey.com/global/content .nsf/International/Media__Press_Release__Renewable_Indices_Q2_2007.
6. Jessica Harris, "Sir Richard Branson," *From Scratch*, NPR Radio, June 2007.
7. Robert H. Socolow and Stephen W. Pacala, "A Plan to Keep Carbon in Check," *Scientific American*, September 2006.

Chapter 1: Big Energy

1. "And the Gas Lines Grow," *Time*, July 9, 1979, http://www.time.com/time/printout/0,8816,920445,00.html.
2. Statistic for number of cars in U.S.: http://www.bts.gov/publications/pocket_guide_to_transportation/2007/html/table_04_02.html.
3. "The Lists," *Fortune*, April 30, 2007, p. 201.
4. The Argyle Private Equity Conference, Union League Club, New York City, June 11, 2007.
5. Geoff Colvin, "ExxonMobil: The Defiant One," *Fortune*, April 30, 2007, p. 86.

6. Elizabeth Kolbert, "Unconventional Crude," *The New Yorker*, November 12, 2007, p. 46.
7. John Carey, "Coal: Could Be the End of the Line," *BusinessWeek*, November 13, 2006, p. 74.
8. Kate Ravilious, "Giant Ocean Tubes Proposed as Global Warming Fix," *National Geographic News*, September 26, 2007.
9. Kelly Hearn, "Plan to Dump Iron in Ocean as Climate Fix Attracts Debate," *National Geographic News*, July 25, 2007.
10. Kate Ravilious, "Fill the Skies with Sulfur," *National Geographic News*, August 4, 2006.
11. Mark Williams, "Cooling the Planet," *Technology Review*, February 13, 2007.

Chapter 2: Green Is the Color of Growth

1. Geoff Colvin, "Chevron's CEO: The Price of Oil," *Fortune*, November 28, 2007.
2. Patrick R. Burtis; Bob Epstein, E2; and Nicholas Parker, Cleantech Capital Group, LLC, "Creating Cleantech Clusters: 2006 Update. How Innovation and Investment Can Promote Job Growth and a Healthy Environment," San Jose, California, May 2006.
3. John Doerr and Bill Joy, "The Blue Sky Project," *Forbes*, May 7, 2007, http://www.forbes.com/free_forbes/2007/0507/082.html.
4. Statement of philosophy of the Free Enterprise Action Fund: http://www.freeenterpriseactionfund.com/release031507.htm.
5. Statement by Tom Borelli of Action Fund Management: Ibid.
6. Christoph Grobbel, Jiri Maly, and Michael Molitor, "Preparing for a Low Carbon Future," *McKinsey Quarterly* 4 (2004).
7. Ibid.
8. Marc Gunther, "Wal-Mart: The Green Machine," *Fortune*, July 31, 2006.
9. Ibid.
10. Jeffrey Goldberg, "Selling Wal-Mart: Can the Company Co-opt Liberals?" *The New Yorker*, April 2, 2007.
11. Lee Scott, memo to Wal-Mart employees, 2005.
12. Stacy Mitchell, "The Hometown Advantage: How to Defend Your Main Street Against Chain Stores and Why It Matters," April 27, 2005. © 2005 New Rules Project.
13. Ibid.
14. GE CEO Jeff Immelt interview: http://www.directorship.com/publications/0707_green_is_green.aspx.

15. Amanda Griscom Little, "It Was Just My Ecomagination," Grist.org, May 10, 2005, http://www.grist.org/news/muck/2005/05/10/little-ge/.
16. Ibid.
17. Anne Kelley of Ceres on GE: http://www.directorship.com/publications/0707_ge_ecopush.aspx.
18. Tom Stewart, interview with Immelt, "Growth Is Process," *Harvard Business Review*, June 2006.
19. GE CEO Jeff Immelt on China: http://www.directorship.com/publications/0707_green_is_green.aspx.

Chapter 3: How Less Is More

1. Andrew Martin, "If It's Fresh and Local, Is It Always Greener?" *New York Times*, December 9, 2007.
2. Ibid.

Chapter 4: High-Rises and Low-Rises

1. Brad Pitt, interview with Ann Curry, *Today*, July 14, 2006.
2. William McDonough and Michael Braungart, *Cradle to Cradle: Remaking the Way We Make Things* (New York: Northpoint Press, 2002), pp. 147–54.
3. Ibid., p. 123.
4. Ibid., pp. 7–8.
5. James Howard Kunstler, *The Long Emergency* (New York: Grove Press, 2005).
6. In 1993 the nonprofit U.S. Green Building Council established its Leadership in Energy and Environmental Design, or LEED, standards for sustainable construction. Platinum is the highest rating, followed by Gold, Silver, and certified, and is based for the most part on how much carbon a building will emit into the atmosphere.
7. Electricity use by buildings: info@architecture2030.org.
8. Energy use in houses: http://www.treehugger.com/files/2006/10/this_house_isnt.php.

Chapter 5: The Car You Are Driving Was Designed by a Madman

1. Job losses in auto industry: http://www.ns.umich.edu/htdocs/releases/story.php?id=1069.

2. Alex Taylor III, "Debunking Auto Industry Myths: *New York Times* Columnist Thomas Friedman Perpetuates Some Convenient Misconceptions About Fuel Economy, and *Fortune*'s Alex Taylor III Calls Him Out," CNN Money, October 4, 2007.

3. Micheline Maynard, "Politics Forcing Detroit to Back New Fuel Rules," *New York Times*, June 20, 2007, p. A1.

4. Union of Concerned Scientists: http://www.hybridcenter.org/hybrid-transit-buses.html.

5. Chang-Ran Kim, "Toyota Says Hybrid Cost Premium to Disappear," Reuters, May 10, 2007.

6. Kevin Bullis, "Lithium-Ion Batteries That Don't Explode: A New Material Prevents Overheating, Making Lithium-Ion Batteries Safer for Use in Vehicles," *Technology Review*, May 22, 2007, http://www.technologyreview.com/Energy/18762/?a=f.

7. David Welch, "Chevy's Volt Has the Juice," BusinessWeek.com, January 7, 2007, http://www.businessweek.com/autos/content/jan2007/bw20070108_195447.htm?chan=autos_hybrids+index+page_news+%3Cspan+style%3D%22font-family%3Aarial%3B%22%3E%2B%3C%2Fspan%3E+features.

8. John Markoff, "Reimagining the Automobile Industry by Selling the Electricity," *New York Times*, October 29, 2007, http://www.nytimes.com/2007/10/29/technology/29agassi.html?_r=1&oref=slogin.

9. Quotes from Honda and Ford executives are from Goldman Sachs clean-energy conference.

10. MQ Wang, "Development and Use of GREET 1.6 Fuel-Cycle Model for Transportation Fuels and Vehicle Technologies," Center for Transportation Research, Argonne National Laboratory, June 2001.

11. Reduction in greenhouse gas emissions (using California energy grid): hydrogen fuel cell vehicle: 39 percent; battery electric vehicle: 67 percent. Source: David L. Modisette, executive director, California Electric Transportation Coalition, e-mail communication, December 28, 2005. See also "Regulations to Control Greenhouse Gas Emissions from Motor Vehicles," California Air Resources Board staff report, August 6, 2004.

12. GM electric car program: http://www.pbs.org/now/shows/223/electric-car-timeline.html.

13. Product liability worries: http://www.automobilemag.com/features/news/0701_2007_volkswagen_gx3.

14. Peter Fairley, "Electric-Car Maker Touts 10-Minute Fill-Up," IEEE, November 2007.

15. Jonathan Fahey, "Hot Air: How a Truck-maker Plans to Lose Money on Each Sale—and Make It Up Trading Carbon Credits," forbes.com, March 12,

2007, https://www.keepmedia.com/Auth.do?extId=10022&uri=/archive/forbes/2007/0312/046b.html.

16. Richard Rogers, *Cities for a Small Planet* (London: 1997).

17. Ed Brock, "On Parallel Tracks," http://americancityandcounty.com/features/government_parallel_tracks/ (accessed November 1, 2006).

18. Hickenlooper interview: http://globalpublicmedia.com/transcripts/618.

19. David T. Hartgen, Ph.D., P.E., and M. Gregory Fields, "Building Roads to Reduce Traffic Congestion in America's Cities," http://www.reason.org/ps346.

20. Alex Taylor III, "Congestion-Pricing Debate Continues," *Fortune Small Business*, November 2007.

Chapter 6: Fuel Without the Fossils

1. GAO, "Aviation and the Environment," February 2000.

2. Jessica Harris, "Sir Richard Branson," *From Scratch*, NPR Radio, June 2007.

3. "Jet Fuel Intelligence," http://www.virgingreenfund.com/index.php?option=com_content&task=view&id=7&Itemid=44 (accessed December 11, 2006).

4. GAO, "Aviation and the Environment," February 2000.

5. Amyris corporate press release.

Chapter 7: The Carbon-Muncher

1. Tim Flannery, *The Weather Makers: How Man Is Changing the Climate and What It Means for Life on Earth* (New York: Atlantic Monthly Press, 2006).

2. "DOE Awards First Three Large-Scale Carbon Sequestration Projects: U.S. Projects Total $318 Million and Further President Bush's Initiatives to Advance Clean Energy Technologies to Confront Climate Change," October 9, 2007, http://www.fossil.energy.gov/news/techlines/2007/07072-DOE_Awards_Sequestration_Projects.html.

3. Matthew L. Wald, "New Type of Coal Plant Moves Ahead, Haltingly," *New York Times*, December 18, 2007.

Chapter 8: Big Sun

1. Martin Green, "Shi Zhengrong," *Time*, October 15, 2007, http://www.time.com/time/specials/2007/article/0,28804,1663317_1663322_1669932,00.html.

2. Janet Larsen, "Coal Takes Heavy Human Toll: Some 25,100 U.S. Deaths from Coal Use Largely Preventable," Earth Policy Institute, August 24, 2004. Copyright © 2004 Earth Policy Institute.

3. A German pig farmer gets 50 cents for every kilowatt-hour he sells to the grid but pays only 20 cents per kilowatt-hour to buy electricity from the grid. From *Nova*, "Saved by the Sun," 2007, http://www.pbs.org/wgbh/nova/solar.

4. Dr. Hermann Scheer, president of EUROSOLAR, "Renewable Energy in America: Phase II Market Forecasts and Policy Requirements," ACORE Conference, Washington, D.C., November 30, 2006.

5. Q-Cells was founded at the end of 1999.

6. David Kestenbaum, "In Japan, Going Solar Costly Despite Market Surge," NPR, October 1, 2007.

7. According to Ron Kenedi, who runs Sharp's solar buisness in the United States, the price of PV before subsidies in Japan started at $66 a watt; when the program was finished it fell to $6 a watt.

8. Scheer, "Renewable Energy in America."

9. *Nova*, "Saved by the Sun."

10. From the Japanese online business newspaper Nikkei.net, November 8, 2006. The figure of 40 percent of U.S. energy needs is based on 2.6 terrawatt-hours of electricity annually.

11. According to Ron Kenedi, Arizona Power System (APS) in Phoenix and some companies in Spain and Japan are testing the concentrators, which will be ready for market within twenty-four months.

12. Michael Peevey, California Public Utilities Commission: http://news.com .com/8301-10784_3-6160098-7.html.

13. Roman solar heating: http://www.californiasolarcenter.org/history_passive .html.

14. John Perlin, *From Space to Earth: The Story of Solar Electricity* (Cambridge, MA: Harvard University Press, 2002).

15. Although solar thermal systems and solar photovoltaic (PV) panels both transform energy from the sun into electricity, they work in vastly different manners. PV panels, which have become very popular in the last five years, split photons from the sun into electrons and positive charges from the sun. The electrons are harvested and funneled into the electrical system of a building or the grid. In general, silicon PV panels convert 15 to 22 percent of the light that strikes them into electricity; mixing other materials into the panels can increase efficiency but also adds cost. According to studies, solar thermal plants are more effective, with efficiencies ranging from around 20 to 40 percent, in part because it's easier to extract heat from sunlight than electrons.

16. Hal LaFlash of PG&E: http://blogs.business2.com/greenwombat/solar_energy/index.html.
17. SunPower Annual Report, 2006.

Chapter 9: Strange Bedfellows

1. Stewart Brand, "Environmental Heresies," *Technology Review*, May 2005.
2. John M. Deutch and Ernest J. Moniz, "The Nuclear Option," *Scientific American*, September 2006, pp. 76–83.
3. The Argyle Private Equity Conference, Union League Club, New York City, June 11, 2007.
4. Clay Sell interview: http://www.cbsnews.com/stories/2007/04/06/60min-utes/main2655782.shtml.
5. Brand, "Environmental Heresies."
6. Felicity Barringer, "Old Foes Soften to New Reactors," *New York Times*, May 15, 2005.
7. Chernobyl radiation: http://www.chernobyl.info/index.php?userhash=25347159&navID=2&lID=2.
8. United Nations Development Programme Report, 2002.
9. Chernobyl radiation: http://www.chernobyl.info/index.php?userhash=25347159&navID=2&lID=2.
10. Rachel Carson: http://www.ccolo.org/lovelock/lovedeten.htm.
11. James Lovelock, *The Revenge of Gaia* (New York: Basic Books, 2006), p. xi.
12. Ibid., p. 15.
13. From BBC interview, July 2004.
14. Lovelock, *The Revenge of Gaia*, p. 3.
15. Ibid., p. 67.
16. From BBC interview, July 2001.
17. David Whitford, "Going Nuclear," *Fortune*, July 31, 2007.
18. Deutch and Moniz, "The Nuclear Option."
19. In 2003 Moniz and Deutch cochaired a major MIT study, "The Future of Nuclear Power," that analyzed the industry and concluded that worldwide nuclear power generation could triple to 1 million megawatts by the year 2050, saving the globe from emissions of between 0.8 billion and 1.8 billion tons of carbon a year, depending on whether gas- or coal-powered plants were displaced. At this scale, nuclear power would significantly contribute to the stabilization of greenhouse gas emissions, which under a plan by Robert Socolow and Stephen Pacala of Princeton requires about 7 billion tons of carbon to be averted annually by 2050.

20. Pebble-bed reactors: http://www.tmia.com/industry/pebbles.html.
21. Nuclear power in Europe: http://www.euronuclear.org/info/encyclopedia/n/nuclear-power-plant-europe.htm.

Chapter 10: A Mighty Wind

1. Warren Buffett and wind power: http://www.midamericanenergy.com/newsroom/aspx/newsdetails.aspx?id=384&type=archive.
2. Iowa wind capacity: http://www.awea.org/news/news030325.html.
3. Warren Buffett: http://www.mindfully.org/Energy/2005/Buffet-Berkshire-PacifiCorp24may05.htm.
4. EU electricity needs: http://www.ewea.org/fileadmin/ewea_documents/documents/press_releases/2007/070201_Statistics_2006_Press_Release.pdf.
5. Denmark wind power: http://www.windpower.org/media(1775,1033)/engelsk_resumé_ea_analyse.pdf.
6. Ibid.
7. Ryan Wiser and Mark Bolinger, "Annual Report on U.S. Wind Power Installation, Cost, and Performance Trends 2006," Lawrence Berkeley National Laboratory, http://www1.eere.energy.gov/windandhydro/pdfs/wiser_data_report_summary_2006.pdf.
8. *The Voices of Tug Hill:* http://video.google.com/videoplay?docid=-7938712870661666877.
9. Wind power noise: http://kirbymtn.blogspot.com/2006/03/french-academy-of-medicine-warns-of.html.
10. Richard G. Jones, "Windmill Cuts Bills, but Neighbors Don't Want to Hear It," *New York Times*, July 11, 2007.
11. Bird deaths by wind turbines: http://www.fws.gov/birds/mortality-fact-sheet.pdf; see also http://www.fws.gov/migratorybirds/issues/towers/kerling.html.
12. Arkansas wind power: http://www.jbs.org/node/5215/print.
13. Denmark, Germany, and Spain wind capacity: http://renewableenergylongisland.org/forums/viewtopic.php?t=82.
14. DC power lines: http://en.wikipedia.org/wiki/Pacific_DC_Intertie.
15. DC grids: http://search.abb.com/library/ABBLibrary.asp?DocumentID=9AKK101130D3006&LanguageCode=en&DocumentPartID=&Action=Launch.
16. DC grids: http://www.economist.com/science/displaystory.cfm?story_id=9539765.
17. Cape Wind project: http://www.capecodtoday.com/blogs/index.php/Op-Ed/2007/05/30/cape_wind_and_tabloid_journalism.

18. Quoted in Cait Murphy, "The Answer Is Not Blowing in the Wind," *Fortune*, April 24, 2006.

19. Offshore wind: http://web.mit.edu/giving/spectrum/summer07/safe-at-sea .html.

20. Ker Than, "Floating Ocean Windmills Designed to Generate More Power," LiveScience, September 18, 2006.

21. Jefferson Tester et al., "The Future of Geothermal Energy: The Future of Impact of Enhanced Geothermal Systems (EGS) on the United States in the 21st Century," MIT and DOE, 2006, web.MIT.edu/newsoffice/2007/geothermal .html.

22. Geothermal capacity: http://www.crest.org/geothermal/geothermal_brief_ power_technologyandgeneration.html and http://www.iea.org/textbase/ papers/2006/renewable_factsheet.pdf.

23. Geothermal projects: http://www.iea.org/textbase/papers/2006/renewable_ factsheet.pdf.

24. U.S. Department of Energy—Energy Efficiency and Renewable Energy, "Drill Problems Halt Australian Hot Dry Rock Geothermal," *EERE News*, July 6, 2006.

Chapter 11: Arnie and Mike

1. Zachary Coile, "Schwarzenegger's Guiltless Green," *San Francisco Chronicle*, April 12, 2007, p. A4.

2. Carol Loomis, "Bloomberg's Money Machine," *Fortune*, April 5, 2007.

3. Michael Bloomberg, PlaNYC, April 22, 2007, NYC.gov.

Chapter 12: The High Cost of Doing Nothing

1. Robert Rackleff, "Voters of Hurricane Katrina," *Carnegie Reporter*, Spring 2007, http://www.carnegie.org/reporter/14/katrina/index.html.

2. Said during Senate debate in 2003 against McCain-Lieberman bill on global warming.

3. SAFE press release, secureenergy.org.

4. Michael Shellenberger and Ted Nordhaus, *Break Through* (New York: Houghton Mifflin, 2007), pp. 1–4.

5. The Office of Energy Efficiency and Renewable Energy FY 2007 budget ($771 million) requests $1.2 billion, $2.6 million (0.2 percent) more than the FY 2006 appropriations. Much of this funding is an integral part of the Advanced Energy Initiative and expands key programs that focus on developing

new energy choices, including hydrogen fuel technology ($114 million); fuel cell technology ($82 million); biomass ($150 million), including research into cellulosic ethanol made from switchgrass, wood chips, and stalks; the Solar America Initiative ($148 million); vehicle technology ($166 million); and wind projects ($44 million).

6. *The Economist*, July 4, 2002.

7. "Energy Crisis Cannot Be Solved by Renewables, Oil Chiefs Say," *Times* (London), June 25, 2007.

8. Edmund L. Andrews, "Panel Supports Tax Breaks for Coal and Non-Oil Fuel," *New York Times*, June 20, 2007, p. C3.

9. Tony Blair, panel discussion, Clinton Global Initiative, September 2007, New York City.

10. Meles Zenawi, panel discussion, Clinton Global Initiative, September 2007, New York City.

11. Mark London and Brian Kelly, *The Last Forest: The Amazon in the Age of Globalization* (New York: Random House, 2007).

12. Eduardo Braga, panel discussion, Clinton Global Initiative, September 2007, New York City.

13. Tom Griffiths, "Seeing 'RED'? 'Avoided Deforestation' and the Rights of Indigenous Peoples and Local Communities," August 2007, http://www.forestpeoples.org/documents/ifi_igo/avoided_deforestation_red_jun07_eng.pdf.

Conclusion: At the Crossroad

1. "Global and Regional Drivers of Accelerating CO_2 Emissions," National Academy of Science, May 22, 2007.

Acknowledgments

This book would not have been possible without the help of many unsung heroes. Charlotte Mayerson provided sharp line editing, all the while challenging my concepts and conclusions. Her contributions raised the book to a higher level, and for that I am grateful. My editor, John Mahaney, skillfully applied his talent for shaping and sculpting books. Beth Bland, a terrific researcher, kept me on track in a field awash with complex facts and statistics. Gib Metcalf taught me how to navigate the choppy waters of carbon taxation. My agent, Mark Reiter, is owed thanks for making this project a reality in the first place, as is Dan Goodgame, who granted me the flexibility to write this book while on staff at Time Inc. Gavin Bromell had the good grace to listen to me lecture on global warming during our long dog-walks and then gave me helpful feedback on my arguments. And thanks to my bike-riding buddies Andrew Heyward and Judy Simmons, who during one long ride on the Putnam Trail came up with the title of this book.

Of course, much love to my wife, Caroline, without whose support I would not have had the courage to undertake this project. Her encouragement, patience, and sharp eye for language were invaluable. And to my children, Paul and Sophia, who inspired me to write a book of hope for them and the generations that follow.

Index

ABOUT THE AUTHOR

BRIAN DUMAINE is the editorial director of *Fortune Small Business*. Prior to that, he was international editor at *Fortune* magazine. He has written dozens of cover stories and devoted much of his editorial energies to environmental issues and, most recently, the rapid rise of the green movement and its impact on capital markets, corporations, and executive thinking.